YOU'RE ONLY
HUMAN ONCE

Grace Moore

ARNO PRESS

A New York Times Company

New York / 1977

Editorial Supervision: ANDREA HICKS

———◆———

Reprint Edition 1977 by Arno Press Inc.

Copyright © 1944, by Grace Moore Parera

Reprinted by permission of Valentin Parera

Reprinted from a copy in
  The University of Illinois Library

OPERA BIOGRAPHIES
ISBN for complete set: 0-405-09666-6
See last pages of this volume for titles.

Manufactured in the United States of America

———◆———

Library of Congress Cataloging in Publication Data

Moore, Grace, 1901-1947.
   You're only human once.

   (Opera biographies)
   Reprint of the 1944 ed. published by Doubleday,
Doran, New York.
   1. Moore, Grace, 1901-1947. 2. Singers—
United States—Biography. I. Title.
ML420.M57A3 1977   782.1'092'4 [B]   76-29958
ISBN 0-405-09698-4

YOU'RE ONLY HUMAN ONCE

Grace Moore

YOU'RE ONLY
HUMAN ONCE

DOUBLEDAY, DORAN & CO., INC., GARDEN CITY, N.Y. 1944

To those best friends—my husband, my mother, and my father—who put up with me offstage, and to those countless thousands on the other side of the footlights who have been the inspiration for this life.

Contents

YOU'RE ONLY HUMAN ONCE

Prelude and Fugitive Thoughts

EVERY PRIMA DONNA has to write her memoirs. It's part of the tradition. It is also a very human wish-fulfillment. Who hasn't thought, when the world kicked too hard, "If I could only write a book!"? There, in repressed defiance, lies the natural instinct to tell the world where to get off: an instinct, alas, that too often takes itself out in the tardy retort framed *sotto voce,* or the year-in, year-out threat mumbled to oneself, "Just wait till I write that book!" Now here, with the retort courteous and the quip modest, is the book I've darkly hinted at writing.

Most prima donnas ride herd on their memories at a ripe old age when no one can say them nay. Then, when the career is all finished and left safely behind in the past, a woman can be as sentimental as she will about her own day and age, giving scorn and damnation to the present. The voices that flourished in the good old days! There was no dancer like Taglioni. No coloratura unto Patti. No champagne, no diamonds, no audiences like those that existed you know when.

The hell with that. It will be a big surprise to me if I ever get old, but if I do I want to sit back and relax. I want my ringside seat to be a comfortable rocking chair from which I don't have to strain to see shadows in the wings. If, at that time, I come around to reminiscing that students unhitched the horses from my carriage and drove me through the streets in triumph—let me, but strictly for home consumption. Now, while I can still wade through my mistakes and while I can still hear the echo of the boys in camp saying "Come on, Grace, come on, encore, encore!"

I want to satisfy this peculiar human and prima-donna-ish itch to scribble my memoirs. After all, one's public, wherever and whatever it may be, certainly sees one's mistakes. They can still say, "Gee, wasn't Grace Moore off last night!" And they can still say, "Wasn't she wonderful!" And they certainly do say, "Why does she do such damn things?"

I don't have to throw dust in the public eye with tales of unhitched horses and hosannas in the streets. The praise is in the current record—so is the blame. I've been hotheaded, ambitious, and Irish; lace curtains one day, the curse of the banshees the next. But I can say a lot about the good fun I've had—the frolic of an era that's quickly burning itself out on a dozen battlefields.

I started as a star, and having been one now for twenty years, I look back on a fine stretch of time. In it the whole scope of opera has changed. During that period, those two Frankensteins of the Machine Age, the moving pictures and the radio, have in turn first isolated living music from its great public and then returned it with a vigor and robustness unprecedented in musical history. Twenty years ago opera had dwindled down to two dominating centers, the Metropolitan in New York and the Chicago Opera Association, with the provinces taking what it could from the annual jaunts of the Hammerstein and Gallo opera companies. Now you can hear *Carmen, Traviata, Bohème, Figaro* in Newark, Hartford, San Francisco, St. Louis, Rochester, and Philadelphia.

Once, if you didn't make good at the Met, was life worth living? Now making good at the Met is still the peak achievement of any singing career, but there are a thousand other ways to make good from coast to coast without even a peekaboo at the gold-flake horseshoe. And not only is the standard repertory flourishing throughout the land. More important are the critical acclaim and the interest in the forward-looking work of experimental groups at the Juilliard, the Eastman, and the Curtis schools and in the New Opera Company.

Twenty years ago you went to Europe to study if you really wanted a career. You haunted the museums abroad to get first-hand material on costuming and *décor*. The study of music was an expatriate profession, like left-bank literature and Grande Chaumière art. Today the young musician keeps her eyes and her voice at home. The faculties of American music schools attract the best teaching talent, both foreign and home-grown. Our museums are crammed with background material for any student who would ferret out the authentic modes of a period. As our writers have returned from Montparnasse, music has come home too. Incidentally, somebody ought to whisper that little secret to the music critics. They are still in the same frame of mind as the old-time Met boxholders, living in the red-plush past. The simple fact of life is that old standards are changing rapidly with the public, and since an artist must reflect what the people want, those standards should be changing with the critics as well. After all, the artist must face both her critical paying audience and her critics who pay off in print.

There is no longer any difficulty for the artist with a simple native name. The unpronounceable jaw-breakers which were once accepted equipment neither add nor detract. I remember that Neysa McMein, who had had her name changed according to the abracadabra of astrology by the famous Evangeline Adams, once prevailed on me to visit Adams myself for advice. Adams read my horoscope solemnly, then predicted that there was a career in store for me, but only if I changed my handle. Her suggestion, arrived at in her own mysterious way, was that henceforth I be called Graziella Morena.

"Is Moore your real name?" she questioned me, looking up from her charts and paraphernalia.

"Yes," I answered decisively, "and Moore it's going to stay. I'll take my chances on it, come what may."

Today Joan Smith has as much chance as Jonina Smithovna. She need no longer suffer the patronizing air that all Italian singers once had towards Americans, an attitude that was so ably (!) stated by Gigli after his last United States tour. That tour had been most unsuccessful, but to add insult to injury, the income taxes he was required to pay further reduced his financial return. These Americans! When he reached Italy he gave out a scathing interview against all the big American names in opera and, amid sneers and barbershop bellowings, declared his resentment at these "interlopers" in what he assumed was a peculiarly Italian sphere.

"American careers in opera consist mostly of taking lessons," once observed Georges Thill, leading tenor of the Paris Opera. A sad, too-true observation then. Where was poor Joan Smith to find an extension of her constant study? The few opera centers in the country remained the stronghold of European direction, and even the public had been conditioned against native talent. It lacked temperament, they were told—Joan Smith had no heritage of fire, passion, pageantry. Her only alternative was to go off to Europe and come back with a fancy name and a shrouded past. Then she would be considered on her merit as a singer and permitted her chance. Now all this hocus-pocus is not necessary. Fire and passion can come out of Oklahoma or Maine, and Joan Smith's heritage needs no excuse.

Quite objectively I can look back on the movie, *One Night of Love*, filmed in 1934, and see what it meant in terms of music. It took grand opera to the ends of the world and brought a new public into the opera houses to rejuvenate and refresh what had become a baronial subscription art. It revolutionized the people's approach to music and sent them from movie house to concert hall whistling melodies they had never even heard before. "It took the high-hat off opera," editorialized the *Daily News* in New York. "The first time in twenty-five years out of the red," said the London *Times* about my Covent Garden debut after the film's great success. Here was not only personal triumph. It meant more than that to me. It meant a new lease on life for the music I loved.

The film made all opera stars movie-minded, and, after it, a diva considered it the greatest sign of popularity if she was asked to go West. Not only did the movies and *One Night of Love* change the hopeful geographical location of all the singers, it changed their girth as well. Because I had to lose, according to the terms of my Hollywood contract, the fifteen pounds I had specifically been asked to acquire before the Metropolitan would give me my contract, Gatti-Casazza laughingly complained that I would be the ruination of the Met.

He had a habit of stalking up and down the Thirty-ninth Street side of the opera building, his thumbs stuck in the armholes of his vest, or his hands caressing his beard. His brows furrowed, eternally clearing his throat, up and down, up and down he went, like an impatiently expectant papa waiting for word on how matters were faring inside. Seeing him so, I wondered if he worried for fear the diet craze had so cut into his private realm of the opera that it might undermine his first-string divas and cause them to collapse at the end of the first act from sheer starvation. The sopranos kept getting thinner and thinner, and even the tenors and baritones would ask me, *sotto voce,* who was that magician who gave me such miraculous massages.

Who ever heard of Caruso being massaged! Or dieting! But see how the world has changed? The divine Caruso could stuff himself with spaghetti for all his public cared, as long as he could sing like an angel. Now they want you to sing like an angel and look the part too.

When I started I had a natural lyric voice, light but with good warm appeal quality. "There's heart in it," said the minister back home. There's no sense in either false modesty or false pride; a pox on both those insincerities if you want to get anywhere. Analyzing what you haven't got as well as what you have is a necessary ingredient of a career. So, because I do have tenacity and an unflinching ambition, I can say this or that about my voice, almost as if I sat listening on the outside. It wasn't a great voice then. There may be some who will still say it isn't. But I do have a voice that has made people listen, that seemed to make people happy and exhilarated. Even with its imperfections, it has been an instrument of communication, which is after all the object of all art. But whatever my voice is, I've gone along with it, and the going has been something.

The tragedy of most stars is that they feel their life ends when the curtain goes down. The antidote is to take time out along the way to live. It is a course that inevitably leads to criticism. The spectacle of the artist who has fun is too much of a good thing for some people to bear. Undoubtedly you end up a "purer" artist if you devote yourself with monastic fortitude and patience to perfection, but there are more things on earth, if not in heaven, than faultlessness. You emerge a human being, subject to all the human errors. And when the curtain goes down, it is just a curtain, and you are still part of life. It's what I have wanted, the way I have wanted to be. Purism may be the breath of artistry to some. To me music, singing, gaiety, love, warmth, people—they are all part of the total spirit, and one doesn't go without the other. Whether people feel hatred or love toward me, I want them, in either case, to know me as I am.

Most careers end in a morass of emptyhearted bitterness. The three most graceful retirers I know are Mary Garden, Geraldine Farrar, and Lucrezia Bori. Professionally, they remain impeccable. Any criticism they may have of present-day stars, they have the good taste to voice in private. Never have they been known to attend an opera performance and, presuming on their prestige, to proclaim in loud voice, from the splendor of a box or of a down-front orchestra seat, their sharp and venomous disapproval. But there are certain ancient and buxom ex-prima donnas who do it continually. One in particular, who for the purposes of this book must remain nameless, has shown uncommon ungraciousness and lack of generosity to the new generation of divas. She fancies that the coldness and the hatred of present-day singers are signs of her ability to intimidate and control their destinies. Since she can no longer sing, she bulldozes the rich, tries to play politics behind the Metropolitan scenes, trumpets against any talent which may emerge. The complete effect is to destroy anything she may once have stood for as an artist.

The personal lives of Garden, Farrar, and Bori remain rich and abundant. Bori has a true Spanish solidity and takes the years as gracefully as a portrait by Goya. With the tireless and brilliant Mrs. August Belmont and other ladies of the committee, she now devotes her time to ceaseless efforts for the Opera Guild. The far-reaching success of that organization must be a completely satisfying note on which to end a brilliant career.

Geraldine Farrar, whom my husband was fortunate enough to sit beside at a recent luncheon given by Clifton Webb, is, as described by him, "still one of the truly great beauties." That's a man's point of view. Mine is to recognize that that continuing beauty comes from an inward serenity to which no curtain could ever write *finis*. Geraldine Farrar has made a place for herself in the present-day musical life of Connecticut and, along with our good friend William M. Sullivan, has done much to stimulate the musical interest and enthusiasm in the town of Ridgefield.

There was a charming story told me by the proprietress of the hotel in Bellagio on Lake Como where I once spent the summer studying opera, and I thought of it the day my husband came home from his luncheon filled with praise for the beautiful Farrar. Some time before I had come to Bellagio, Geraldine Farrar and Antonio Scotti had come together to that same enchanted spot to rest and study their roles in *Madame Butterfly* or *Carmen*. The whole village, enthralled with the romance between Farrar and Scotti and reverent of their position as great artists, took the two to their hearts. Everyone in Bellagio turned out to meet them, my hotel proprietress told me, and as their steamer landed at the little wharf, roses were strewn in their path. They were symbols to the town's inhabitants, and the adulation was as much for the love between the two as for their renowned artistry. Is it any wonder that Farrar, who has known the applause of the world as well as the happiness of being a beloved human being, could carry the grace of living into her later years of retirement?

And as for Mary Garden—my adored and gallant Mary Garden—she writes in a recent letter from Aberdeen that each afternoon she serves tea on her front porch to the boys from the mine sweepers who daily risk their lives off Scottish shores. Mary Garden, after a lifetime of performances, now gives the best performance of her career each day on her front porch to an audience that includes her amazing mother and sisters and those grim-faced young lads. She will not return here until victory comes to the Allies.

Such women, who spelled glamour for their whole era and who brought outstanding talents to opera, remain charming and fascinating women without the finery of scenic props and the blood and thunder of the libretto.

Natural flair is more important than any other thing. That is true not only in making or breaking a career; it is true in the simple, yet complex, maddening business of just being a woman. Next in importance to natural flair is perspective—which is just another word for sense of humor. Perspective gives you the ability to stand off from yourself and discover certain talents and qualities within, sometimes quite by accident, so you can say, "Keep it; that's interesting, worth playing up all you can." If highly developed, this perspective adds up to astute showmanship—and whether for femininity's sake or career, is an invaluable asset.

When you are forming your ideas of being an artist, everything counts. Singing is just part of it. Even as a young girl I felt that one should think of one's talents as a service, as a means of reaching out to people and bringing them happiness. The mistake of many artists is that they develop an egotism before they render that service, and this pride of self weakens and flattens what they finally have to offer. I have always sung for people—to reach them, to touch them: not for cold, printed critical notices.

Just as I reach out instinctively to people from the platform, so have I made people part of my life. My friends never change. I have had them for years. What is more, I've liked them for years. The friends of my Broadway days, the friends of my Hollywood experiences, the friends I made in Europe and here, the good friends who have made the music, painted the pictures, written the books, and colored the amusements of the last two decades—who have done all these things but whom I like primarily because they have heart and wit—they are a dear and fixed part of my life that I would not change for any amount of wealth or power. And why should I? Who could ask for better ones?

I have my own approach to the people I meet. I want to get at them, even flirting with them across a dinner table if that paves the way. I am irresistibly drawn to self-made people, persons who have worked up from the bottom of the ladder. In my experience, so many of the people who have inherited wealth have been the worst-mannered, the worst-educated, the most unintellectual stuffed shirts, making a fetish of gaucherie. I run from them as from long-winded bores. With self-made people I have a warm and immediate sympathy, but only if they have acquired or kept good manners. I do not necessarily mean the standard "Yes, please," "No, please" variety—but rather the breeding that comes from having gone through the mill.

The saying goes that when you begin to reminisce, it is a sign of old age. But of course I don't feel that way. I have always been sentimental about friends and the things that have happened to me. And being southern and full of sentiment, I have spent all my money and time collecting and preserving tangible memories of my life. My Spanish husband—my one and only husband, to whom I have been married for more than a dozen years and whom I quite frankly adore—cares nothing at all for possessions. Like all Spaniards, he has the ability to simplify life to the essentials. He twits me about the nonsense of holding onto every scrap of paper, every letter, every inherently valueless bibelot or costly gift ever given me. That's the difference between Hibernians and Iberians—and Val forgives me, as a racial characteristic, my little brown trunk stuffed full of souvenirs.

That little brown trunk, now safely stowed away in our home in Connecticut, still has on it the faded sticker of the Fabre Line, dating back to the boat that sailed from Brooklyn on my first Mediterranean cruise. Jostling that sticker is another from the Grand Hotel at Sorrento, where I stood at the window of Caruso's suite, looked out over the Bay of Naples, and heard the peasants on the hillsides singing the familiar Italian folk songs as they picked the grapes. I felt quite unashamedly like crying because the world, at that moment, was as lovely as it was. There are stickers from the South of France, the North of France, England, Sweden, and high points east and west. And inside are mementos and letters with which I shall never part. Best of all, that little brown trunk is a constant reminder that there are many things yet remaining to go into it.

Naturally one's reminiscences aren't always sentimental, although it is curious how time lends a gloss to even the most ludicrous and humiliating experiences. Now I remember, as if I were glad it happened, the night I sang on a mountain crag at Carmel, New York, and couldn't see the audience for the fog. The fireflies flew into my mouth, and I sang standing in deep wet grass. The wind kept blowing the music off the piano, which we had borrowed from Billy Sullivan. Humphrey Doulens, traveling companion and manager of many concert tours, who is now serving in the United States Army, had gotten lost. The management asked would I mind if they announced the next week's bill, whereupon they introduced Blanche Yurka, who boomed out in her great elocutionary way for about fifteen minutes, while I stood shivering behind a tree.

All that kind of thing goes into a singing career. That—and Chautauqua concerts and being hypnotized in a store window and staying in dreadful hotels. The trials and tribulations of "the road"—terrible in the early days because of lack of money, again bad on account of wartime conditions. Opera at the Met, with all its intrigues and complications. The Opéra Comique in Paris; the opera houses of Liége, Deauville, Cannes, Rouen, and Bordeaux; Covent Garden in London. Concerts in Sweden, Norway, Denmark, Holland, Rumania, Poland, Mexico, Brazil, and other South American countries. Impromptu concerts everywhere—harmonizing with Charpentier in Montmartre, with Noel Coward as my accompanist in Paris, with Heifetz playing the piano for me aboard ship, barbershop quartets with Alec Woollcott and Charles MacArthur and Scott Fitzgerald.

This is the book of memoirs I have always wanted to write. My friends know me for simple spontaneity, no matter what the cost. It was Yvette Guilbert who once said to me: "It is not only our errors which ruin us, but our way of conducting ourselves after committing them." I want to tell the errors, but also the before and after. I want to talk about music, men, and making the most of what there is. I have found there's a lot. I do not like much of the world today and want it changed. Singing at camp shows, talking with the men who have returned from the front, convinces me that there has to be a shift in mind and spirit. But I have an incurable love of living. It's an aberration I was born with, in Tennessee. It looks, from the way I have lived my life, as if I shall never get over it.

By the Old Mill Stream— But Not for Long

I was born in Slabtown, Cocke County, Tennessee, only a few miles from my mother's family farm at Del Rio, Tennessee, in what I fondly like to imagine was a rose-covered little log cabin. My family insists that, picturesque as that may sound, it isn't true. "It was an ordinary modest shingle house," says Father, "the like of which you can find by the millions throughout American small towns. Don't go making it anything else." Well, Papa is probably right, but I *remember* it as a log cabin. There is no disagreement about the roses. Mama's greatest passion has always been her garden, and she has the true "green finger," with a genius for making things grow around her.

When she met Father, Mother had been something of a belle, with the slenderest waistline in Cocke County. He came riding out of the East, from Murphy, North Carolina—a knight on horseback selling dry goods and notions. From all accounts he was the handsomest traveling salesman who ever caught the eye of a farmer's daughter. The farmer in this case was William Stokley, prominent and respected veteran of the Civil War, who was not any too pleased when his daughter up and eloped with the stranger. However, reconciliation came after I was born and after Grandfather saw how conscientiously Papa settled down to run the general store in Slabtown (or, more recently, Nough) and provide for his family.

That general store had a sawmill on one side of it and a village church on the other. It was as typically American as hominy, and I can still catch, buried in the past, the whiff of calico as it flapped out of the bolts (there's a special odor to clean, unused cottons), the feel of sawdust under my bare toes, and the *chug-chug* of the old mill as it turned in the mountain current. Mother washed, cleaned, cooked, and tended her roses. Papa pursued his business of being a merchant with the same ardent concern he shows today as owner, with my brothers, of Loveman's Department Store in Chattanooga, Tennessee, which I call the Saks Fifth Avenue of the South (free advt.).

Papa has Scotch-Irish determination and ambition, two stalwart traits which have come down to me. Whatever "drive" I have is from him—as whatever gaiety, love of life, appreciation of and desire for beautiful possessions come from Mama. She is the most feminine of women, extravagant, generous, loving; he, the most forthright and stubborn of males, with persuasive charm which he can turn on or off at will. He started in at the little store in Slabtown with a tenacious belief in the American dream that to work hard, be honest, and take advantage of opportunity made anything possible for a young man. He was one whom that dream did not betray.

The visits to the Del Rio farm of the Stokleys were crammed with the kind of simple, satisfying experiences that flower into the most lasting memories. The Stokley family was a large one, and the big family dinners served on the vast oak table in front of the open fireplace, where most of the cooking was done, were full of noise, laughter, grownup farm talk, and our own childish conversations. At harvest time the noonday meal, served on the porches that circled the house, was heaped on platters in the middle of the table. Second and third helpings of fried chicken, homemade bread, fresh milk, butter from the spring house, and deep-dish apple pie were conveniently at hand. Grandma sent me to and fro, from house to porch, fetching this and that, and I remember, even at three, being worn but happy because I had taken part in the hospitality.

Harvest time always ended in a grand finale with the square dances, when the best fiddlers rode down from their mountain farms, the front parlor was thrown open, and everybody took part in the fun of "swinging your partner." The first songs I ever knew were "The Cherokee Girl" and "The Lost Indian," taught me by my Grandfather Stokley; and from Uncle Estel and Aunt Laura I learned how to call out the square dances with such abandon and gusto that, even at three, my shrill excited voice could handle the figures as well as an old-timer.

Wash day was another great event for me, no matter how blue a Monday it was for adults. We hauled a large wooden bucket filled with homemade soap that smelled strongly of lye and cleanliness down to the old sycamore tree by the side of the creek. There we would soap our cotton underwear on the big rocks and rinse them in the creek, letting the water bubble over the white garments till they rose and puffed up like sails in the wind. As a *reward* for what was the most delectable occupation in the world anyway, we were allowed to jump naked into the cool, purling waters of the creek.

Another wonderful chore was to ride the horses bareback through the fields at sunset, rounding up the cows for their homeward journey and the milking. We always kept our fingers crossed about getting home before dusk, because we had to pass the old family cemetery where relatives and slaves of the old days were buried. We were certain that "hants" roamed among the white headstones, brushing lightly and quickly through the tall grass, waiting only for us to pass, when they would lunge and force us to join them in nameless, unspoken horrors. There is a little cemetery near our present farm in Connecticut, and I never go past it after dark without remembering the old childish terror, and I quicken my steps to reach the front gate and safety before "they" get me.

Of all the Stokley aunts and uncles, Aunt Laura was my ideal. She had so many beaux, was always so popular and gay, that I thought to be like her would be the most enchanting thing in the world. She understood me, too, for she let me trail along with the grownups. In a sense I was her chaperon then, as later she was mine, and I learned a lot from her about the art of listening to a story, as well as the technique of telling one in turn.

Those days on the farm were so warm and filled with endless delights! Box suppers, when the taste of the miracle mixture in stuffed eggs was more delicious than any other food ever since tasted; the family gatherings in the front parlor, when everyone sang, off key and on, "The End of a Perfect Day"; earning my weekly stipend by pulling out the gray hairs from Grandma Stokley's head, five cents for every ten pulled. . . .

When Papa moved us to Knoxville, Tennessee, where he had gotten a much better job selling for the Daniel Briscoe Company, I had to say good-by to the farm. I was heartbroken at leaving behind all the familiar friends and animals. I hated my new city clothes and the awful city shoes—the first I had ever worn. I was certain I was going to loathe everything that had to do with this change.

I was almost five and aware of Mother's great pride in Papa's advancement, but even the new home, with its splendid heavy mahogany beds and divans and its upholstered rocking chairs, did not make up for the homeliness and comfort of my grandmother's high goose-feathered bed. I missed the goose feathers for another reason. I had been told that a feather pillow kept the lightning away. What was going to happen to us all if a bolt came down from the Knoxville sky? Today, when I can do, or not do, as I wish about superstitions, I prefer to take a little feather cushion with me on all my travels. After all, one never can tell.

The city soon took on other complications when I was sent off to my first school day at the kindergarten. Mother had done me up with the biggest pink bow she could find and a dress so starched that when I sat down the whole class tittered at the noise. I began my academic career in confusion and humiliation as I heard all the giggling around me. But the despair of that first embarrassment vanished in my adoration for my teacher. She was lovely and gentle and wistfully tragic, like a sentimental song about aching hearts and lovers' tears. She dressed in various shades of lavender, kept a bunch of violets on her desk, spoke always in subdued throbbing faraway tones, and wore a gold chain and watch around her neck which I was sure concealed the portrait of a long-ago sweetheart. Her fragility and paleness aroused my compassion, and when she died, at the end of that first year, of heart failure I was certain it was of a broken heart instead.

Knoxville was only an interlude, for we soon moved again, this time to Jellico, Tennessee, sixty miles away, in the heart of the lovely Cumberland Mountains. Although it was a much smaller town than Knoxville, it was a giant step up in Papa's career. He was now a partner in the Baird Dry Goods Company on the Main Street, and he could do much more for his rapidly increasing family than ever before. We were four children by then—Martin, the twins Estel and Emily, and myself. Perhaps I ought to mention here that I was christened Mary Willie Grace.

Working with a single-tracked purpose, his routine never varying from departure to the office at seven, home for dinner at noon, inevitable fifteen-minute nap, off again until supper at six, and back to the office until late at night, Papa was able, by the time the family had grown to eight children, to buy the big white Macombe house on Jellico's nicest street. It was the first place that was big enough to house us all, and our first real home. We still keep it, and today my mother loves nothing better than to sit on the porch and welcome the tourists who, as they approach the lovely valley of Jellico, are greeted by the sign, "This Is the Home Town of Grace Moore."

Everything in my life has been a long way from Jellico, yet everything starts there. I always felt a little apart in my own family and in the town, and I created a terrific imaginary world to sustain me. Economically my childhood was comfortable but modest—with not enough money to hinder freedom, yet not too little to hinder growth. I have been shaped by the "little" important tragedies that come out of the prejudice of a small town as well as by wholesome small-town fun.

The greatest handicap of the southern town was its prejudice. There was always the turbulence that came out of having a Catholic problem, a Jewish problem, a Negro question. Papa brought us up not to be anti-anything, and the hatred in which such a small town was steeped seemed to me strange. The one thing I watch with greatest pride about the South is its gradual but persistent change. All along I felt that all people were born to equal opportunity because that is the way my mother and father lived their lives. And I don't mean opportunity handed out on a silver platter, but opportunity that was there without social or racial strings for anyone who had the initiative to reach and hold.

The first Jewish friends we had in Jellico were the Garbers, and Goldie Garber remains one of my mother's dearest companions to this day—in addition to being one of my greatest fans. For the Catholics I had a warm and atavistic sympathy—a feeling that lurked in my Irish ancestry. One of the great prides of Jellico was being able to take visitors to one side of the town and say "Look, put one foot there, another here—see, now you're half in Tennessee and half in Kentucky." Right over the line in Kentucky was a tiny Catholic church. Rather shabby, ugly, and ramshackle on the outside, it held the mystery of a strange, other world within. I would come into it in awe; then, falling solemnly to my knees, would say a quick little prayer and run away, back to the Baptist solidity of Tennessee. Today I am married to a Catholic, and that kinship for the warm, passionate pageantry of the Church still holds.

On the hill back of our new house was the colored Baptist church, and the first time I ever remember being impressed by music was when I went there with our nurse, "Aunt Willie," and heard the colored minister "pray a spiritual." "Let us all pray," said the minister. Then his voice rose in song: "Our heavenly Father, on this day we thank Thee," and a swelling chorus grew around him as each brother and sister answered "Amen, amen." Finally everyone in the congregation had lifted his voice, had woven his part into an uninhibited contrapuntal masterpiece. Swept up by the spontaneous emotion, my young tremolo voice joined in with "Praise the Lord," and I found myself singing, for the first time, from a deep inner need. From the musical faith of these simple colored people, music crept into my blood and became part of my faith too.

The greatest difficulty I had in adjusting myself to Jellico was in my superabundance of what one might call animal spirits. I was always getting into the most outrageous messes—innocent childish messes that unfortunately led to disproportionate censure and then to an inferiority complex which has hung on through my whole adult life and made for me most of my enemies.

I was a skinny, long-legged ugly girl, good at sports, much disliked by the other girls, but a pal to all the boys in the neighborhood. That was a result of the coaching given me by my brothers. Emily, my only sister, was lovely and feminine and not energetic. Her seeming fragility, however, hid a firmness of will that played ducks and drakes with us all. We waited on her hand and foot and were all proud of the admiration and praise which were always given her. Since the softer side of the family was well represented by Emily, I was able to join with my brothers in the more energetic phases of Jellico life. We roamed the mountains, camped and cooked out during vacation days, and sometimes made our own vacations when it was too lovely outdoors to be tied to a desk inside. I became skilled in copying Mama's handwriting and delivering little "please excuse" notes to my adored teacher, Miss Mabel McSweem. She loved me enough to trust me.

On one such hookey excursion I wandered down to the violet field a few miles from the school, picked huge bunches of the little flowers, and waded in the creek. Presently, tired from my pleasant exertions, I went to sleep on the riverbank under a bridge. As I slept, the rain fell, the river rose over its banks, and I woke up to find myself struggling in the water. I was soaking wet, hungry and worried, but I waited until dark so I could sneak home through back streets, into the back door, and—I hoped—out of sight. My plans fell through when I was caught sidling in through the kitchen, and I was thoroughly switched for all my misdeeds—including everything from forgery to forgetfulness. I went up to my room, sore but not chastened. The restlessness, the longing for freedom, which has dominated most of my life was strong in me even then as I rubbed my backsides. I figured that the afternoons of elbow room I had had out in the fields and away from school were compensation enough for the momentary humiliation of a spanking.

Even when I achieved the limelight of captaining the basketball team, I came a cropper from too much Irish ancestry. The fatal climax to my career as head of the Jellico Bear Cats was brought on by a red-headed girl with an Irish ferocity to match my own. We were playing on our home ground, and she came with the visiting team. It was a great day for the family, and they had front-row seats to cheer me on. All was going well until the red-headed opponent tripped me up and then violated all laws of basketball and Hoyle by tickling me. I was definitely not amused. I was hopping mad. I took her by the beautiful head of red hair, she grabbed me by the waist, I pinched, she kicked, the two teams joined in, I lost my dark blue bloomers, and the game was called off.

Poor Mama and Papa! As their neighbors rose indignantly to leave, demanding their money back, they muttered to my family, "What can you do with Grace?" I heard the complaints and they didn't calm me. Standing bloomerless, with legs straddled wide apart, I shouted, "Well, if the game is over, it's not my fault and to hell with it."

Mama and Papa managed to get me home, where they read the riot act to me about being a lady. I promised I'd try, and I lay awake all night wondering how one went about it. Apparently no thunderclap or visitation came to me in the darkness, for soon afterwards I was again a public scandal (and definitely no lady). The circus had come to town, and my brothers and I, playing hookey, set out for the big tent. We were so caught in the aroma of sawdust and romance that we became dissatisfied with being merely onlookers and went to work for the circus for the sum of ten dollars apiece and glory.

Our jobs were wonderful. My brothers were hired to be clowns and I to ride an elephant during the big parade called for ten o'clock. A razzle-dazzle blonde took me in hand, painted my face, hung a spangled dress on my uncurved length, put a tall hat with waving plumes on my head, and squeezed my feet into gaudy shoes with rhinestone heels. When she was finished with me I looked enough like an electric-light bulb to be given the biggest elephant at the head of the parade. Waving a flag in one hand and a horn in the other, through which I boomed at intervals, "Follow us for the Big Show starting at one o'clock," we set out. What magnificence! Trumpets blared, the band noisily huffed and puffed at a Sousa march through crowded Main Street, the curbs were lined with everybody I knew. I waved and signaled proudly to my friends, calling, if anything, even more attention to my un-Jellicoish position. Suddenly I found myself in front of Father's store. Even the elephant was stopped short by the stony look of horror on my father's face as he looked out and saw me.

"My God," he screamed, "it's Grace."

Not being a man to hesitate when principles are involved, Father flew into the street, reached up and yanked me off the elephant, trying all the time to cover my face with a handkerchief in the hope of disguising me from the possible neighbors who had not yet been treated to my superspectacle. I was pulled, kicking and screaming, into the store. I was outraged and humiliated not only at having been swept from my elevated perch with such vigor, but also because I realized that once again I had failed to master the A B C's of proper Jellico behavior.

Recently in Charlotte, North Carolina, I saw my first highschool teacher again, Mrs. Rebecca Reid, who with her short bobbed hair and intelligent face would look, if she had a few more pounds, like the image of Gertrude Stein. When I told her I was writing my autobiography, she said with a smile, "You may not be naughty now, but you certainly were then."

A momentous happening of my childhood was when I won the first prize for a chocolate cake I baked for the county fair in Jackson, Tennessee. All southern girls learn to cook, and I was no exception. At that same fair I won second prize for singing and third prize for spelling, but the first prize for the chocolate cake was the Congressional Medal itself. I might add that one of my greatest prides is still my cookery. I love to cook, studied the finer points at the Cordon Bleu in Paris, and continue to experiment today with all kinds of recipes, herbs, and pure imagination; but no matter what wonderful dish I concoct, I take no more joy in it than in that chocolate dream that took the cake in Jackson, Tennessee.

Religion came to me through music. There was no music outside our church singing, except for the occasional hay-ride outbursts of such sentimental numbers as "Down by the Old Mill Stream." I loved hymns and dreamed of getting into the church choir. I wanted to sing because singing made me feel alive and happy, but I never thought of song outside the church. My religious fervor mounted as I took more and more joy in the music. I was baptized and at peace with myself and the world. Then a young minister came to Jellico from work as a missionary in China. Because I found him the best-looking and softest-spoken man in the whole of my world, and because too of the stories of Chinese struggle and sacrifice for Christianity, I felt a new humility; I decided to be baptized again.

One Sunday, when the call came for repentant sinners, I rose and marched proudly down the aisle in complete disregard of the fact that I had been saved only a few weeks before. As I neared the front pew where Father was sitting, he reached over, caught my pigtails, and hauled me over to the side. One honest baptism, he believed, should be enough for any soul—and here I was, once more making a spectacle of myself.

I must confess there was even a third baptism—this time Father was not on hand to pull me aside before the deed was done. My final conversion came when the colored Baptist church had a public baptism in a creek near Newcomb, Tennessee, and my brothers and I went out to watch it. The passion and tumult of Brother Johnson's plea for sinners, the great waves of mass singing that swept over me, proved too much for my soul, and again I sought salvation, finding it this time in the muddy waters of the local Jordan.

The adolescent fervor of my religion, occasioned not by sin but by a need for dedication, took a practical turn. I decided to be a missionary to China. There were many of the neighbors who said I had so overplayed the baptismal business that I apparently didn't know what I was doing, but I felt I did. I wanted to give myself selflessly and completely to religious work. I headed a Sunday-school class, sang in the church choir, became president of the Baptist Young People's Union, and to polish off a full Sabbath of sanctified activity, attended the Sunday evening service. Then, after one year of diligent application, I received my diploma from the Baptist Seminary College in Louisville, Kentucky. I felt that with this certificate, plus my high-school diploma (I had graduated from Jellico High School), I was prepared to learn missionary work in the Orient.

Tragedy awaited me—classic tragedy compounded of nemesis and inevitability. My nemesis, as always, was the small town's prejudice. Inevitability was implicit in my too great love of life.

It was the rule of our church that no dancing was permitted its members. Even the game of "rook" was frowned on from the Baptist pulpit and considered fit only for Presbyterians. I knew all this, had already felt the impact of the blue code of community procedure. But knowing does not always put a brake on impulse. One night I ventured a few dance steps at a social gathering. This cataclysmic scandal was reported to the church deacons the next day. The Jellico *Sentinel,* the town paper, followed with an editorial about certain young church members dancing on the road to perdition. My blameless slide-slide-and-waltz, which had taken all of five minutes, turned the town into an uproar. There was a flutter of lace curtains as I walked down the street. It took a brave heart to speak to me. The disgrace and shame became more than I could bear. I agreed with my father that Brother Martin's request for a public apology might be for the best and prepared myself for that ordeal at the next Wednesday prayer meeting.

That Wednesday night is one I shall never forget. It takes first place in my life in intense mortification and torture. The people filing in solemnly to their places—each face so reserved and sure of itself. Then the young faces—of the girls and boys (mostly boys) who were there to stand by me because my disgrace was a symbol of what they wished they dared demand: the right to dance without wickedness as the young should dance. My mother, my father—their faces sad with suffering. At the appointed time I rose and asked forgiveness for my innocent infraction of church discipline and pleaded for a return to the church's good graces. Scattered amens came from this corner and that, and I scarcely heard the final hymn as my father led me quietly away.

This was torture beyond youthful endurance. I was shaken with it, shaken with its pettiness, its mercilessness, its inhumanity. I determined to run away from home. Packing what I thought necessary into a large kerchief, I ran—as far as the hilltop near Jellico, in the opposite direction from the railroad station. There I sat, under the full moon, in grim adolescent thought, trying to come to some conclusion about myself, my inabilities to fit into Jellico, and the world at large.

I still wanted to be a missionary because, in all sincerity, it represented an escape that no one could criticize me for. But the harshness of the church discipline had driven an iron into my soul. Life was so difficult to understand, so hemmed in, and I ached so to give it wings. (I was only fourteen—how tragic everything is then!) I knew what I really wanted, and there, on that hilltop, I admitted it to myself. I wanted to be a missionary through my music. I knew that, to attain music, I had to study it. I had mentioned the possibility before to Father, but he had dismissed it as a passing interest which I might indulge if I wanted to, but not to the exclusion of other, more "normal" interests. Now the conviction of what I really wanted steadied me. Instead of running away, I would return to Jellico and plead with Father once more. I knew he felt it might be wise for me to go to some kind of school until I reached the sedate and ripe age of sixteen, at which time I could marry the beau I had in the offing. Contrary to present-day headlines from Tennessee, anything younger than sixteen was considered too early for marriage. I wanted to study music, with music—not marriage—in mind. I still had two years in which Father could send me to school without questioning my purpose.

Ward-Belmont College in Nashville had a department for the study of voice, piano, harmony, sight reading, and French. Father had just been appointed to the governor's staff, and I thought it would make everything simpler for him if I suggested to him that I attend Ward-Belmont. He agreed, poor man, probably with a silent prayer that all might go well. Although I was never permitted out later than nine-thirty and never met my beaux farther from home than the garden gate, where all of my trysting was done, I knew that Papa would not rest easy until I was safely married. I considered his permission for me to go away to school a kind of momentary triumph.

My life at Ward-Belmont did not last long. I loved working with my vocal teacher and felt, for the first time, an excitement in the use of my own voice. But I was lonely and restless. I found it difficult to make friends and couldn't make a niche for myself anywhere because I tried so hard to fit in everywhere. Mrs. Rose, the girls' dean, would call me in daily for a lecture on the meaning of right and wrong, trying to impress me gradually as if she despaired of ever making me understand. (Two years ago, when I returned there to sing, Mrs. Rose again called me into her office, closed the door and said, with a twinkle in her eye, "My dear Grace, do you now know the difference between right and wrong?" My answer then, as it unconsciously must have been always, was a quiet, "Do you?")

These constant interviews with Mrs. Rose came to an end when I sneaked out one night, with another girl, to go to a dance at Vanderbilt University. Misfortune again. Here was my nemesis. I never did anything deliberately wrong unless there were pointless restrictions which caused my rebellion. According to the rules of the school I was doing wrong, but because my own concepts told me I was doing right I proceeded with the little adventure. The next thing I knew I was back home in Jellico—where the more malicious neighbors pointed fingers and crowed, "We knew she'd never come to any good."

Ward-Belmont had not been, as I saw it, a total loss. It had given me a point of view. It convinced me that I wanted a singing career above all else. Before I went, I had known about the musical world only through the *Musical Etude* and a limited number of phonograph records. The sounds of the voices coming through the horn of "His Master's Voice" seemed beyond human accomplishment. In the class at Ward-Belmont I had heard my own voice, for the first time, reaching and prolonging fairly high clear notes. The shock had nearly stunned me.

From the first day my teacher had treated me with special concern and started guiding my young enthusiasm in the right direction. He gave me special work in piano, harmony, and sight reading and encouraged intense study of French and English literature. Even though I "prematurely" returned home from Ward-Belmont, I felt that I could, perhaps, sing myself out of the narrow restrictions of my life into a bigger, more generous world. I was determined to try.

War against Germany was declared by President Wilson the day I returned to Jellico. I must admit it was merely a newspaper headline to me then. I started in on the "serious" business of checking up on music schools, determined to get into one if I had to work my way through. Father argued, but found me obstinate. This was my one chance, my passport. I battled Papa with all the persuasion and stubbornness I could muster. Then, because he seemed immovable, I decided to go off by myself to the Wilson-Greene School of Music in Washington. I borrowed the money from a family friend to pay my fare to the capital, packed my trunk, and announced to my family that I was off to the station. Father knew, as he looked at me, all dressed and ready to go, that I was as adamant as he. He gave in, returned the borrowed money, and deciding to put the best face on my departure to save further public display of my difficulties, set out with me for Washington.

We arrived in the capital in a flurry of snow and walked the last two blocks from the streetcar to the unimpressive main building of the school on Connecticut Avenue. A uniformed butler let us in. Another crisis almost resulted when, as we passed the front hall, we saw a group of girls in a side room playing billiards.

"This is no music school," said Father, stopping short at the sight, "and I am not spending my money to send you away from home to learn to play pool."

Fortunately the directors of the school, the Wilson-Greenes, appeared, took Papa in hand, and in an hour had charmed him into a state of affability with a liberal administration of Irish blarney. As Papa said good-by to me that night I felt a pang of tenderness and pity. He had wanted so hard to understand me, as I wanted to understand him, but we were both stubborn and determined in our convictions. Undoubtedly it was the warring of temperaments which resulted in my desire to make or break my own future. Papa left me with a final warning. This was, he said, my last trial. "You are to get an education along with your musical studies and then plan to marry some nice fellow and raise a family." This was his idea of making good (and a fine one it is too, although it was not mine at the time). "If you don't," Papa warned, "you are on your own."

I worked hard at the Wilson-Greene School. I absorbed the seven hours of daily study like a thirsty sponge. I liked the girls, some of whom were rich and merely dabblers in music. They were all so attractive and gay. Best of all I loved the concerts and theaters to which we went, heavily chaperoned. They opened up a bright, heady world, far from the straitened one of Jellico.

Alma Gluck was the first great star I ever heard. I shall never forget the way she glided onto the stage. Nor shall I forget her slim figure draped in gold cloth, her poised head and friendly smile. She had had a baby a short time before, and her voice was warm with tenderness, especially when she sang a lullaby as part of her brilliant program. We were all taken backstage to meet her afterwards and were struck with her dark beauty. Years later I was to meet her once more, introduced to her by Frank Crowninshield at supper in the old Knickerbocker Hotel. Again, as when I was an excited schoolgirl in Washington, I was surprised at how beautiful she was. She wore her black braids wrapped peasant-madonna fashion around her head. Her brown eyes, deep as velvet, were warm with kindness. I couldn't help thinking, when I met her later, of what all the girls in Washington would have thought if they could have seen me then leaving the restaurant with Crowninshield and Condé Nast and being driven away in Alma Gluck's Rolls-Royce. The vision of my school friends' popping eyes held as the footman put the mink rug over my knees, and I almost nodded to them across the years as I sank back into the luxurious upholstery and tried not to show how impressed I was.

Then I asked a peculiar question. "It's such a lovely car. Does it cost much money to get one?"

I said it as much for my own benefit as for back-through-the-years information for that former schoolgirl group.

"My dear," she answered, not at all put out by the impertinence of my question, "I just paid for it today with twenty thousand dollars which was part of a hundred-thousand-dollar check for royalties sent me by the Victor Company."

The fact that there was that much money in the whole world or that one could earn it by singing was still a secret of the future that night in Washington. What impressed me most when I first heard Alma Gluck was the real affection the audience showed for her.

The most important event of my life that year was hearing and meeting Mary Garden for the first time. In Jellico I had swallowed word for word every story the *Musical Etude* ever printed about her. She had been the shining lodestar of my dreams. When we were taken to hear her at her concert in Washington I was trembling with nervous excitement—until I saw her come onto the stage. Then I knew I was not to be disappointed. She had flaming red-blonde hair and a face and body so alive they were music themselves before she sang a single note. Years afterwards when I grew to understand Garden's art, I realized that her moments of silence on the stage were as pregnant with her artistry as the sound of her voice.

The whole group of girls from the school was taken backstage to meet Garden after the concert. Face to face with her, no words came from my tightened throat. Impulsively I threw myself on my knees and kissed her hand. Her astonishment was covered with an embarrassed laugh, but her eyes sought me out as the line of girls faded past. She beckoned me over to her. Mrs. Wilson-Greene, who was the Washington concert manager for most of the musicians who came there to sing, introduced me to Garden and to Garden's manager, Charles Wagner.

I stood before her, quivering. She smiled and asked me if I was a young singer. "Yes," I blurted out, "and you are my goddess." She took the extravagance graciously. Patting my cheek, she looked at me with a long, penetrating glance and said, "We shall meet again one day."

I went home that night with my inner dreams for a career now fortified by a new resolve. I *had* to meet the wonderful Mary Garden again. I *had* to sing to prove to her how much she meant to me. My purpose became so strengthened that suddenly the school seemed lacking in seriousness. I became restless and dissatisfied because there wasn't more work demanded of me. I asked for a conference with Mrs. Wilson-Greene and mumbled something of my desire to her. Her answer was a promise that the next season I would be given opportunity to try my wings as the assisting artist on one of the programs which the visiting concert stars gave under her management. Since my second-year course was to end the following June, this concert could be my graduation program.

I returned to Jellico for the summer vacation happier than I had been for a long time, but boiling with secret hopes. Wandering on the hills near home those months, I went over and over again in my mind this new serious approach to a career in music. The war, curiously enough, had meant little to me in Washington. I felt it now in Jellico, where the absence of so many of the local young men, the tension of their families, had personal meaning within the circle of a small town. I knew that the war would interfere with my outspoken wish to be a missionary. Why had I wanted to be a missionary? I tried to answer my own question honestly. There were two reasons. One, I had a joy in living and a sadness in living that I wanted to bring to and share with others. Two, I had sought escape. But now, I thought, art is a way of service too: not merely through the singing in which I myself took joy, but because it was an extension of self, a giving, through music, of everything one took from life. And a musical career would mean escape—not only would it free me from the humdrum existence of middle-class life in a small southern town, it would free me to be of greater use because I myself would take more joy in living. I came to the conclusion, that summer in the hills of Jellico, that it was, in all humility, what I wanted to do more than anything else in the world.

I returned to school that fall with nothing said to my family of these ambitions, but with one purpose in view—serious preparation for the promised concert on which hinged the door to a definite beginning.

The Armistice was signed in November. The world went mad that day, but I, always the sentimentalist, remember only a little restaurant where I had gone with school friends and a chaperon and in a corner at an upright piano softly played and sang "Rose in Bud" (of all things) as I gazed into the eyes of my best beau, Fisher Hepburn. He was a major assigned to an important defense job whom I had met in Washington. He was much older than I, but gay and charming, and one of the best friends I ever had. Until his tragic death in a fire at the Union Club in Cleveland he used always to send me violets or sweetheart roses each day. He was romantic, trustworthy, gallant, and it was he who helped me hurdle the first obstacles from Washington to New York, after the promised concert.

One morning Mrs. Wilson-Greene took me to the National Theatre where, on the gloomy badly lit stage, I auditioned some songs for Charles Wagner, Garden's impresario. He agreed to let me be the assisting artist at Giovanni Martinelli's forthcoming appearance. I worked night and day, with feverish consecrated intensity, towards the great event. The afternoon finally came. A full house awaited the famous tenor, but the only people aware that this was the biggest moment of my life were the girls from the school, my teachers, and loyal Fisher Hepburn.

Martinelli sang magnificently, and I can still remember him, as I stood quaking in the wings awaiting my turn, with his lion's head of electrified gray hair and his enormous joviality. As I crept unsteadily out on the stage that dismal February afternoon and let out my small soprano in the sententious aria "Ritorna vincitor" from *Aïda,* it must have seemed like a ludicrous squeak after the soaring Martinelli voice. But the audience was friendly and tolerant and I could hear their kindly applause as I left the stage, half unconscious with the effort, strain, and excitement. The next morning when I read the criticism (a pernicious habit I have never overcome) one paragraph engraved itself on my mind, and the last three words gave me the courage I needed.

"Yesterday," it read, "at the National Theatre a concert was given by a lion and a mouse! The lion was the famous tenor Giovanni Martinelli—the mouse, a young lyric soprano from Tennessee *who showed promise."*

After that concert all the girls at the school accepted the fact that I was headed for a career. I did not agree definitely in words, but my attitude confirmed their suspicions. Mr. and Mrs. Greene, seeing the turn of events and aware of my family's opposition to any thought of a career, sent for Father. He came—and there followed, in the private Greene living room that afternoon, a terrific scene which disrupted the whole school. For the first time I openly declared my intentions. Papa was shocked and horrified. How could a southern girl of any "standing" even dream of going on the STAGE! He stormed and threatened, fighting this disgrace. Fuel was added to the hostilities when a little love poem from Fisher Hepburn, stolen from my bureau drawer by a sneaking maid, was thrown at me. Here was added proof, claimed Papa, that I was out for no good.

I was furious that something which had nothing at all to do

with the principle involved should be introduced as evidence. I was furious—and chagrined. Eager only to end the whole shameful session, I promised to finish the term and think over my decision during the next summer vacation in Jellico. Papa returned home, and I was left under careful guard at the school, with only one confidante and friend, Blanche LeGarde. Blanche, who was from Virginia, was studying piano and dancing at the school, and she now became the intermediary between me and Fisher. It was to her, and through her to him, that I announced my decision to break my promise to return to Jellico. I felt that the promise had been torn from me under duress, with the whole school listening in the corridors. I feared that once I was back home the family would beat down my resolve. It was now or never to me, and I determined to break away at once.

Blanche and Fisher became my unwitting and rather unwilling confederates in crime. They were worried about my decision to leave the school so informally, but, once they saw my firmness, were stanch enough to stand by. Leaving the school building was easy enough. One night in the rain I just walked out. I drove to the Poinciana Hotel and registered under the plumes-and-grease-paint name of Genevieve Morena. I locked myself in the tiny room, called Fisher, announced my escape, and requested a loan. Finally he agreed—but tempered the loan with a sharp lecture on the evils of being headstrong and the need for caution. I took both money and advice with a promise of early future repayment.

Because I had no idea of how to get around in New York, and was secretly panicky about trying, the plan was that I should wait in Washington while Blanche obtained a legitimate release from the school, which would take a week. She would then go ahead to the big city and signal me to follow. I spent that intervening time in solitary confinement while private detectives, hired by school and family, combed the city.

I knew what my family's consternation at my absence must be. I was saddened by the thought. But my own conviction that they would never willingly be reconciled to my plans held my filial emotions in check. One day the call from Blanche came, and with my borrowed three hundred dollars and my courage, I found myself on a train headed for New York. Blanche met me at the station. She was by that time not too sure herself where I was headed for, so she had enrolled me at the Martha Washington Hotel, a female hostelry down on Twenty-ninth Street. We went there from the station. As I walked through that austere, sinless lobby of white-haired grandmothers and clear-conscienced teachers, and was shown to a tiny room with white iron bed, two straight unbending chairs, and a washbowl, I was glad for all that solid, unflamboyant simplicity which gave me a sense of old-maidish security in the midst of the frightening New York City noises.

First days in important places have always been great days with me. That first day in New York two people came into my life who remained there through the years. One was Ruth Obre, sister of Arthur Obre, an Annapolis midshipman friend, who met us for luncheon at Schrafft's. She was a private secretary in fabled Wall Street who was later to marry three famous husbands, the last, André Dubonnet of the French apéritif family. Ruth is now the chatelaine of a great French château. I wonder if in her present isolated splendor in a temporarily Nazi-occupied France with which gossip says she has collaborated, she sometimes longs for the good easy live-and-let-live days and her live-and-let-live ·American friends. That first typically tourist day (luncheon at Schrafft's, matinee at a musical) also brought Clifton Webb within the scope of my experience. It was that afternoon from behind the footlights that he first danced his way into my admiration. That admiration, coupled with affection, still holds today after almost twenty years of friendship.

The plan of campaign organized by Blanche and Ruth was that I should set out to look for a job early the next day. They recommended the Packard Agency. Taking their advice, I showed up there bright and early the next day. Bright and early the day after that. And after that! I camped there for most of a week. Finally I did get inside the boss's office. He put the inevitable question: what was my experience? I was prepared. Confidently

I answered that I had been touring the West Coast in the operetta, *The Lilac Domino*. He looked me squarely in the eye and answered simply, "That ain't so, for that's our company." After a week of waiting to get in, I now waited to get thrown out. Instead I was permitted to sing. I sang.

"Nice voice, good figure, pretty in a fresh country way," was the laconic verdict, voiced in a cold, unimpressed voice by the boss, as if he were picking melons for a market. "Take her name," he added to the secretary.

I went out jubilant. Imagine having my name taken! I was so encouraged that I wrote my family at once, telling them of my whereabouts and emphasizing my determination to stay in New York and seek a career. I realized, I wrote them, their heartache and worry: I asked only for time and belief in me.

The answer was the appearance of Father, early one morning, storming the bastille of the Martha Washington. I was summoned to the lobby by a terrorized clerk who announced Father's presence below. I came down to meet him in such defiance that two of the "old girls" fled the lobby in alarm. Anxious to keep things as quiet as possible, I steered him out of the hotel to the nearest Child's restaurant. There, over coffee and doughnuts, I made a final compromise. I agreed to try to do only the "classics," such as Shakespeare, since at least these were more ladylike. I promised to apply to David Belasco at once for the leading role in *Romeo and Juliet*. And I also made clear to Father that I was so set on this way of life that as long as I pursued it I would never ask him for one cent to help me out.

When Father returned South that day, I'm certain he was a shaken man. I know that I too was shaken. Now, at last, I was free to take up my ambitions and turn them into a career. But for the first time I was completely on my own. At least it was the Age of Innocent Optimism. The year was 1919, life was good, and the future had been saved for democracy.

From Black Cat to Broadway

NOT LONG AGO Val and I had luncheon at Ludwig Bemelmans' apartment overlooking Gramercy Park. Our friend Jules Bache, a great raconteur in his own right, was also a guest. Bemelmans has a mad, ingratiating sense of humor, a way of announcing himself to the telephone operators at my hotel as the "King of Bavaria" that invariably throws them into a dither, and a five-year-old daughter who identifies me as the lady who sings Mrs. Butterfly. She is a remarkable child. As memory goes bad with Bemelmans, he turns to her and asks, for example, "What was the name of the man in Quito who had the old Hispano-Suiza filled with polo mallets but no horse?" Barbara always knows.

I hadn't been to Gramercy Park in a long, long time. I leaned out of the Bemelmans' window, from which the statue of Booth, hedged in by many colored tulips, could be seen, and felt a surging return of old memories.

"Why so pensive?" asked Bemelmans.

"Well, you know," I said, pointing to a red brick building at the corner of the square, "see those large windows? That's my girlhood over there. I haven't been back in years. That's where I started in New York."

Bemelmans stuck his round Puckish head out the window and looked to where I pointed. "Really? Those windows?" he said. "Isn't that funny? I tried to get that studio for myself. But it's a music school for little girls. The nearest I come to it is that Barbara is a pupil there."

The thought of young Barbara going one-and-two-and-three in

the same studio where Blanche LeGarde, Ruth Obre, a sculptress named Lilian who joined our ranks, and I put in such a wacky happy time seemed somehow very funny and curiously apt. With Blanche tossing her seven veils around in "the dance," Lilian in another corner pushing and patting a lump of clay, Ruth in and out with an eye always on the main chance, and I bellowing at the top of my lungs in a series of disastrous scales—we were not so far in spirit and unhardened hope from the present-day music-school fledglings.

With my first job I found the courage to leave the austerity of the Martha Washington Hotel. That job, while it was not grand opera, brought food and fun. It all came about one night when we were strolling around Greenwich Village. Blanche, Ruth, and I often went downtown for our dinner as much because it was inexpensive as because we were impressed by the desiccated candle-lit romance that went along with the food below Fourteenth Street. Leaving the little restaurant where we had dined, we walked up the street past the "Black Cat." It was so gay and crowded that out of wistful curiosity we stopped and looked in. A talkative master of ceremonies was in the process of offering a little vanity case as prize for a winning song sung by any girl in the place. There was a great deal of horseplay as various girls came forward and sang. Suddenly Blanche, in a wild-goose mood, dared me to try, virtually pushing me through the entrance onto the floor.

There I stood. The M.C. dangled the little vanity case before my eyes. There was nothing to do but sing, so I sang Herbert's "Kiss Me Again." Everything went off splendidly until I reached the last "kiss me, kiss me," when the final "again" was stifled by a young man who stood up with an "I sure will" and kissed me. Whatever it may have been as a kiss, it was certainly a marvelous punch line on the song, and the "Black Cat" howled with pleasure. The manager, pleased with the applause, hustled the three of us into the back room and offered me a week's trial as the club's singer, at thirty-five dollars, with dinner and supper and a guarantee of no kisses. He also introduced me to the young man who had helped me bring down the house—and a job: Walter Dean Goldbeck.

Walter Goldbeck was to become one of the best friends I had in those early days in New York and later the first husband of Ruth Obre. He was a brilliant portrait painter, with a personal charm that was to exert a strange and powerful influence on my thinking. He led me down the garden path of Freud and got me all mixed up with symbolism and portents. "Your dreams," he pointed out, "are more important than you think." Later he got me to analyzing those dreams of mine, and in despair because I couldn't find the importance Walter talked about in them, I wrote to Mother, suggesting that, if she was depressed, she write down her dreams at once and send them to me. *I* would settle the depression in no time. I'm afraid Mother linked my attachment to the venerable Sigmund with the other evils of theatrical life and answered, by fast mail, that I ought to stick to Shakespeare.

Walter, in addition to being a fine painter, was also the possessor of an excellent voice. He introduced me to his Italian music teacher who was "good and cheap," he said, and suggested I take lessons from him too. Walter's own curious personality, Freud, and the Italian music master who was cheap but *not* good were later to prove a combination too tough for my Tennessee simplicity to handle; but I have always been grateful for the experience that did come of it.

With a job, food guaranteed, and a music teacher, I felt permanently on the way. Blanche, Ruth, and I found a fourth to chip in on a place to live, and the Gramercy Park studio-and-alcove apartment was the result. Now I was working in earnest. Each night I sang to pay my share of the expenses. Each day I bellowed out scales as Walter's Italian music teacher instructed and because I knew no better. It was a good life and the whole world was covered with a rosy glow.

I did remember the promise to Father to do something about the Immortal Bard. The family felt that if somehow I stuck to Shakespeare the taint of theatrical life would be rubbed off. Since my only Shakespearean stock in trade was the classroom interpretations of Juliet's more tender passages—with a southern accent—I tried those out on my studio mates. They agreed that only the great Belasco could fathom the depths of my histrionic art.

There was nothing to do but go see Belasco. I had met Morris Gest one night in the studio Walter Goldbeck shared with his mother. That brief meeting gave me justification in my own mind —without Gest's acquiescence—to use the magic Gest name in getting past the receptionist in Mr. Belasco's outside office. I preferred to ignore the receptionist's peculiar look when she asked me in what connection I wished to see Mr. Belasco. I replied that I had come to read Juliet for him in the hope of doing it under his management. After waiting for two hours, I was finally ushered into the Belasco presence.

At this point I almost bolted and ran, for here was the first really imposing person I had met on Broadway to take the starch out of even my youthful brashness. He sensed my ebbing courage and gently asked me to sit down. I did. Then, when he asked me to read Juliet's passage from the balcony scene, my knees trembled so I could not move from the chair but stuttered the opening phrases from its enormous upholstered depths, southern accent and all. Mr. Belasco was kind but frank—and very firm. He didn't throw me out the window as I deserved, but gave me some candid advice instead. He guessed that I was a young singer, for he said I vocalized each word. He told me to approach Shakespeare through music and recommended that I learn Gounod's music for *Romeo and Juliet*. Years later, when I was to debut as Juliet at the Metropolitan, David Belasco and Morris Gest had orchestra seats and came backstage after the performance to offer their congratulations. But that first trip to Belasco's office had many, many years to bear Shakespearean fruit, and Father's hopes for a career in the classics had a long wait ahead.

I took the return bus downtown, reported to my studio mates that I had *not* been given the lead in Juliet, and threw myself completely into my vocal studies—which, with Goldbeck's music master, meant shrieking at the top of my lungs for many hours each day. My voice had grown; that I could feel. But something was wrong. For though it was strong in the high range, it was virtually non-existent in the middle. I know now that what was happening to me is what has happened to so many eager young trusting students who have come under the tutelage of the wrong teacher. Instead of permitting my voice to grow and become enlarged naturally, I was being forced into a terrific vocal fatigue. Furthermore, my friendship with Walter Goldbeck was producing psychological overtones that strained my nerves, produced confusion, and left me thoroughly exhausted. The result was inevitable. One day, in the middle of a lesson, my throat muscles tightened and I could not sing a note. I tried, tried again, but all there was in the studio was a deathly gloomy silence. My teacher was completely unalarmed. Closing the piano, he patted me on the shoulder and advised me to rest for a few days. Then he departed, his job well done!

As I stood there, completely sunk, Walter walked into the studio. I told him what had happened. He begged me to marry him at once and promised to take care of me. This was the final complication. I wasn't in love. I wanted to sing. With my voice gone, the future stretched bleakly before me. I put Walter off, asked him to go, and promised to let him know what I should decide to do. Instead of emotional *Sturm und Drang* I wanted protection and sound advice. I was to turn to old friends—not new ones—to get them.

Orme Campbell, from Atlanta, Georgia, whom I had known in childhood, was in New York. He and his family had had a summer home near Jellico, but now, I knew, they had a camp up in Canada on a lake near Montreal. I telephoned Orme. He offered me a cabin in his Canadian camp for as long as I should need and want it. His family, he told me, was in Europe. I should be alone up there, with only the caretaker's wife to look after me, and, blessed news, it wouldn't cost me a penny. "You'll get lonely and depressed," he warned, "because the summer season is over, but if you want peace and quiet, that's the place to go. You're welcome to it." What luck! I accepted the offer post-haste and prepared to leave.

Before going off I went to see Dr. Marafioti, then the physician for most of the Metropolitan Opera singers, who had been recommended to me. It is often so difficult to point to this person or to that event and say, "He [or it] wielded the greatest influence in my life." But Dr. Marafioti certainly was a great influence in my life then, and I desperately needed his forceful directing genius. Not only did he train my voice, he guided my mind and emotions. He was dominant not only as a singing teacher but as a man who knew that music sprung from the human source. Only today, after hearing all voices and seeing various methods of teaching, do I recognize that for basic training which lasts, none is better than Marafioti. Because he was the throat doctor at the Metropolitan, he was never taken seriously by the Italians there who tried to underestimate his value. How could a man, they argued illogically, who knew so much about the structure of the throat have any interest in what came out of it? But the logic is that because he did understand the throat so well, he should know about the manipulation of sound and resonance or what, in operatic parlance, is called the focus of a voice.

On my first visit to his office, Dr. Marafioti studied my throat thoroughly and in a casual professional voice said: "Signorina, you may never sing again. Acute laryngitis and severe strain are apparent in all the cords of the throat. Your future recovery lies in rest and complete silence. Even one word may endanger any chance of recovery. Come back to see me in three months and *boco allupo*."

Before I left his office he gave me *Jean Christophe* to read. "Take that with you," Dr. Marafioti said. "It will give you courage. Music is a hard road."

Today I do what Dr. Marafioti so wisely did to me then—I give *Jean Christophe* to any young music student who comes to me for advice. Romain Rolland has caught the passion and torment of the musician with all his pain and hope. It is a book that gives heart where heart is needed, yet never offers false inspiration. It is a book that meant a great deal to me, and it remains alive and robust in my memory to this day.

I stumbled out of Marafioti's Fifty-ninth Street office completely desolate and for a moment without hope. But after all, when one is young, healthy, terrifically ambitious, and possessed of a few real friends, hope comes bouncing back. I returned to the Gramercy Square apartment, packed my bags, said good-by to my studio friends and our carefree bohemian life and wished them luck with the new girl who was coming to take my place and share the studio's expenses. For Walter, who was to take me to dinner that night and receive the answer on his proposal of marriage, I left only a note. I could not face his dominating and persuasive personality.

Ruth Obre delivered my note to him and took my place on the dinner date. Later she wrote and told me that she had fallen in love with him and hoped that he, in time, would love her too. I, she hoped, would surely find my voice and through it a career: but she, unlike me, wanted only to live through the career of another—in this case Walter Dean Goldbeck. They were married a year later.

Meanwhile I retired to my Canadian retreat, where for three months I lived a solitary and silent existence.

It was a shattering and make-or-break experience. In my enthusiasm for life and my drive towards a career I had overlooked many things. Now I had to come face to face with myself. The silence, for a person of my volatile temperament, was a terrifying ordeal. The loneliness and uncertainty crushed my spirit. So often I wanted to give the whole thing up, forget about a career, go back home to Tennessee and take what that life had to offer. But day by day the immense silence and the very routine I had established of writing little notes to the caretakers became a kind of security. I was following instructions, I had been told if I did so there was hope for me—in these thoughts I took comfort and peace. Even if the chance to sing again hung by the slightest thread, as long as it hung at all I would stay quiet and solitary while the chance ripened. The conviction that it was worth it was all I needed.

I fished, read, wrote endless letters, and very occasionally rowed over to the adjoining island for fresh eggs and raspberries. The island was owned by a gigantic white-haired, white-bearded Belgian political refugee who read French philosophy from a great book while his numerous family sat under an oak tree and ate cakes. He had two Indian wives, one for "indoor" work and one for "outdoor," and babies everywhere, indoors and out. There was such good spirit all around that it made one question the usual state of monogamy. Seemingly the old Belgian had sensibly settled the riddle of a happy life.

As the end of my three months of enforced silence drew to a close, I prepared to return to New York and Dr. Marafioti. Fear haunted me: fear of the doctor's verdict, fear that the treatment would fail, fear that my ambition would die abortively; but I wanted nevertheless to have the answer. In a growing panic I left my Canadian camp and returned to New York.

Dr. Marafioti looked at my throat in silence, then took me to the piano and asked me to repeat after him the Italian words "Io, ti segui come iride di pace lungo le vie del ciel." As he played the music, he cautioned me to speak softly, with no effort. I did so slowly, hesitatingly, like a child learning its first steps. We repeated this exercise several times, then he asked me to return the next day. From then on we started a daily regime, sometimes twice each day, at the Fifty-ninth Street studio. I never sang, but only recited Italian poetry or the words of songs as the doctor played the musical notes on the piano in varying keys.

Just to hear the sound of my voice again, if only in speech, sent my hopes soaring, but Marafioti was taking no chances with a quick decision. Day after day he had me repeat the rich-voweled Italian words that were like a vocal massage. I was learning to speak Italian well, since it was the only language I used at that time, and then only in his studio under his guidance. I was permitted to see no one else. I lived in total loneliness, in a little one-room apartment a few doors from the studio, with only one goal ahead, the sound of my own voice in a full round ringing, singing tone. I had hardly any money and had most of my meals at Marafioti's, where he and Clara and their cook Maria filled me on the best spaghetti in the world.

After three months of this speaking experiment, Dr. Marafioti had me start vocalizing, and then, one day, we began, in a simple, almost speaking voice the "Ah quell' amor" aria from *Traviata*, pitched by the doctor in a lower key than the original, and worked up to the original little by little. Thus I became used again to the emotional excitement of hearing my voice once more. I learned also an enduring, invaluable lesson—the "color" and flavor of the words themselves, their meaning and emotional impact apart from the music. It has given me, throughout my career, an understanding of the psychological story involved in a libretto or a song that leads to a greater and more intense direct communication with one's listeners.

My throat muscles were growing stronger each day. I could now sing for one quarter-hour in full voice. Finally one day Dr. Marafioti took me by the shoulders, looked at me long and earnestly, and said, "I believe you are safe now. With discretion you can begin your career. I know you need money desperately, and a friend of mine is bringing Mr. F. C. Whitney, who managed *The Chocolate Soldier,* to hear you sing."

Mr. Whitney arrived in the friend's tow and, after hearing me sing "My Hero," signed me to my first Broadway contract. Having lived in such fear through the long months of silent worry, the relief that came as I held the contract produced an avalanche of tears that lasted through the night. When I examined the contract the next morning I found that I had been signed for the ingénue lead in the Whitney play *Suite Sixteen,* at seventy-five dollars per week, rehearsals to start at once! Manna from heaven! There were no more tears. I was on my way—or so I thought.

I have always been dogged by the paradox of being a star before I was a beginner. I have had to go through all my apprenticeships in full public view and with top billing. What was true in musical comedy was later to be true when I made my debut in opera, in the movies, over the air. I played a lead in each field without preliminary training, outside of singing, and in escaping the basic theater approach to these métiers I found myself in even more complex difficulties: the necessity of working for perfection while being expected to have it.

Here I was, the ingénue lead in a musical, but with the limitations of a novice in a high-school play. It was apparent in my costumes, my dancing, my acting, and my singing. Mr. Whitney and his wife were charming and kindly people, determined to launch me in a big way. They dragged out of storage the lavish, glamorous finery that had been used in *The Chocolate Soldier,* and I was so impressed with it that when I was given a hand in the costumes for *Suite Sixteen,* I used Kitty Gordon and the famous Irene Castle as prototypes, forgetting that being an ingénue meant being "young, ingenuous, fresh." I learned to speak my lines, but with an awkward, stilted unnaturalness. I even learned a few dance steps as the accompanying rhythm to my leading song, "First You Wiggle—Then You Waggle." I also kept my fingers crossed and hoped.

We opened in Syracuse. I was on hand early, before the curtain went up, in order to have plenty of time. With the actual performance right at hand, I suddenly realized I did not even know how to put on a proper theatrical make-up, and dashed from one dressing room to another, getting pointers. When I finally appeared on stage to await the "curtain time" cue, magnificent, as I thought, in an ermine daytime coat and with the longest, heaviest-beaded eyelashes professional Broadway actors had ever seen, I was greeted by an ominous silence. It was clear, from the look of consternation on all the faces, that instead of being the dear sweet ingénue called for in the play, I looked like a cross between a Barbary Coast belle and Bert Savoy. Not a trace of Jellico, Tennessee, was left.

The Whitneys rushed me off stage and into a dressing room. They had trusted my judgment too far. As Mrs. Whitney swapped my ermine coat for her own plain tailored one and slapped cold cream on my face to remove all traces of my gaudy "glam-moor," I could hear, through the closed door, the stamping impatience of both audience and waiting actors, who made no bones about how they felt about the stupidity of giving beginners too much leeway. What a beautiful way to start! When I appeared, thirty-five minutes later, looking like a misguided choir singer again, the manager gave me a sour look, made his good-luck speech with certain pointed asides, signaled the overture to start, and the curtain went up.

I was not a howling success. The rest of the company did its job, but I only seemed to cover a lot of stage space to no particular avail. It was only when my role called for a change from pure young wife to a bit of sham hanky-panky that I managed to make any impression at all. I lit into my song, "First You Wiggle—Then You Waggle," with complete abandon. Syracuse responded with thunderous applause. I was surprised and pleased at my success, although a trifle irked that it came from hip-swinging rather than from more solid histrionics. Was this art? However, art or not, I continued to do my wiggle with energetic liveliness whenever the show played, adding the "subtle" touch of saving the last big wiggle for my exit. I was a riot in the college towns, and there was no stopping the boys in the front row from whistling for repeated encores. My colleagues were not amused by my display and openly showed their disapproval, but since our fortunes were tied up together, anything that would keep us touring was tolerated. I learned from that first company the important lesson of never counting too heavily on one's associates for undying friendship.

We were booked for one-night stands, and life became a jumble of day-coach jumps when no other train connections were possible, of sleepless nights in baggage trucks, of hurried railroad-station meals, third-rate hotels, and dirty theaters. Nowadays when I become tired and fed up with the strain of long concert tours I have only to look back on that endless round of one-night stands to realize how my fortunes have changed. But such is the vigor of young ambition, all the fatigue of that trip only added to the excitement.

Our play, alas, went from bad to worse. Neither the excellent company nor my wiggle-waggle could bring the clink of honest coin into the box-office till. One Wednesday night we were called together, told that Mr. Whitney had returned to New York, and the show was to close the following Saturday. Those were the days before Equity demanded the two-weeks' notice. When Saturday night arrived we were each given a return ticket to New York and twenty-five dollars in cash, with a promise that the rest would be paid later. Mr. Whitney, it seems, had taken a flier in Wall Street, had been wiped out, and we were left with the leavings. Christmas, to make the whole thing just ducky, was only two days off. We were a sad and defeated lot as we streamed through Pennsylvania Station the day before Christmas, and our holiday greetings had a hollow ring as we separated to go our various ways.

I was met at the station by Blanche and Lilian. Lilian, who had always had a longing for the sea and was periodically in love with every branch of the maritime service, had just returned from a brief honeymoon with the captain of a tramp steamer. Apparently the charms of being rocked in the cradle of the deep had quickly palled, for she was remarkably reticent about the whole matter and joined now with Blanche and me in our search for an apartment.

We decided that Christmas in a hotel room was just impossible: misfortune had gotten us all down far enough without pushing us to that level. We also decided that we were permitting money—or the lack of it—to play too great a part in our plans. We owed it to ourselves to trust more to luck. So, set in our recklessness, and finding ourselves on West Sixty-seventh Street in the famous Artists' Studio Row, we asked the manager to "show us something." He ushered us into a two-hundred-dollar-a-month suite just vacated by my dream girl, Kitty Gordon. When I heard her name I felt it was a portent. I had worn her cast-off ermine from *The Chocolate Soldier,* hadn't I? Why not this apartment?

I said we'd take it—it was just what we wanted—and signed, then and there, a six-months' lease. That poor landlord must have been stuffed full of Christmas spirit to have taken our meager hundred-dollar advance, scraped from the bottom of our three purses. When he left, with all our money and that incriminating lease, we turned and looked at one another in wild panic. Then the whole situation was suddenly so crazy and reckless that we collapsed with laughter. Here we were, with a great apartment, an empty icebox, empty pocketbooks, and the holiday upon us. We were certainly *in* the trenches for Christmas.

When the laughter had subsided, Blanche remembered that she knew someone called Ginsberg who lived across the way at the Hotel des Artistes. She telephoned him to wish him a Merry Christmas, whereupon he invited us all over to share his roast turkey, especially prepared, we were told, by the Reuben of "from a sandwich to an institution" fame. Blanche turned from the telephone and asked if we would go. No, I said, I wanted none of it. I'd rather have no turkey at all than spend Christmas with strangers. My telegrams to my family were filled with clichés on success and happiness to cover up the shock of this first Christmas away from home. I was desperately homesick and determined to have my holiday with at least one friend in front of our own expensive fireplace. If the nice and hospitable Mr. Ginsberg had a Reuben's turkey, why not we? We decided to telephone Reuben for a dinner on credit, and I was commissioned to charm him with my most melting southern accent.

I called his number and plunged right in, saying that we were friends of Mr. Ginsberg just arrived in New York, the banks were closed for the night, we had very little cash on hand, would he be a dear and send us over a little order on credit? Reuben was no fool. He guessed the blarney at once, and in acting as if he believed my tall tale, he was being kindly as well as charitable. He sent over everything for a gala dinner, enough even for the traditional leftovers, which lasted for days, and when I signed my name to that credit blank, it began a loyal and long-lasting friendship. Years later, when my opera debut was announced, the first purchaser of a box for that matinee was Arnold Reuben. He had followed my career with pride and a personal satisfaction that he had lightened my first homeless Christmas, and he knew I remained always grateful. It is a great gift to have the instinct to know which person to trust and then to trust him all the way. Arnold Reuben had it and on it built a fruitful life.

We practically lived for days on the leftovers of that Christmas dinner. With a half-full tummy to help matters along, I again started the rounds of Broadway booking offices. Each evening I reported to Marafioti's studio for a lesson while the good doctor tried to scrape the wiggle-waggle song off my vocal cords. One of my daytime calls was made to the offices of the Aborn Opera Company, where a fat-faced man sat with his feet on the desk and leaned back in his chair to look me over.

"The voice may be okay," he said, "but lift your skirt, girlie, so I can see the legs." I gave him a smart smack across the cheek and left with what I hoped was a telling exit line: "I don't sing with my legs." Now, as I look back on it, I've had quite a bit of leg trouble. Managers seemed never to consider the voice as a separate entity from what went on below.

My next stop was at the audition theater where they were casting for the George White *Scandals*. I waited my turn on the empty stage and when it came gave the sheet music for Fritz Kreisler's "When You Are Free" from *Apple Blossom Time* to the young man at the piano. He took it and played it so well that I sang the song better than ever before. When I finished he asked me for my name and said, "You'll hear from me. It's too late for this show, but I'm writing another and can use you. My name is Gershwin, George Gershwin." I never did do a Gershwin show, but we often did that song together in the homes of various friends. The year before his sad and untimely death he sat at the piano at one of Elsa Maxwell's soirees on the Waldorf-Astoria roof and played it for me for the last time, and, as always, so well that I sang the better for it. His death robbed the musical world of a great and vital talent, a talent which had brought remarkable change but which could have gone even further in leaving a final and lasting impact on the music of America.

After the audition for the *Scandals,* I was sent over by a mutual friend to see John Cort. Because Cort believed in his friend's judgment, he gave me a singing role in a play called *Just a Minute,* which lasted about that length of time. I did learn, however, from that momentary experience to walk across the stage in time with the music. While the pianist hammered away at the theme song, big lumbering John Cort would lead me, in time with the melody, back and forth across the boards. We later discovered that my prodigious awkwardness was due mainly to the fact that I was stumping around on the highest pair of spike-heeled pumps this side of Broadway. After the Cleveland opening night, some friends of Fisher Hepburn's, Mr. and Mrs. Mike Foster, not only sent me an invitation to supper but made up a collection at the supper table to buy me a pair of respectable shoes.

Just a Minute went as far as Pittsburgh, at which time I found myself minus show and bank account, but with some valuable theater background. I also met in Pittsburgh J. Frederic Byers and his wife, who remained among my loyal friends. Fritz Byers gave me a letter to Charles Dillingham, master showman and producer of the then current *Good Morning, Dearie,* which I took over to the Dillingham office on my return to New York. Charlie Dillingham was a remarkable fellow—brilliant, charming, faithful, a gentleman of the old school of theatrical tradition. I suspect he was first impressed by my social connections, but he also said I "hit" a pretty musical note and why didn't I go see Joseph Gates, who was doing *Up in the Clouds?*

Up in the Clouds netted me another leading role and some more opportunity to travel. However, this time our travels skirted us awfully close to Broadway. We played the subway circuit, and Bob Benchley of *Life* got up to see us. His review was worth a dozen orchids. "There are two young people," he said, "in *Up in the Clouds* who will one day be stars: Grace Moore and Skeets Gallagher." In spite of Mr. Benchley's personal encouragement, the show faltered in Brooklyn. The cast got together for that kind of riotous closing-night celebration that always reminds me of a jolly wake, and going on stage after the hilarity, the tenor got so confused he kept speaking and singing my lines all night.

I returned from Brooklyn to the Dillingham office again. Mr. Dillingham continued kind. "If you would hop a train to Boston," he said, "Raymond Hitchcock could probably find a little role in *Hitchy Koo* for you."

I hopped—with a new hat and a coat with a fur collar bought on credit. Raymond Hitchcock, *Hitchy Koo* with Julia Sanderson—this was big time to me, and worth going into debt for. I got by the stage door of the Boston theater and into the wings, where Hitchcock, who was on stage rehearsing, spied me. I waved to him. He boomed out for them to send in the little blonde girl, and I started across the stage towards the great man. In order to get to him I had to wade through a group of statuesque beauties, typically clothed in long-trained cloth of gold and icy stares. Unfortunately, in my shambling progress I crashed into the golden train of one of the tallest and most willowy of the blondes, and as she stepped forward, the whole tail ripped off, leaving her exposed in very pretty lace panties. She turned on me with a shriek: "You greenhorn, can't you lift those club feet?" Mortified by my unhappy entrance, I stood silent and gauche, not knowing whether to go forward or turn and run. But Raymond Hitchcock paid little attention to my stormy entrance; his life was probably a constant round of baleful stares and exposed panties. He signaled me forward, took my note from Dillingham, then shrieked to the stage manager, "Take Gracie Moore out to sing for Jerry Kern."

Jerome Kern is not only a great master of melody, he has an inexhaustible enthusiasm for the novice and a helping hand that stays out. After I sang for him, he gave me his lovely and amusing song "Oh Moon of Love" for my special number in the show. However, neither of us reckoned on Julia Sanderson, star of *Hitchy Koo* and undoubtedly an estimable woman, but firm in that fine old tradition that would permit no one the possibility of overshadowing her. It constituted a virtual palace revolution for Jerry Kern to wiggle the song out of her reach that day and into mine. I sang the romantic melody about the magic of the moon while eight of the famous golden beauties stood behind me and with dead-pan faces chanted, "What the hell do we care about the moon!" Julia could do nothing about it, and we were one of the hits of the show. My boosters, Dillingham, Kern, and Hitchcock, were delighted—indeed, Kern was so pleased that he composed a new number for me for the New York opening. Called "The Wedding Cake," it was a wonderful song for a spectacle number. It used a giant white wedding cake, I was dressed in the most ravishing white finery as the bride, and the show girls, as bridesmaids, were given a chance to really show off. At our dress rehearsal of the number in Boston, Julia Sanderson sat in the dark theater, watching. Suddenly we were stopped in the middle. Jerry Kern scurried down from the stage and went into deep, solemn conference with La Sanderson. Finally he returned to the stage and with apparent suffering announced that Miss Sanderson wanted that number for herself and he regretted that I could not yet be a bride even in name only. I burst into tears and dashed off the stage.

The blonde with the amazing fiery blue eyes whose tail I had ripped off turned out to be my greatest comfort and remains one of my firmest friends. She's now Jane Draper, married to Duncan Draper of Boston, but back in those ladies-of-the-ensemble days she was known as Nette Thomas. She was then—as now—quick-tongued, "savvy" and generous. As I sat crying in my Boston dressing room after having "The Wedding Cake" snatched out of my reach, she patted my shoulder and consoled me with snappish tenderness. Her report on the dressing-room gossip *re* La Belle Sanderson was etched in acid and had better remain untold, but it cheered me no end at the moment. At least, in losing the song, I gained the cordiality of the chorus line, which had been prone to regard me as high hat until my downfall.

Hitchy Koo was taken on to Cincinnati as part of its road tour. In the audience—but not out front—was Father and the family, their first glimpse of me on the professional stage. Father arrived at my dressing room, a shy stranger in the world of grease paint, costumes, and make-believe. We tried to talk in embarrassed intervals between stage calls, and somehow at one point I missed my cue. Hitchcock started calling frantically, "Where's Gracie?"—and soon, above the din of Father's advice, I could hear the whole audience in chorus, "Where's Gracie, where's Gracie?" I quieted Father and got onto the stage, inwardly feeling that I was forever doomed to make the most undignified entrances. Later, Father and I thrashed out *Hitchy Koo* versus a southern girl's social station. He relented far enough to admit that the music was pretty, that I sang rather well, and Hitchcock seemed like a nice fellow—*but!* It was an endless circle of protest and counter-protest. I started all over again to present my point of view. Poor Father, again he retreated before my determination, and by the end of the evening he and *Hitchy* were on reasonably friendly terms.

New York opening night, at last. It was not the Metropolitan Opera, but it *was* the New Amsterdam—and only two blocks away from my goal. I was not the star, but I *was* the star's understudy and had a song hit of my own to sing. It wasn't until Thanksgiving, when Julia Sanderson got indigestion from too much turkey dinner, that I was given a chance to replace her for that night and thus made my first starring entrance on Broadway. But I was happy in what there was and felt that the *Hitchy Koo* opening was my real New York start.

The Fritz Byers and hurried telephone calls filled the front rows with New York's leading eligibles. After the performance I was introduced to T. Markoe Robertson. Tommy Robertson invited me to go along with him to a supper being given the show girls of *Hitchy Koo* in that famous club on Madison Avenue where the town's Beau Brummells gathered. Not being one of the show girls, I wondered about taking him up on his invitation, but since he urged me and I liked the girls, I agreed. At least I wouldn't be alone on my opening night on Broadway.

It was a fabulous party, my first taste of the big-time show world. The champagne flowed like water; there was a thousand-dollar bill under each plate; the gaiety was electric and high-pitched. I was suspicious of the champagne, and as for the thousand-dollar bill, I couldn't understand getting money you hadn't worked for. If this was New York night life, it was a long way from home.

At the party was Whitney Warren, Sr., famous architect who had to his credit the Grand Central Terminal, the restoration of the Louvain Library, and many other renowned American architectural wonders, who was introduced to me by Tommy Robertson. Mr. Warren was of the school of gentlemen who had learned how to combine courtesy and breeding with bohemianism. Taking me under his wing that night, we sat at the head of the red-carpeted stairs while he gave me a little lecture on how to be an artist and human being rather than merely a frustrated "lady." He paid me a great compliment before he died recently when he said to his son, "She's worked out her life well, because you know she's always a lady although you can feel the artist coming through." Incidentally that son of his, Whitney Warren, Jr., is an enchanting person and loyal friend and a great credit to his father. Whitney Junior is on the board of directors of the San Francisco Opera, runs a vast peach ranch, and was the first private employer during this wartime crisis to take on labor from the Folsom prison ranks. It is a tradition that whenever I go out to sing in San Francisco, it's Whitney who gives me my supper afterwards.

After the *Hitchy Koo* opening, life became a whirl of wonderful people and new friends. Tommy Robertson was the center of my new group of friends, and one night at a party at Alma Gluck's house I met a friend of his, the Philadelphia painter George Biddle. Tommy was pleasant and convivial, George a bit more on the solemn side, but both took a great deal of interest in me as a person and tried to bring a little cultural sweetness and light into what they considered the dark potential of my mind. Tommy was an enthusiast of Walter Pater's and turned me into an enthusiast too. I know Pater is considered old hat by the literati. Somerset Maugham once wrote that he thought that Pater, egardless of his exquisite style, represented the depth of decadence. Who am I to quarrel with the dean of English letters? But I still feel a debt of gratitude to Tommy Robertson for the loan of his books on Pater and the spontaneity of his interest.

I was often invited into the world of serious musicians. Whether it was at Alma Gluck's or the John McCormacks', there was a magic new world for me of the great names in music. Mischa Levitzki would sit and play Chopin for me. He was melancholy and romantic and we were happy and imagined ourselves in love.

One night Samuel and Pauline Chotzinoff gave a party for Alma at which Heifetz, Zimbalist, Paul Kochanski, and another violinist whose name I cannot remember played an endurance contest, using the Paganini "Concerto" to drive themselves and everyone else divinely crazy. It wasn't enough to go through this extended bit of virtuosity once—the trick was to see how long violinist, violin, and audience would last, to say nothing of Mr. Paganini.

Neysa McMein and Dorothy Parker had a studio on Fifty-seventh Street and Sixth Avenue, where I first ran into Alec Woollcott, F.P.A., Heywood Broun, Marc Connelly, Bob Benchley, George Kaufman, and Bob Sherwood. They made up what was then known as the Algonquin Round Table, so called because they all lunched together at the Hotel Algonquin and tore the world apart and put it together again loudly and pungently along with their food.

F.P.A. became a great friend who always referred to me in his column as his "dream girl, Gracie Moore." No thing of beauty he, Frank Adams had enough charm and personality to make up for any lack of handsomeness. Furthermore he added to his appeal by taking me occasionally to luncheon at the Round Table. There I not only was amused but caused hilarious amusement, mainly because of my terrific southern accent which hung on in spite of my Italian singing lessons. Once when I said to Frank, "Well, I don't know what was so funny about my remarks," he answered, "My dear, it isn't that, they were far from funny. It's just the way you say them. Nobody can understand one word, and you will have to do something about that southern accent."

Mostly I sat back at the Algonquin, drinking in every word and swept up in hero worship of these men who were so much a part of the life of that day. I didn't always understand their particular. brand of wit. They seemed to slash at one another constantly, and the more terrible and vindictive the verbal attacks, the more hilarity there would be. The group was inseparable. They stimulated and amused one another and rarely permitted the outsider to break them up. Once Herbert and Maggie Swope gave a buffet dinner where the actual round table from the Algonquin was moved into their front parlor so the boys would feel at home! Once I said to F.P.A., "I don't know what would happen to these fellows if they ever found themselves with another group of people. Do you think anybody else would understand them?"

The farthest they would go in leaving their beloved Main Stem was out to Great Neck, Long Island, where, at this period, most of the week-ending went on. Once at Neysa McMein's place Alec Woollcott ducked my head up and down in the dirty Long Island Sound, all in the spirit of fun. Three hours later I was on the way to New York with a rapidly mounting temperature, a touch of delirium, and an incipient mastoid condition. Fortunately nothing came of it, except an infection at the back of the ear which had to be lanced. Later, when I showed Alec the scar, he looked at me with scorn, but he felt keenly about the matter and resented having been responsible. We both carried a chip on our shoulders over the incident for a long time after.

Those Broadway days in the early twenties were made up of many farewells. From the topmost peanut gallery of the Metropolitan Opera I heard Geraldine Farrar sing her last Carmen— a "first" for me, since I had never before been inside that shabby, magnificent plush-and-plumes building. Rector's, which I had heard about for years as the symbol of New York's gaslight and carriage trade, was gone and the gay spot was the Palais Royale where Paul Whiteman played while his Rhythm Boys, including

Bing Crosby, burbled along. Reisenweber's got the theatrical supper crowd; and Mae Murray was the dancing queen of Broadway at the Merry Gardens.

Caruso's serious illness had begun, and I never did hear him
sing at the opera. However, I did get to hear him in "person" in
spite of all. Down in the basement of the old Hotel Knickerbocker was a little chiropodist's office belonging to Lilian Blynn.
Lilian, brave and good, who still takes care of me today, had always had an enormous musical clientele. I started going to her
as much because I needed tending as because I was music-struck
enough to want to get closer to the musical great even if through
a mutual chiropodist. One day I was really rewarded.

"I can't take you now, Miss Moore," said Lilian. "Caruso is
coming, and I have an appointment."

"Caruso!" I said, my mouth hanging wide. "Oh, Lilian, please
let me hide behind that screen and just get a peek at him."

Lilian was a little skeptical about the ethics, but I finally prevailed. I hunched behind the screen and waited. Soon the great
man came in. Afraid to reveal my presence, I didn't dare peek
around it to see him, but it didn't matter, because I *heard*. He
seated himself on the chair, took off his shoes and stockings, and
then in his wonderful voice, in clear rising golden tones, chanted,
"Lily-yan, Lily-yan, feex my leetle toes."

When *Hitchy Koo* closed I was given a part in the Ned Wayburn review called *Town Gossip*. It had an accordion existence in
Boston, both opening and closing there. I remember it for a number of things. Among them Vinton Freedley, who was its leading
man. When Vinton turned producer, the stage lost one of its best
potential matinee idols. Vinton was good-looking, ingratiating,
romantic. It wasn't his fault that the show collapsed.

Another member of that cast was Edythe Baker, who played
the piano in the show, and one of the bitterest fights in all my
theatrical life was with her then. She accused me of distracting
the audience from her piano-playing act by flirting with the bald-
headed men in the front row as we all sat around as part of the
scene, listening. I heatedly told her that the front rows were filled

with Harvard boys, and if my eye wandered occasionally in their direction or vice versa there was certainly no bad intent. We scuffled verbally, were pulled apart several times before the fatal blow, came to no decision, but apparently both found it rather ridiculous, for years later, when Edythe and I met on the Riviera, we laughed and joked about it and set it down to the tension of a show that wasn't going over.

Ned Wayburn had staged *Town Gossip* with his usual good taste and a lavish hand and had completely gambled his whole bankroll on it. When it definitely looked as if the venture was a failure, he had no money left to get the chorus girls back to New York. One hard-luck story after another was told to me. I had no alternative but to telephone my friend Bernard Baruch. He had been kind to so many people that I felt I could appeal to him for aid. With his usual generosity, Barney Baruch saw that the chorus got back to New York. Then for years after he kept getting checks repaying him, sent through Actors' Equity. For one who has sat up front in two wars and done a magnificent job in both, Barney Baruch has never lost the simple kindly touch that makes a human being.

I came back to New York after the Boston fiasco, flipped through my bank roll, and decided that with the few hundred dollars on hand from two years of work I was ready to taste the joys of travel. I had no intention of waiting until I could "afford" it. Now seemed the logical time.

The First Time I Saw Paris

WHEN I STARTED WRITING THIS BOOK I wondered how to begin my story of France—the France I have loved so dearly and for so long—the France of the Riviera and Paris and Normandy and the Wine Country—the France of second-rate provincial opera houses and magnificent music—the France I have known from north to south and across. So much of my life has been bound up with my experiences there that it seemed hard to find an opening wedge to talk about. My mind always floundered for a beginning—should it be the France of hard work, of Charpentier and *Louise,* of constant study, of the Opéra Comique and Mary Garden? Or should I begin with Paris and the gay, talented, wonderful friends I made there from the very first moment I arrived? Or should it be the Riviera and my little pink villa at the Hôtel du Cap and later my marriage and the happiness Val and I found there?

"You have two countries," the saying goes, "your own and France." Not along ago in Colorado Springs, deep in the heart of the U.S.A., an opening gambit for the story of my life in France came to me. And with a nice, certain logic, it starts me right back at the very beginning.

I was on a concert tour with a stopover at Colorado Springs. There I was given a dinner at the country club by the wonderful group of people who have brought such flair and flavor to that western enchantment spot: the Maytags, for instance—handsome and witty Bud, who made his fortune from a washing machine, retired when he was young enough to enjoy it, and now

57

plays a distinct part in the civic and cultural life of the West, and his wife Catherine, an attractive and charming hostess, whose father was one of the founders of the famous Mayo Brothers' clinic, and a vivid personality in her own right; Ethel Carleton; music-loving Julie Penrose, whose husband pioneered most of Colorado Springs and built the stadium for our summer concerts; the Menarys and the Blairs—all of them persons who, while typically American, have the Continental approach to living and a feeling for good taste and warm hospitality. The belle of the ball at that dinner turned out to be Mrs. Walter Paepcke, who was the girl whose cabin I shared on my first European trip. In Colorado Springs, six thousand feet high, where native Coloradans think nothing of saying, "Come on, let's run up to the mountains for dinner," and then take you to a luxurious log cabin some four thousand feet higher, Pussy Paepcke and I exchanged old gossip like two giggling schoolgirls, and we regaled ourselves (and sometimes our surrounding friends) with so many tales and anecdotes of that boat trip on the Fabre Line, when we sailed from Brooklyn in May 1921, that the whole past came back to life with all the fun and laughter of everybody on board.

"Remember," said Pussy, "your chaperon, austere, white-haired Jessie Harrison, whom you took along to add an air of respectability to the presence of your best beau on board?"

"Yes, and remember everyone on the boat thought I was his model and he was taking me to a desert island to sketch me in the nude?"

"I'm telling all in my book," I promised Pussy.

"For heaven's sake," she said, "don't dodge the issue then. You've got to tell with what fanfare you came on board in Brooklyn. It's a good story on you," and Pussy added slyly, "You don't want to give the impression you were prunes and prisms just because you're writing a book. It wouldn't be you."

It seems, Pussy reminded me, that somehow I had gotten listed as a "schoolteacher," and when Pussy came to her cabin she expected some nice proper companionable girl who would be a quiet, steadying influence throughout the trip. Instead the cabin was filled with flowers and quantities of luggage and farewell telegrams, and the *pièce de résistance* was a large heart-shaped wreath pierced with a bleeding red arrow and flaunting a painted banner inscribed, "To My Sweetheart."

"Some schoolteacher!" Pussy said she remarked to herself. "I wonder what school *she* comes from."

By this time enormously curious, she went on deck to see if her cabin mate had arrived. Then, she says, suddenly she saw a moderately tall, stringbeany blonde girl dashing up the gangplank with a very dapper, *Esquire*-ish-looking gentleman in tow. They made for the Moore-Paepcke cabin.

"My heavens," thought Pussy, "if Grandfather could see the schoolteacher, he wouldn't be so sure I was nicely set for my cruise."

"Hello," said Pussy to me, coming into the cabin, "I think we share this together. That is, if you're Grace Moore."

"Yes, I am Grace Moore," I seem to have bubbled, and Pussy says she didn't know what floored her most—the fact that I was wearing two corsages, one of orchids pinned to my left shoulder and one of gardenias on my right, or the lavish gesture with which I turned to the elegant Beau Brummell in the cabin and said, "This is my fiancé. Good-by, my dear," and whisked him out.

We were both at the rail to wave farewell to the descending fiancé when there was a jab at my elbow. Pussy and I turned. There stood a gawky, distinguished man, in a strawberry tweed suit, grinning at us.

"Oh my God!" I said to Pussy, and peeked over the railing to wave a last good-by at the departing beau to speed him on his way. Then, seemingly having cleared the decks below, I introduced the newcomer with another flourish. "Meet my fiancé," I said to Pussy without blinking an eye. "This is George Biddle."

"After that," confessed Pussy in Colorado Springs, "I never knew what you were going to do next. But it did turn that nice cultural trip into a lark."

I took that trip in 1921 long before I could really "afford" it because that was precisely the time I wanted to take it and couldn't wait until I had enough laid neatly aside to do it in style. With all the money I had in the world I bought a round-trip ticket for a Mediterranean trip lasting thirty-one days each way, with enough stop-offs to cure any fervent Cook's tourist. Being completely unknown, I had no compunctions about reserving a double cabin to share with a stranger, which brought the fare to $365 all included. George Biddle popped up unexpectedly on that trip because he was determined to put our engagement to the acid test of thirty-one days of cramped shipboard living. George couldn't have picked a better litmus paper. By the time we had reached Marseille, both he and I had been willing on two or three occasions to commit the other to a watery grave and would have done so if not for the intercession of kind friends.

Our cruising ship made its first stop at Ponta Delgada, in the Azores Islands, where Wagner had once lived. The house craze which I have inherited from my mother and father took possession of me when I saw Wagner's former villa. I wanted it. I wanted to buy it. I wanted to live in it. I immediately opened negotiations for the purchase of the place, with no funds, of course, to back them up. My friends who had come ashore with me and knew the state of my finances teased me for even broaching the proposition to the man in charge. I became adamant. I would buy it on the installment plan, a system of payment which I ordinarily hate, and attach my future to paying it off. The late Murray Nelson, the great Chicago criminal lawyer who was in our party, seeing that I was on the verge of buying without money, made a very feeble offer to buy the house for me. I'm afraid my refusal was just as feeble. There remained only twenty minutes in which to return to the boat. Fortunately some of the people who had returned to the ship reported that I was remaining at Ponta Delgada to buy a house. In the nick of time, like a Perils of Pauline thriller, there arrived a message from the ship's captain. People, he said, didn't buy houses on the island. People ran away from Ponta Delgada. Beautiful as life might seem, the place was subject to annual epidemics of the homely and bothersome scourge of boils. Having no appetite for the life of Job, I canceled all negotiations and returned to the ship a somewhat chastened prospective realtor.

George Biddle came into his own when we reached Marseille. George was an intelligent and sympathetic man who felt that I too had possibilities. He taught me to appreciate what was the best in art and architecture, putting me under his serious tutelage on tour and, with the help of a Baedeker, dinning into my head every known fact about church, gargoyle, or steeple. He was no pedant, but tender and concerned about my acquiring knowledge. He dragged me through the mistral heat to see the murals of Puvis de Chavannes, the paintings of Poussin, and the Château d'If. We ate bouillabaisse at the Basso Restaurant on the waterfront. Ardent epicures say Marseilles is the only place in the world you can get real bouillabaisse, because even if you have the authentic recipe and follow it, the fish and sea food itself must come out of the Mediterranean and be used at once to give the authentic flavor. I saw for myself the freshness of the fish, for I went out on the barge with the fishermen who brought in the tasty catch.

After Marseille, we motored to Bandol, where at the Grand Hotel I first tasted the paradise *en pension* of the Riviera which could be had for two dollars a day. We motored up the Riviera through a coast like our own chamber-of-commerce California: eternal sun, palms, lush vegetation, and semitropical trees, with always the henna-colored rocks jutting over the cobalt Mediterranean. At Cassis we ran into an artists' colony which had never heard of the rich international set that had supposedly made the Riviera its own. Here again life was sweet for that same *prix fixe* —the inevitable two dollars. At Beaulieu I saw Mary Garden's villa for the first time and ogled it like any small-town fan peeping at the home of a favorite heroine. We went up to St. Paul in the mountains back of Nice, with its walls that date to Francis I, and met Billy Grimm, the painter, and Florence Lucius, who is now married to Jo Davidson. Mr. Roux, who kept the hotel, was a friend of artists, and although his charge was the same two dollars a day, he took, as token of exchange, work instead of cash. Even today his dining room is covered with many a poem and painting that paid for *l'addition*.

Our typical tourist cruise took us to the North African coast, and in a 1911 Ford, we set out for Oran and Algiers, complete with guidebooks, for a trip through that part of the world that has meant so much during this present war. There was no fighting then—only the stark white houses that shone clean against a burning blue sky.

When we visited Palermo, we were greeted by a serenade of "Old Folks at Home" and "Marching Through Georgia." George showed me the wonders of the seven-hundred-year-old Monreale Chapel, with its famous Byzantine murals of Bible stories. I ate finochio for the first time, taking it from one of the gaily colored painted carts that lazily clop-clopped over the cobblestoned streets. When we left Palermo, the parting salute was once more American: the strains of "Home Sweet Home" followed us as we left shore.

After this thirty-one-day taste of Mediterranean life, I became incurably hungry for more of it. From the sunset on the Rock of Gibraltar to sunrise on the Bay of Naples, it stretched like a land of dreams. But I had to return to New York with the cruise in order to go back to work to replenish my funds and provide enough to take me back to France the very next summer. I could hardly wait, but at last the next year found me again across the Atlantic where I wanted to be. This time, however, I headed straight for Paris.

Somehow Paris has stayed separate in my mind from the Riviera, and through the years, one time here, another time there —New York, the Riviera, Paris—interlinking one happening in my life with another, still the spirit of each has always remained distinct and apart. When I think of the Riviera, I draw a curtain between lapses in time and pool all the feeling I have for it in one corner of my mind, while into another goes my love for Paris.

I have always been an American in Paris. Through all the

years I lived there, and with the many people I learned to know in France, I was still essentially the American whose home base remained across the Atlantic. I studied in France, sang there and all through Europe, and got the social whirl of my life in Paris— yet I never took on the color of an expatriate. My friends belonged to that set with citizenship in various countries who were at home everywhere. Elsie De Wolfe, Noel Coward, Bea Lillie, Elsa Maxwell, Heifetz, the Cole Porters . . . Parisian by virtue of their love of beauty, freedom, art, fun and laughter; but though I too was Parisian, it was in a limited sense only, with my other foot always on native soil.

I think that to get under the surface and really appreciate the beauty of any country, one has to go there poor. I was poor, all right. I tossed all my worldly wealth into the jackpot for a chance to live and study in Europe. I was treated to a taste of the social hospitality of Paris that was doubly surprising when you consider how young and uncelebrated I was.

My social life in Paris started from the very first night I arrived. Never was there such a happy beginning. Frank Crowninshield and Condé Nast came to my *pension* near the Bois de Boulogne to take me to dinner immediately I came to town. The pension, run by a typical bourgeois family, had been recommended to me by my friend Margaret Case of *Vogue,* both for its inexpensiveness and the fact that, since the family took only one or two paying guests, I should quickly learn how to speak French in such an intimate atmosphere *en famille.*

Frank and Condé, as a welcoming treat, gave me my choice of restaurants. I picked La Pérouse on the Seine because I had read that it had been, in all its quiet red-and-gold elegance, the favorite eating place of Oscar Wilde and Marcel Proust. Elsa Maxwell was there too that night, and on the sidewalk after dinner we ran into a friend of Condé and Frank, a Mr. Tornquist, from the famous banking family of Buenos Aires. It seemed we all had the same invitation for the evening to a supper party given by Captain Molyneux at his beautiful house at Maison

Lafitte, and Mr. Tornquist whisked us away in great style in his highly colored Rolls-Royce.

It was an important party for me, for it was here that I first met not only our host, Edward Molyneux, but Elsie De Wolfe, Cécile Sorel, and Millicent Hearst—persons who were to become an intrinsic part of my life.

I also met my very first duke, a handsome Spaniard who had a charm I instinctively knew would turn out to be unreliable. The duke invited me to drive out with him the next morning in his yellow Mercedes so he could show me the sights of Paris. I accepted without wasting coyness, because having someone with both the time and the means to show a newcomer around was a find; I would take my chances on his unreliability. The first morning stretched into a succession of excursions, and each day we would start out, first to St. Cloud for an apéritif on a terrace leading to the Royal Park, and then off to a tour of historical spots, which the duke always accompanied with great detail about the past lore of France. He was not at all interested in the history of his own country, Spain, but knew all the oddments of information about the places we visited. This beautiful idyll ended when I discovered that he had put two of the most vicious police dogs I had ever seen outside my hotel-room door and then installed himself in a room at the corner of the corridor, where he could observe my comings and goings. I called the police and asked them to remove both dogs and duke and sighed as I thought that at least I had gotten quite a bit of sight-seeing done before the duke had gone to the dogs.

The first night party at Captain Molyneux's also brought me an invitation to a dinner given by Cécile Sorel. I arrived at her magnificent apartment overlooking the Seine, where I was taken to powder my nose as I sat at the foot of Mme. du Barry's bed. We dined from a solid gold table around which breezed some spirited dinner conversation mainly concerned with Sorel's beautiful *poitrine*. I looked cautiously over at Sorel's décolleté, which was so modest that I wondered how *all* the guests got the positive information to discuss *l'affaire* with so much authority. Some-

time later I was given the opportunity to get first-hand enlighten-
ment myself at the Quatre-Arts Ball when Sorel, lifted onto the
backs of the students in a triumphant parade, had her dress pulled
off to her waist during the height of the revelry, while people
cheered. I saw then that although Sorel's face might have been
only interestingly ugly, the rest of her, in spite of her half-century
or more of years, justified the dinner conversation at which I had
been somewhat naïvely surprised.

Another happy by-product of that first party in Paris was an
invitation from Elsie De Wolfe to spend the next week end at
her Villa Trianon in Versailles. Elsie was an American who was
accepted as completely Parisian by the French. In her guestbook
in the entrance foyer of her fabulous house were names known
all over the civilized world for urbanity, achievement, distinction,
and power. She had the most amazing facility for mixing people
and could do it better than anyone else I know. She had a charming light touch which made her guests feel immediately at ease.
If you were a stranger she would always acquaint you at once
with the people to whom she presented you, so you escaped
fumbling about for the tiresome first approaches. "Mr. So and
So," she would say, "is interested in music," or, "This is the most
popular young woman in London who gives the best political
parties," or, "This is Mrs. X, who edits that famous fashion
magazine, and you two should know one another."

The minute you met people under Elsie's tutelage you had a
skillfully executed vignette that enabled you to get along. She
was always thoroughly unmalicious and never said an unkind
word about anyone. If you were there, in her house, it was because she enjoyed having you for yourself.

Elsie De Wolfe's one concession to the mounting years was
always to wear white gloves in the house in order to conceal her
hands. She was my friend in spite of the fact that she was stone
deaf to music and heartily and frankly admitted being bored with
it. It was a relief to me when she married Sir Charles Mendl of
the British Embassy staff, a fine musician himself with a passion
for *lieder,* which he sang with great style and feeling. He was

known for the parties he gave for musical people, and he once advised me to stick to the Italian school of operatic training and not take up the French school. "You ought to capture the French theater style," he said, "but sing in the Italian manner. The French school whitens the voice, but French acting is intense and superb. That kind of eclecticism would be magnificent art." Sir Charles, who knew Duse, nicknamed me the little singing Duse because he said I looked so much like her and, like her, was "an interesting but difficult person to understand."

After Elsie's marriage I felt more at ease when she, out of courtesy to me, came to the Comique to hear me sing. At least now she had Charles with her, who loved the opera and who could explain to her when she was supposed to listen and when not. In spite of Elsie's allergy to musical tone, it was in her ballroom at Versailles that I made my French debut. It was strictly a private and social debut, and my accompanist was that strictly private pianist, Noel Coward. Noel was then a young man known only to a few cronies who loved to hear him sing and play his own songs. Not until Noel took Elsa Maxwell upstairs and read to her the manuscript of *The Vortex* did he give the first inkling to his friends that he was not just another ingratiating young man who composed attractive melodies and was always generous enough to play the piano at parties. When Elsa came down the stairs in the De Wolfe villa after that reading, she was completely convinced of Noel's genius and warned, "Watch that boy." How right she was!

Elsie Mendl's white gloves remind me of another famous American hostess in Paris, my friend Lillie Havemeyer, who was supposed to have started the vogue for wearing short white gloves during the days when she was the only woman in society who took up the great craze for dancing which had swept in the wake of the Castles. Because she occasionally danced with professional dancers in Paris, she was looked upon as an eccentric. I could never understand why—since, if you love dancing enough and are impatient with the shufflings of simon-pure amateurs, only the accomplished partner makes it really fun. But at any rate, Lillie always wore the little white gloves when dancing with those not in her set, probably to denote to her friends that she still recognized class distinction.

Lillie had a talent for houses, a wonderful collection of friends, and a piercing wit. Wherever she lived—whether in her distinctive mansion on the Avenue Gabriel, or in New York's Sutton Place,—there was never a house like hers for its perfection of a unique, highly personal taste. She has now retired to secluded splendor in Rhinebeck, New York, but she left her affectionate mark on the between-wars Paris.

Of all the Americans that went to Paris, Cole Porter probably had more fun than anybody else I knew. He had the capacity to make himself a part of every phase of Parisian life. He was serious and artistic, gay and frivolous. He has always had an enormous zest for enjoyment, which springs from the fact that he was—and has remained at heart—the boy from Peru, Indiana, who reached hungrily at life. Like me, he looked towards a career as an escape from the small town into the abundance of the metropolis.

Linda and Cole Porter had a beautiful house in the Rue Monsieur and gave parties that were the talk of Paris. I went there one Christmas escorted by Chato Elizaga, and I remember carrying on a terrific and aimless flirtation with Duff-Cooper, who suggested, with as little intent as I accepted, that I go with him on a trip to Spain, which at that moment appealed to me beyond discretion. I think it was my friend Howard Sturgis who then, as often afterwards, steered me clear of impulsive "train catching."

Linda Porter has always been one of the great American beauties. Originally from the state of Kentucky, famous for its race horses and women, Linda was the Kentucky Belle of banjo-strummed songs and story. She had a rare kind of face, the bone structure pure and well defined, marked with an unusual graceful femininity. She and Cole made an unusual couple. She was loyal and gracious. Cole had an irrepressible gaiety, a naughtiness that made you always feel that, lurking behind his broad grin, was a roguish kind of wickedness you'd like to know about.

It was good to be part of Cole's fun, and because we both had pretty much the same sense of adventure, we constantly found ourselves involved in the same scrapes. I remember that when my sister Emily came to Paris for the first time, I determined to give her a party the first night that would equal my own introduction to the city. I was the possessor of a red-plush two-room apartment at the time and invited all of Paris to crowd into it. My friends, co-operating with my desire to make Emily's introduction memorable, had each arranged some contribution to the evening's gaiety. One was bringing an act from the Folies Bergères, another had invited a *diseuse* from a Montmartre *boîte,* a third had presented me with a little Negro boy called Snowball to usher the people in.

I read in the Paris *Herald* about a group of singers called the Icemen Yodelers who had just arrived in town after a sensational splash singing before all the crowned heads of Europe. I called Mr. Hill, the editor of the *Herald,* and breezily said I should like to invite the Yodelers to come to my party to sing for distinguished guests. The editor didn't know whether he could get in touch with the group but said he would let me know. Later he called back and told me that the Yodelers had accepted my invitation with pleasure and would be at my apartment at ten o'clock.

I proudly announced at dinner that the Icemen were coming to yodel for us after a triumphant tour of Europe. Cole went on to describe them for those who were out of touch with the American scene. "They'll be the men with the green gloves," he said. "Watch for the workshirts and checkered caps."

After dinner, Cole and I haunted Snowball at the front door to see if our Icemen had arrived. We didn't want them sent to the back entrance and lost on the way. At ten sharp the doorbell rang and Snowball opened it, with Cole and me peering round his shoulders. There stood twelve handsome young Americans impeccably dressed in white tie and tails. Thinking they had the wrong floor, I asked them whom they were looking for. "Miss Moore," they said. "We've come to sing. We're the Icemen Yodelers."

Cole rolled his eyes up at me and groaned, "My God, Grace, what have you done now?" I quickly recovered from my astonishment and ushered the twelve huskies in. With great aplomb the young men arranged themselves in a neat little group and began to sing. Their technique was as finished as their appearance, and it was apparent they had not been practicing in a shower room. It was not until later, after their concert, that I discovered they were twelve of America's most prominent young bankers who had organized this tour, which had included command performances before royalty, as an easy and amusing approach to getting around Europe together.

I made another friend in Paris that first summer about whom I find it as difficult to write as she must find it hard put to talk about me in her column. Elsa Maxwell has remained the same today as she was then. But being so close to her all these years, I have lost sight, as one does, of the details that go into the making of a particular human being and find it difficult to separate them from the career that meets the public view. Elsa's career is part of her character. She has always had an enormous pride and appreciation of the famous people who have come into her life, and they in turn have been drawn to her because of that appreciation, so they are usually at their best when in the orbit of her enthusiasms. She stands alone in her contribution to what was called Cosmopolitan Society in Paris. There was always a grandeur about Elsa, who has never been known to have a bank balance, which never belonged to anyone else, no matter how fabulously wealthy—whether it was at a party at her studio, where it was not unusual to find Stravinsky or Milhaud at supper; or at a luncheon for Kreisler that she gave at her villa on the Riviera, just above the hills of Cannes, which she had acquired as a gift across the luncheon table from the handsome and lovable Eric and Eleanor Loder; or at the famous birthday party she gave at the Ritz-Carlton in Paris, at which she politely declined a birthday gift from Cartier's presented by one of her rich friends who did not know her aversion to jewelry, and asked if she might swap the diamond pendant for a Rubinstein-Kreisler recital which she might share with her friends . . . and then crowded all her most intimate cronies into the Ritz ballroom so they could have with her the pleasure of listening to the inspired music of these two great virtuosi, and outside afterward Diaghileff brought all his troupe to dance among the pink hydrangeas on the Place Vendôme side of the hotel and her best friend, Dickie Gordon, sang *La Bohème* arias.

In 1921 Elsa and Molyneux opened the first fashionable night club ever started in Paris. The European tradition had not included night clubs as part of *faubourg* Paris entertaining. Society entertained at home. There were *boîtes* in Montmartre and Montparnasse, but they were the "naughty" places, certainly never to be considered by a reputable hostess. The night club sponsored by Elsa and Molyneux sprung at once into social favor. Called "Les Acacias" for the street on which it was located, it was opened with Clifton Webb and Jennie Dolly as the main attractions. Molyneux financed it, Elsa was social overseer, and such a success did it become that all international celebrities flocked to it, partly out of curiosity, partly in the hope of enjoying themselves, but mostly because "everybody" was going. There was always a famous artist or diplomat or visiting nabob on the balcony above the dance floor, and as a great person entered, the band, to save the obvious vulgarity of a spotlight, would strike up the favorite tune of the incoming notable. Nothing, of course, could have been more attention-getting: for the band might be in the midst of a tango but would switch immediately to a waltz if a waltz was the signature of the entering celebrity—and· everyone on the little dance floor would stop, turn, and look, much to the arrival's delight.

Molyneux created a new gown for Jennie Dolly every night, outdoing himself for the opening with a slinky cloth of gold with the cape covered with real gardenias, which Jennie would pluck and toss out to the men as she danced around with Clifton dur-

ing the introduction music. Webb had two little black boys, like
nineteenth-century Nubian figurines, who waltzed around with
him, holding two baskets filled with corsages which Webb handed
out to the ladies as he danced. On the closing night of Les
Acacias, Rosie Dolly escaped to Paris from the private yacht of
some wealthy friends and joined Clifton and Jennie for her first
Paris appearance. That night saw the first version of the Pony
Dance, which was to become the theme of the Dolly Sisters' success, improvised by Clifton, who charioteered the two around the
black-carpeted dance floor on the inspiration of the moment.

Shortly after Les Acacias was opened, Molyneux and Elsa
opened a second place to siphon off some of the crowds from
the first. This second place, "Le Jardin de ma Sœur," had as its
stars the new Paris oo-la-la, Josephine Baker, and two dancers,
the great Maurice and Eleanora Hughes, the lovely American
who became an overnight sensation and a legend. One of the
typical stories told about her concerns a Spanish marquis who
was madly in love with her and threatened to jump out of the
window because his suit was spurned. She answered, so the story
goes, "All right, dear, go ahead and jump. But since the room
is only two stories above the ground, I'm not the least impressed
by your bravery."

Elsa continued her party-giving along with her night-club
life. It was at one of her soirees that the Princess Marina, now
the Duchess of Kent, first gave international society a glimpse
of her beauty. At another time Elsa turned over her Montmartre
studio to "Les Six," the six great modernist composers that included, among others, Milhaud, Honegger, and Stravinsky. Elsa,
with sly audacity, invited at the same time the formidable traditionalists, Rubinstein and Heifetz. Those two, hugging tradition
close, refused to be introduced to any of the Six, and when the
modernists were asked to perform, the two intransigents sat on
the side lines and carried on a potpourri conversation in Polish,
Spanish, and French that they felt might, if all went well, drown
out the barbarous noises afloat in the room. However, as the
music began to impinge on them in spite of their chatter and

the determined will not to listen, they began to cock their ears little by little to the unexpected rhythms until they were reduced to complete silence, absorbed in this new and unbelievable world. At the end, the traditionalists rose and kissed the cheeks of their former modernist enemies, swearing eternal friendship.

So through the years Elsa's friends have loved her and consumed and enjoyed her sumptuous hospitality. They sometimes sigh over Elsa's blissful ignorance of income tax and rent bills as she tosses money away with such largesse on the splurge, but it is only a momentary worry, a kind of mental aside, "My God, Elsa's spent her whole salary again," for the worry passes when the memory returns that somehow, somewhere, now as always when Life balances, there exists some magical exit for her.

In spite of the gaiety, I led a double life that season in Paris. I lived frugally in my little *pension,* devoting most of my days to work and study. I had looked desperately for a good teacher and through a letter from Farrar had been able to present myself to Trabadello at his little *pied à terre* on the Left Bank. He was then an old, small thin man with an artistically rouged face that peeked maliciously from beneath a marcelled toupee. Balancing himself on his high heels, he looked me over very carefully, slowly, from head to toe, then asked me to sing a few scales. This I did with no comment from him to break up the interludes as I went on and on, singing scales through sheer embarrassment and not knowing how to stop. The climax came when he asked me to push the baby grand piano from one end of the highly polished parquet to the other while I sang "Ah." Not satisfied with a single performance, he made me repeat it three or four times. Then he said, "Very good, mademoiselle, your diaphragm is in good shape." *Well,* I thought, now we're getting somewhere. We were.

He sat down at the piano and played parts from two or three arias which he asked me to sing. I did so. Then he gave out his decision. "If you will sign a contract with me," he said, "in which I am given complete and absolute control of your artistic career for the next five years, I will make a great star out of you."

I was exhausted and suspicious and confused. Instead of refusing immediately, I promised to think things over and see him the next day. Perhaps I made a mistake in turning M. Trabadello's proposition down, but during the night I decided there were better ways to develop one's diaphragm than by moving pianos across floors; besides, five years was a long, long time. I sent a thank-you note and a "no" to Trabadello and started searching again for a music teacher. Through some friends who advised me, I became a student of Roger Thiral's. M. Thiral was an ex-artist from the Comique who specialized in French diction.

He came every day to my *pension,* and often I went to his studio for a second daily lesson. It was there one day, in the midst of my eighteenth repeat over some of the phrases in "Après un Rêve," that I looked up and saw, standing by the inevitable maroon-colored draperies between the folding doors that exist in every French living room, a medium-sized, middle-height, middle-weight man with a ruddy glowing face. I interrupted the song, wondering who he might be.

"Perfection," said the stranger, "is a difficult thing, mademoiselle, but the only artistry left is the pursuit of it."

He greeted Thiral, then sat down at the piano and played the song for me himself, and in some way all the hitches that had limited me earlier disappeared. Without nervousness or intimidation, I sang the song with the corrections it demanded, feeling a communication with the authority of the man at the piano. My teacher, who was his friend, introduced us. It was Gabriel Fauré.

I learned something that day. It seemed to me then that when you were in the presence of genius, things righted themselves and obtained their proper balance, because genius gave authority. I have since discovered that the more difficult things are, the more that is expected of me, the more I can give in return. I have never been intimidated by difficulties. I have been inspired. And I realized that all too infrequently have I, and most singers today, had the tutelage of truly great masters.

I saw Fauré frequently after that. Sometimes we had only purely social discussions of music around the tea table, enlivened with his reminiscences that covered an enormous span of French music; but sometimes he would run through various of his songs for tempo or emphasis, or he would sit at the piano and improvise. He was intensely serious about music, and his wonderful dry French wit never made light of the art to which he had devoted his life.

As a young student I found this period of Parisian life full of intellectual ferment and inspiration. Diaghileff and his ballet held balletomanes enthralled night after night, as much by the magic of the choreography as by the imaginative *décors* of Berard, Picasso, and Leon Bakst, and the music of Stravinsky. There were the great private balls of Comte de Beaumont, Baroness Rothschild, and the Princess Polignac, who was the reigning queen of one of the great musical salons of the day. There were galleries to visit, so many the stronghold of this wing or another of the controversial art cliques—the surrealists, the abstractionists, the intransigent impressionists, and the dadaists. And of course there was always the Opera.

I must admit that my first visit to the Paris Opera was different from my original trip to the Metropolitan, where I had to climb to the top of the Peanut Gallery to see Farrar in her great Carmen. My first sortie to the Paris Opera was made in great style with affluent friends who invited me to share the center box in the golden horseshoe.

I'd like to say here that never have I underestimated the importance of my rich friends, because they have given me the opportunity I might never have had to feast at Lucullan banquets, to learn the rare bouquets of vintage wines, and to sit in the assembly lines of jeweled women who hold down the golden horseshoes of the concert halls of the world. You may not hear nearly as well in the horseshoes as in any other part of the house, but you sometimes do love the tremendous splash. I have always had an affectionate gratitude toward the people who have taken me. There are many who find the rich boring per se. But I have never made that mental reservation. Whatever may have been their appreciation of the things I myself love, they have held out the means for me to enjoy them. I feel a kind of foolish protectiveness for the rich. I know they are supposed to be fading on the political scene, probably heading for class extinction—and, some say, with justice. But I refuse to analyze or criticize the engaging hospitality that has provided me with so much happiness. Economic determination is one thing, the mouth of a gift horse another.

That's why, even as a poor student, I remember the lights and sparkle and elegance of the Paris Opera. I love that place, with its magnificent staircase, the high-domed ceiling with its blazing chandelier that makes me think inevitably of Cinquemodo and De Maupassant, and the courtly solemn custom of the bejeweled circle that moves constantly to the right in a slow processional during intermission. Opera becomes really grand when sung here. It has an inevitable destiny in this huge place. All the tragedies, the big booming calamities of the opera repertoire, find a fit sounding board in the walls, echoing from the maze of its cellars to the top of its haunted roof.

I had wanted especially to hear Fanny Heldy. There was always so much gossip about her, so much talk and adulation. In addition to being the ranking French star, she was also the top female jockey in France and rode her own horses at the tracks. Heldy was not a woman of gigantic voice, but she possessed great acting talent and allure. In recent years I remember seeing her in *L'Aiglon* and marking how, as she walked across the stage, there was a tenseness, a thin, poetic strain of suffering that transformed her from Heldy, the singer, into L'Aiglon. She *was* L'Aiglon before she ever sang a note. Everything—movement, emotion, sorrow—was there in her body, and that body became an instrument of passion that inevitably foreshadowed the song.

Fanny Heldy reigned supreme in the Paris Opera for many years, not only because she had as champion an influential man whom she finally married and who was interested enough in the Opera to lard over the deficit each year—but because she had the temperament and flair of a supreme singing actress. Fanny didn't need a rich "friend." She was exactly the kind of prima donna the French adore. The French have never demanded virtuoso voices from their prima donnas. What they insisted on having was a perfection of acting artistry ingrained in the music. They also were partial to good looks. They demanded chic and beauty and the credible illusion of enchantment. All of my musical work in France, all of my allegiance to the French techniques, springs from my own sympathy towards this approach to opera, and because of this conception, I have found the Opéra Comique the finest training school an opera singer can have.

About this time Neysa McMein joined me in Paris directly after her marriage to Jack Baragwanath. The papers had carried, the story of the marriage, and when she was seen with me in Paris there was considerable comment and buzz-buzzing. The explanation was very simple (as it usually is in such cases). Jack, handsome son of an American minister, who looks more like a dashing Spaniard and has more Latin spark than a native Don Juan, had been called down unexpectedly to South America immediately after the marriage. Neysa did what so many movie people do—she saved the honeymoon for later and joined me rather than linger alone, pining for Jack in New York. Before her departure, Neysa had asked Woollcott and Heywood Broun for the name of a good cheap hotel. The two wags recommended the Hôtel Opal, near the Boulevard des Italiens. I was then at the Hôtel Mirabeau on the Rue de la Paix, where I had been able to make a special inexpensive arrangement.

The first night of Neysa's arrival, Cole Porter called for me to take me over to Neysa's, and we would all have dinner. We arrived at the Opal and put in a call for Neysa to come down and meet us in the lobby. We plumped down in a room off the little entrance lobby, there to wait. Suddenly it dawned on us as we sat there that something queer was afoot. All the other chairs in the lobby were filled with the most succulent collection of blondes and brunettes, dressed to the teeth, and treating us to the most amazing performance of rolling eyes, hip wiggles, and insinuating gestures. I looked at Cole, he looked at me, we both tried not to look at our neighbors. When Neysa came out of the elevator we grabbed her and rushed her into the street. There Cole broke the facts of life to our young bride, adding that a brothel was no place for her to get them. Sending Neysa there was a typical practical joke of Woollcott's and Broun's.

The freedom, the Rabelaisian merriment, the typically Parisian ability to turn art and sex and living into a bubbling Olympic jest came to a head each year in the Quatre-Arts Ball. On that occasion the whole of the city was turned over and belonged to the students. The police heard no wrong, saw no wrong, reported no wrong. If anyone objected, the motto was, let them stay home. On that night the creative imagination which has made Paris the dream city for artists all over the world runs riot.

As much a part of the traditions of the ball as the ball itself were the little private dinners given by the various ateliers before the main event. Thanks to Jascha Heifetz, Neysa, Dudley Field Malone, and I not only got to the ball, but to one of these very select little dinners that preceded it. Jascha managed it by distributing a pocketful of concert tickets as a bribe, pleading with tears in his eyes, and a few well-placed falsehoods. He told the arrangers of the dinner that Neysa was America's greatest painter, I America's great dancer, and probably that he—well, they knew who he was: an artist loved by the Parisians. That was his admission fee. At any rate, we got in. It was quite a sight. There were fifty men there, immediately resentful when they saw Neysa and me. They apparently wanted no women—not, to put it baldly, because it was stag but because it was drag. The sullenness clung to the room until festivities started. Let me telescope that part of the evening by saying that I ended standing on the table singing "Madelon," while Neysa and the fifty men in various treble ranges of voice toasted the U.S.A.

After the dinner, Neysa, Jascha, Dudley, and I joined the merry throngs on the sidewalks of Montparnasse, undaunted by the rain, which was streaking our Pompeiian make-up and wilting that dab of chiffon which made up our costume. We went over to the ball proper at Luna Park. Knowing that there were arbitrary rules about the costume, we had dressed accordingly. A kind of censorship in reverse abided—if you came to the door and you or your costume were found to be not to the committee's taste, they would direct you *"à gauche"* and you found yourself right out on the street. For the in-betweens, who were neither rejected nor accepted, a black cross was painted on the back to indicate that the costume was not entirely authentic. This particular Quatre-Arts Ball had as its subject "Scenes from Old Pompeii," and when we finally got up to our box and looked down below, we saw a fantastic bohemian world that seemed more like an animated picture from an unexpurgated Lucius Apuleius than a scene out of modern Europe.

Condé Nast was supposed to have been in our party, but the last glimpse we got of him that evening was as he, arrayed in correct white tie and tails, was being turned away from the door by the police, who warned him that no one so respectable could survive the bedlam within. We had been wiser and less restrained. Malone, the Paris *Herald* said the next morning, looked "like a Roman senator escaping the volcano's lava." I was supposed to look, according to the *Herald,* like a blonde vestal come down to take a peek at such goings on. Jascha was described as "Al Jolson with leprosy." Neysa was a Pompeiian queen of easy virtue. All of us were found to be very much in keeping.

Surrounding our box were the exhibits put on by the famous ateliers, which were having a public *vernissage* of their prize models displayed as living paintings. It was startling to see the famous beauties of Montmartre and Montparnasse, who were so familiar on canvases in galleries throughout the world, here in the flesh.

Below, the crowd swirled in a mad, riotous display. But it was a pageant of beauty. It was at this ball that I saw Sorel hoisted, in the half-nude, on the shoulders of the students to the delight and cheers of the crowd. One costume was more revealing and more irreverent than the next, and the horseplay was on a par with pre-reform Minsky's. We decided to leave as they were getting ready to put Lady Godiva on her white horse. Later we learned from Jascha, who had stayed to see all the fun, that everyone had gone swimming in the Place de la Concorde, much to the consternation of the Americans who looked down from the Crillon windows and murmured, "Ah, Paris!"

Neysa was leaving Paris on the early boat train the next morning, and we managed to get back to the Hôtel Mirabeau about an hour before she had to catch it. We had stopped on the way to buy baskets of fruits and flowers to give her for the long trip home, leaving little time to pack and get ready. In the scramble to get off, we found we couldn't remove the Pompeiian brown paint. We tried with sponges and with soap, but it resisted our pressure with the same tenacity as the real Pompeii had stood off the decay of ages. Neysa finally made her exit from the Mirabeau looking as splotched as if she had a scrofulous disease, wearing two stockings but only one shoe, no hat, and heavily laden with a basket of strawberries and flowers. A fine sight she was too! Later I found the shoe under the tub, but Neysa had gone.

Caruso and I again brushed elbows at about this time. Some friends had arranged an excursion to Mont St. Michel, and we started out by car from Paris. We stopped in Dijon in a little restaurant Aux Trois Faisans and had dinner in the beautiful courtyard under the trees. We lingered long over dinner and arrived late at Mont St. Michel.

It was an amazing night, heavy with black shadows, a full moon, and the witchcraft beauty of the huge pile of stone that leaped to the sky. The night watchman of St. Michel would not let us in. No, he said, it was too late—we could come back tomorrow. But, we pleaded, we had motored five hundred miles and had to start back almost at once—couldn't he let us walk around and see one room? Probably because he was lonely he let us in. He led us through the great main hall and then into a little refectory room off to the side, brilliantly lit by moonlight.

"This room," the caretaker told us, "has the best acoustics in the whole world." I went to the end of it, onto the little stage, and did a few bars from "Ave Maria." Yes, I agreed, I had

never before heard a place where one could sing with every
subtlety and variety of voice and know it would come back perfectly distilled. We thanked the caretaker, gave him his *pourboire,* and started to leave. He stopped me.

"You know, mademoiselle, you have a pretty voice. Too bad
you don't use it professionally. The only other voice I remember
vividly here was when a big fat man came and sang here just
this way, to test the acoustics. I never heard such tones. Magnificent. As he left he gave me a big, generous tip and said in
funny French, 'Good luck, my friend. Don't forget me—I am
Caruso.' I never have."

One night, at a dinner given by Dudley Field Malone, who
had such an international practice that he had set up an office
in Paris, I met Mary Garden again, for the first time since the
Washington schoolgirl episode, and she remembered me! There,
under the chestnut trees in the gardens of Armenonville, where we
watched the enchanting Irene Castle and Billy Reardon dance, I
had my first opportunity to talk to her about my dreams and ambitions. She was so alive-looking, with bright red hair and a face
that could never be old because the eyes dominated it with such
an intense and enormous intelligence. She told me I ought to
study *Louise,* inquired about my plans, and promised to arrange
an audition at the Comique for me. She also gave me a letter
of introduction to a friend of hers, Edward Herman, a man of
solid critical judgment and friend of many musicians.

I presented myself later to Herman, whose enthusiasm was
important, and when he heard me sing he told me I needed a
good deal more training, but that my voice was beautiful. One
day, at Garden's request, he took me to a rehearsal room at the
Comique to sing for Albert Wolff. With us went Roger Thiral,
my coach, and Cécile Satoris, an American known throughout
musical circles in Paris.

Wolff was at the piano and played for me himself. I stood by
the side of the upright on the empty stage of the Comique and
sang "Depuis le jour" from *Louise* as Mary had advised. When
I had finished singing, Wolff looked up at me and said, "My

dear, you have a beautiful voice, but you don't know what you are singing about. Go out and live and then come back and sing it for me, and I will tell you what career you shall have."

That incident stuck in the back of my mind until the morning of the rehearsal with orchestra that preceded a concert at Ostend in 1937. I had by that time sung *Louise* many times with success, but Wolff had never happened to be at the baton. As I finished the rehearsal of the aria he turned to me and said: "I don't know what you have done since I spoke to you last, but you have exceeded expectations." (After all, Mr. Wolff, a girl should have a chance to get around in that number of years!)

My friends were pleased with Wolff's enthusiasm about my voice and felt certain, they assured me, that my life would take care of itself. Now, they said, if I just kept working hard and followed the regime I had laid out for myself, I would achieve the operatic career which I had so definitely in mind.

However, there was an unexpected detour directed by the state of my diminishing bank balance. The 1923 version of the *Music Box Revue* was being cast in New York, and I was recommended for the prima-donna lead by Bob Benchley and Hassard Short. Irving Berlin, on a trip to Paris, called for me at the pension, took a good cagey look around at my unpalatial surroundings, and invited me out to Ciro's for lunch. There, across a glass of red wine, Berlin offered me the role in the show. Whether because of the unexpected ferment of the wine, Berlin's charm, or the knowledge that my money wasn't going to last much longer, I agreed to join the cast of the *Revue*. The contract was signed on the tablecloth in Ciro's—for which the headwaiter insisted that Berlin pay.

My friends, who had been so elated over my audition at the Comique, were bitterly disappointed when I signed the contract with Berlin. But I saw no other way. I had to go back to Broadway to work and save. I said good-by to Paris and sailed for home.

Music Boxes and Round Tables

My RETURN TO NEW YORK for the first *Music Box Revue* was the drawstring that pulled my whole life into shape—it laced my friends, ideas, ambitions together and caught the scattered pieces in one pouch. I felt that now I was really going forward: that here was Broadway at its best, and that in being given an opportunity to sing Irving Berlin's simple, lovely songs that suited my voice, I had found the right niche at the right time.

Irving Berlin and I sat up until dawn the night the *Revue* opened and waited for the morning papers. He read the notices aloud to me, and I remember trembling with excitement and nervous indigestion. When he came to Alec Woollcott's criticism: ". . . hats were thrown in the air and cheers resounded from one end of Broadway to the other and a new star was born," I broke down and cried. Irving was sweet and understanding— and audibly patted himself on the back for having guessed right when he persuaded me to give up study in Paris for this Broadway appearance.

Irving was happy for himself too. He was so much in love with Ellin Mackay and was up against the toughest resistance Clarence H. Mackay, her father, could maneuver. Success was important to him, because it could bolster his resistance against the tycoon who was using every avenue to kill the romance. The songs in the Music Box were love messages from Irving to Ellin, and I never sang them without thinking of the two. In a way I was Irving's "singing telegram" to his love—in defiance of Mr. Mackay's Postal Colossus.

How the tables have turned! Just recently when I saw the dress rehearsal of *This Is the Army,* I thought of how proud and honored Clarence Mackay, if he were alive, might well have been to know that the little Jewish boy who used to sing at Nigger Mike's, and who has made one of the greatest single-handed contributions to morale in this war, is his son-in-law.

My associates in the Music Box were troupers of good, long tradition—among them the stars John Steele, Frank Tinney, and Florence Moore.

Irving Berlin had written some of his most lasting and beloved melodies for this *Revue.* There was the melancholy, nostalgic "Remember." There was that sweeter-than-blue "All Alone," which remains the loneliest song in all American popular music. There was the plaguing, heartbroken "What'll I do?" For the "Orange Grove" number the stage was full of orange trees which wafted perfume to the audience. I loved the music and was happy in singing it.

The *Revue* was staged by Hassard Short, with imagination and his usual-unusual good taste. I found, however, in the first rehearsal that he expected, as they always do on Broadway, that because I could sing I was a dancer too. Not only was I to carry the lead singing role, but I was also to hoof it with the entire ensemble in the finale of the first act. Determined to make a go out of this new part, I struggled through most of the first day, went home, turned back the rug, practiced the little dance routine most of the night and showed up the next morning with fingers crossed that I would get by. But, in the good old Broadway tradition, when I arrived on stage for rehearsal, I found that the whole dance had been changed. I gave up, and so did Short. We decided that I should do the singing, let the dancing fall where it may.

Florence Moore used to talk of me and introduce me as "the little sister," and many people at the time thought that I was. The nip-and-jab gossip claimed that Florence did this only after I became a success, so that it would show her generosity in giving the other little girl of the family a helping hand. Each time she made any reference from the stage about "the little sister" there was applause from the audience, and I must admit that it sometimes annoyed me.

Frank Tinney was a roguish, lovable soul but too often in his cups. He came of the genus *joker practicalis* too—which some people can take or leave alone. I'm the last named variety. I had a devil of a time escaping the cute electric-shock chair that he used to put in all the odd corners backstage at the Music Box where one might want to sit for a bit of momentary relaxation between scenes.

John Steele, the star tenor of the *Revue,* had a wonderful voice. Its quality and timbre were very much like that of Felix Clement, who had been a noted opera and concert star earlier. But to round out his lyric voice, John Steele had some of the worst characteristics to go along with a tenor. He was extremely jealous of my success and made it clear from the first. For instance, on the opening night when I took an individual curtain bow as cheers rose throughout the house, I made the little curtsey to the audience which I still continue to use as a thank-you today. It was my first Broadway success, and I was so overcome with emotion that, as the applause continued, I seemed paralyzed in that curtsey. Suddenly I heard behind the curtain the voices of Florence Moore, Frank Tinney, and John Steele, who said, "Well, why in the hell don't you get up, are you going to stay there all night? Let us out there too."

I was too inexperienced to cope with the jealousies and intrigues backstage—such as the stepping on my toe just before I had to take a high note, or the upstaging that almost sent me into the pit. But I was not too wide-eyed to have any of it escape me. However, all these petty incidents put the company in an uproar, which was climaxed by my receipt one day of an anonymous letter which attacked me personally and viciously.

I knew the whole business was a childish explosion of backstage jealousy, but it got under my skin none the less and churned up my nervous system. For instance: For the first number of the show, I sat in an enormous wicker ·chair surrounded by lovely girls all dressed in their nighties, while I sang the opening song, "Tell Me a Bedtime Story." After many months of this petty backstage business there were times when I would hold onto the chair desperately but could not finish the number. The curtain had to be rung down while I tried to pull myself together for my next appearance on the stage.

Irving one day brought me a letter of apology from Steele, and sensing my unhappy and nervous condition, he and Sam Harris insisted that I take a ten-day vacation. As I didn't know where to go, Irving suggested that I try Lakewood, where, he said, the food was good and it would be quiet. I went off and found the place ideal, comfortable, with excellent food, and really quiet as Irving had claimed. I felt my spirits rising. I liked it so much that I wrote Jane Thomas to join me. She arrived, looked around and said, "Why, Grace, I didn't know you were Jewish."

I looked at her in surprise. "Why, I didn't either," I answered.

"But after all," she explained, "this is a place where only Jewish people go and only kosher food is served."

I'd been there for ten days and hadn't noticed the difference! Even with the men wearing their hats in the dining room. Irving and Sam Harris laughed when they met me, rested and happy, on my return, and said they didn't know I'd be able to stick it out, since I was unaccustomed to kosher food. Apparently, they pointed out, the laws of the Old Testament had been laid down for me too.

Those were happy, eventful days. Is there anything more gala than being a young star with her first taste of success and fame? To my three-room apartment on West Fifty-ninth Street, which Jessie Harrison shared as my duenna, came some of New York's most fascinating people. They would overflow from my smallish living room into the bedroom, to which I gave the look of propriety by draping the beautiful Venetian bed with a heavy cover of dark green brocade. The very first day that Beatrice Lillie and Gertrude Lawrence landed in America they were brought to my apartment to tea by Will Stewart. Dorothy Parker, Cole Porter, F.P.A., George Jean Nathan, and Elsie De Wolfe were on hand to greet them. June Walker and Marc Connelly did a tap dance on the two-by-four parquet around the piano, and Bea and Gerty sang a duet, off key. Johnson and Leighton, the colored team that was the rage of New York at the time, did the honors at the piano. Sam Goldwyn brought Jack Dempsey, then at the height of his fame as the Manassa Mauler, who spent most of the afternoon telling me what a fine "type" of woman I was—just the type to marry.

Often I would come home after the show and find Jo Davidson and Augustus John waiting there for me for supper. Those two would get into such violent arguments that I frequently went off to bed and left them, only to find both on hand for breakfast. They had become so exhausted in the small hours of the morning by the pros and cons of their artistic views that they had collapsed on a couch or a chair in the living room to sleep off their rage. One night I overheard them ranting loudly against the rich and insisting that the only legitimate excuse for permitting people to build up fortunes was to give them the means to patronize artists like Davidson and John. Wealth made sense only if the wealthy shelled out the necessarily high fees to have their vanity perpetuated in marble and paint. A neat economic theory, I thought, as I drifted off to sleep.

One night, I was asked to sing at a benefit performance, sponsored by Minnie Maddern Fiske, for the S.P.C.A. Bea Lillie appeared too, and it was the first time I realized what an incomparable clown she is. She had only to come out on the stage, lift an eyebrow, and she brought down the house before a sound had been made. She had a genius for comedy that was implicit in every movement of her face, her hands, her body. Bob Benchley contributed to the hilarity—and the good cause—with one of the first of his now famous monologues on the sex appeal of the baby. The whole affair, at twelve-fifty a seat, was an enormous success, even if Doug Fairbanks didn't come. When I had approached him in advance to buy some tickets, he said that rather than pay twenty-five dollars for two seats it was better to buy a horse and be kind to it!

High finance also came into my life—briefly—at about this time. I had joined the Riverside Church, where I went each Sunday. Recently when I accepted Mr. Rockefeller's invitation to sing at a special service there, I dropped my purse, and as the coins fell from it with a dreadful clink-clink that seemed to reverberate to the tower, Mr. Rockefeller, who was sitting in the next pew, got down on his hands and knees, crawled around under the pew, and helped pick up my scattered belongings— powder puff, lipstick, mirror, perfume bottle, and comb. With each retrieved belonging he looked up at me as startled as a young March hare. As he handed back nickel after nickel, I had a comic sense of vast fortunes changing hands with the blessing of heaven.

I continued going every day to Marafioti's studio for vocal lessons. There I would meet other students. One was an associate of mine at the Music Box. He was an electrician at the theater, with operatic ambitions. Another one of the students drove a taxicab at night to support his family. A third was perpetually broke because he devoted his life to those touring opera companies that bravely crossed the country, season after season, without winning public support.

The great Emma Calvé was then going over special vocal exercises with Marafioti too. I met her at the studio, where she had the hour preceding my lesson. She was fascinated by Marafioti's method of teaching and often was so carried away by her enthusiasm that I found myself sitting in the little anteroom while the minutes allotted to my own lesson ticked away unheeded. One day I became so exasperated with this continued waste of time that I interrupted Calvé and Marafioti and declared to both that my lessons were much too important to *me* to share them even with Madame Calvé, and that I was not rich enough in bank balance or experience to do so. Calvé was incensed at the interruption and flounced out of the studio indignantly. Marafioti turned on me furiously. Suddenly I realized what I had done, and I thought I should die with mortification. The whole business proved most expensive—because I had to go out and buy an enormous bouquet of flowers and send it with a note to Madame

Calvé. Luckily she was primarily an artist and not a resentful woman, for she changed the hour of her visit to the one following mine and often would come in during the middle of my lesson and wait in the anteroom listening, and on several occasions she came quietly into the room where I was having my lesson and sat silently in a corner until we were finished. Her interest in me was chiefly as the instrument for Marafioti's voice method.

When Calvé and I met in Paris years later and became friends, she would tell the story of how I burst in on her visit with Marafioti. She always ended by saying that she had secretly admired the impulse that had prompted me—if not the style of delivery.

My lessons were dominated by Marafioti's concern with the life that is in the word. He felt that an artist must know the meaning of a word before it can be colored with vocal sound. "Emotional powers," he insisted, "are the greatest asset, but, unless controlled by intelligence, one will never achieve real distinction."

Marafioti also worked on the conservation of breath. We used to take a lighted candle, which I held before me as I started to sing. If the light flickered I was pushing the voice, which meant it was not nearly as big or resonant as when I used it to recite the words. I had to learn to sing with the same ease and fluency as in speaking, so the light would burn without a flicker.

One Sunday night at the traditional Marafioti spaghetti dinner I met Montemezzi, the famous Italian composer of *The Love of Three Kings*. He had been to the *Music Box Revue* to hear me and asked me to sing a little song that night for the party. I did. He fanned my hopes by saying, "You know you have definite operatic talent." He told me that I must learn to concentrate on singing as a natural spontaneous function. "Singing right," he said, "is the easiest thing in the world, and singing wrong the hardest."

Roberto Moranzoni, then the conductor at the Metropolitan Opera, was also a frequent visitor at the Marafioti studio, and he became a wonderful friend with whom I later worked in Milan on my preparations for *La Bohème*. He had loved Maggie Teyte very much at one time, but they argued continuously. One night we all got into a verbal free-for-all on the emotional intensity an artist had to feel on his side of the footlights in order to communicate the mood to his audience. Moranzoni said that an artist should feel twice as much emotion as he wanted an audience to feel, but should know when to conserve it. Maggie Teyte's point of view was that only the illusion had to be given—it was not necessary to steep oneself in the emotion itself. Later I remembered this discussion when Mary Garden said to me: "A woman doesn't have to go around destroying and cutting off men's heads to play Salome or be a strumpet to play *Resurrection* or a virgin to play Marguerite or a great amoureuse to play Manon, but she must have imagination—the thing that colors all vocal sound, regardless of one's private life and emotions. Melba was a great holder of her men but cold on the stage, but Calvé was a passionate siren on the stage and couldn't hold a man!"

One night early in 1924, at a dinner at Sir William Wiseman's, I sat next to Otto Kahn. He seemed a rather pompous, dignified man, interested in too many things to get a great sensation out of any one of them, but he did sound most proud of his chairmanship of the board of directors of the Metropolitan Opera. I asked him if he ever fell in love with the Opera's prima donnas, and he answered that when it came to opera stars he found himself completely indifferent. "The Opera itself is too important," he said simply. Kahn had a real passion for art, and his death a few years ago took one of the few true patrons of the arts that this country has ever had—a man who devoted himself and his fortune to the theater, the ballet, and the opera with all the intensity of a Lorenzo of olden days. He had, in addition, a capacity for loyal friendship, as I myself discovered through the years.

I knew that he had been to the *Music Box Revue* opening and had expressed enthusiastic approval of my voice, for his opinions had drifted back to me through the grapevine of mutual friends. Now, at this dinner, we spoke of my operatic ambitions, and with a generosity I shall never forget he said that if I was really serious he would arrange a meeting at the Metropolitan. One day at five o'clock I met him at the Met's stage door. He introduced me to

Mr. Gatti-Casazza and Mr. Ziegler, and I was invited to hear parts of auditions which were being held that afternoon. I remember how quietly bored Gatti-Casazza looked and how seemingly cold was his "thank you" after each singer had done his little stint. But I felt I could hardly blame him, because there was not one good voice to listen to that day. My own audition was arranged before we left, and I dashed over to Marafioti's studio to begin work in earnest.

I chose an aria from Montemezzi's opera *Giovanni Galurrese* for the audition, and Montemezzi himself coached me at the piano, day after day at the studio. April 10th at four-thirty was the crucial moment, and all my energies were directed toward it. Finally it came and I stood at last, for the first time, on the great stage of the Metropolitan, waiting for Wilfred Pelletier, at the piano, to strike the opening notes. My ability to make a quick recovery from a panicky situation helped me in that crisis. I started off in a trembling, hysterical voice—and I could feel it get away from me. I looked down at my little audience—Mr. Kahn, Gatti-Casazza, Ziegler, Bodanzky, and other directors— and could sense their nervousness and restless inattention, and I knew that very soon they would get bored and walk out, one by one, as I had seen them do to others the day of my earlier visit there. But fortunately it has always been characteristic of me that the tighter the spot, the more effective the results. I pulled myself together, and singing better than I had sung at any time or place before, I finished that first audition with success.

Everyone was most charming and enthusiastic, and Mr. Gatti-Casazza told me that I had the potentiality of becoming a Farrar but that I had to work to achieve it. I left the auditorium determined that since the master had said I had the possibilities, I would work, work, work to realize them.

I was up in the clouds that night at the Music Box. Irving's lovely and simple songs were suddenly not enough—they lacked the soaring notes I wanted—but I was happy to be where I was, making money and able to study every day. I had only one ambi-

tion—Opera—but I did not underestimate the Music Box as a
financial provider and stepping stone toward it.

Now that Gatti-Casazza had compared me to Farrar, I became
passionately interested in her. But it was that same season that she
sang her farewell performance as Zazà at the Metropolitan. I
went to hear her, and was swept up in the most affectionate
theater farewell that I have ever seen. The whole house, backstage and out front, was dissolved in tears. You could hear the
weeping rise in great waves and flood onto the stage, where the
incomparable Farrar, surrounded by enormous quantities of
flowers, took bow after bow. The "Gerry-Flappers" who crowded
the house were the most doleful-looking group of girls in the
world. Geraldine Farrar had been their idol: her dress, her style,
her manner had colored and influenced their lives. Now with
reddened eyes and swollen noses they snuffled and wept openly
and unashamedly because the one they loved was no longer to
lead them. Years later in Hollywood, Edward Knopf's wife told
me she had been a Gerry-Flapper and could never understand
why she and her friends didn't "just break down and die."

A mass commentary on the transience of human emotion was
made to me when I went with Condé Nast, not long after, to hear
Maria Jeritza make her debut at the Metropolitan in *Die Tote
Stadt*. The same audience which had melted in sorrow at Farrar's
exit was now swept in a paroxysm of joy at Jeritza's entrance.
Jeritza had a big rich voice, a robust personality, and a sure instinct for domination on the stage. She knew how to be a "star."
As to her art, there has been much controversy. I heard her do a
beautiful Elsa in *Lohengrin* and once, in Paris, heard her do such
an appallingly bad Tosca that the French audience hissed. But
Jeritza was always a great showman, although she never had the
subtlety or beauty of Farrar's art.

My work began to pile up. I made my first actual public appearance at the Metropolitan in late April of that year, singing
"What'll I do?" at a benefit performance for Equity. There was
the routine of the *Music Box Revue,* constant study, and the
persistent undercurrent of my ambition. Soon the strain began to

tell. I became nervous, confused, and unhappy. Marafioti thought I ought to try a new "cure" just coming onto the market. So he sent me to a friend of his for psychoanalysis. This doctor was a specialist in nervous diseases and had a great reputation throughout the medical profession. Psychoanalysis was in the early stages of its development, and this man was doing pioneer work in this new field. I took Marafioti's advice and presented myself to the doctor.

It seemed to me a wacky experience. The doctor had two hypodermics—one Italian, the other French. On the days he administered the Italian one, we spoke in Italian. When he used the French one, we chatted in French. "What is he up to?" I wondered. "Does he want to see which Latin inspiration I react to most effectively?" He told me many things about myself —some of which were apt, some confusing. I was six women in one, he said, ranging from six to sixty, and would remain like that. Because of this conflict I should always seem apparently simple to understand but should be really complicated not only to myself but to everybody else. He also said that I was happy only if I had someone in love with me or was giving affection— but the answer to that is, who isn't? The doctor finally confessed that he knew me but could not unravel me: that although he saw that my interest in men was superficial and causing a great deal of my nervousness because I was sublimating it in a burning ambition, he himself had psychoanalyzed me to the point where *he* had fallen in love. I now had the new little problem of helping the doctor to pull himself together. Those were indeed the early days of psychoanalysis, and the art of who sublimates whom hadn't been perfected.

That spring, after his final proposal by cable, my engagement to George Biddle was publicly announced. He suggested that I join him in Paris directly after the closing of the *Music Box Revue*. The announcement made front pages of the newspapers and headlines in Philadelphia. George's mother came to New York to visit me and was very gracious about the whole matter. "If you and George are really serious," she said, "and feel you will go through with it, I will run over to Paris to put the finishing touches on the arrangements." Francis Biddle, our present Attorney General, also called on me. He was charming but outspokenly dubious about the whole thing and said he didn't know how George and I were going to manage two careers in the same family. He added that he had two categories of advice to offer. As a lawyer, he could only point out that I was still pretty young to know just where I was headed for or what I wanted. As a friend, he could only say, "If you really love him, go ahead and take the consequences." I felt that here was a nice judicial weighing of the evidence.

Irving Berlin had a business slant on the whole thing—box-office sales, he said, had shown a terrific increase since the announcement of my engagement to a Biddle. So, with a little of this and a little of that to determine my judgment, I sailed for Paris and George.

That summer in Europe after the first *Music Box Revue* was a holiday jaunt. I trotted around Paris from museum to museum, studying the costumes. I believed that good singing had to have its place in a cultural background in order to be truly meaningful. The world of color was not too far removed from the realm of coloratura, and I felt that the student of one must know something of the other. Painting has always seemed to me to be most closely related to music. Its tones, its harmonies, its symphonic arrangements are like the point and counterpoint of musical composition. I know that according to purist theory it is anathema to haul in one art in understanding another. A painter can make no more scathing remark about a critic than to say he has a literary approach to graphic art. Perhaps the musical approach is just as outlandish. But it has always had validity for me—and the old saw, "I don't know much about umph but I know what I like," is not all poppycock. I had been a devotee of the Louvre and haunted the damp-smelling Cluny which stood shrouded in grayness on the corner of the Boulevard St. Germain. Now I had my first glimpse of the moderns at the Michel—Gauguin, Matisse, Mary Cassatt. I became acquainted with Toulouse-Lautrec and even went so far as to buy a Marie Laurencin for 175 francs. George and I, in our wanderings on the Quai Voltaire, found a little Rembrandt engraving, tattered with age, which we bought for 150 francs, *à bon marché*. Today that Rembrandt, now magically put together, my first Laurencin, a small but excellent collection of etchings, lithographs, and drawings of Toulouse-Latrec, an original each of Whistler, Degas, and Gauguin all hang on the wall of the music room in our farmhouse in Connecticut.

That summer I saw my first entire performance of the opera *Louise*. Given at the Opéra Comique with Rosie Elsie singing the name role, it was a most unimpressive affair. Perhaps it was the heat which produced tepidness on the stage, for the cast marched through the acts with a lackadaisical disinterest. I was so disappointed. *Louise* had not been given at the Metropolitan since Farrar and Caruso, and I had never before had a chance to hear it in its entirety. This was hardly the enchantment I had expected. But in spite of the offhandedness of that cast, I was so caught up in the music and spirit of Charpentier's masterpiece that I determined that the singing of *Louise* would be the goal of my operatic ambitions. I felt despondent, as I often did that summer, that I had to return in the fall for another *Music Box Revue*. I wanted to stay on in Paris and study, especially to study the role of Louise. But there was the constant question of money, and I knew the Music Box had to continue as a bulwark towards a bank account.

Jane Thomas joined us, and we went off to the Lido on my first trip to Venice. George and I were beginning to tiff, and our quarrels made a little background pattern to that whole visit. George was—and is—a darling, and although he said in his autobiography that we had done a lot of slugging, it was pure mental fisticuffs carried out verbally. We never came to a real knockdown-and-drag-out decision until Venice—which is, incidentally, as fine a place to end a romance as it is to start one. George accused me of being impressed with the "slick Menjou type," but that was because I objected to the strawberry-colored tweed for which he had a passion. George also loved cats and had them snuggling and brushing up against him constantly. I am no cat hater, but neither am I a cat lover, and I felt I was being displaced in the Biddle affection by the most feline of the species.

Nevertheless that trip to Venice and the Lido was a happy one. I was fascinated by the pictures, the people, the place. I "did" the galleries seriously and unashamedly like any tourist, with my guidebooks. Otto Kahn and Rudolf Kommer arrived in Venice and were joined by Bodanzky and Max Reinhardt. They took me on as their unpaid guide, and with Jane Thomas to round out the party, we went from picture to picture. One day Kahn took me to the palace of the two Giovanelli princes where Giorgione's "Tempest" had a suite to itself and for which, rumor had it, Kahn made a fabulous offer each year. Together we stood for almost a quarter of an hour before the canvas without saying a word. Then Kahn said, "You know, this is one of the few things in my life that I have been unable to buy. Everything has its price but this."

I learned to admire Otto Kahn more and more that summer. Once, admitting that it sounded like the talk of an old man, he said that we were all living on the vitality of our forefathers and leaving very little to give the coming generation because of our nervous confusion. His age troubled him—not because he himself was old but because he liked living so much and age was the beginning of the end. One day I saw him looking depressed. I asked him why. "I feel the romance of Venice," he answered wistfully. "I only regret I'm not fifteen years younger and you ten years older."

The two women who turned the Lido into an international summer resort were the fabulous Countess Nina Morosini, redheaded and vixenish friend of the Kaiser who was always a tricky card player, and the fantastic Princess di San Faustino, American-born Jane Campbell, who held court among the Italians like a Medici, wore a Mary Queen of Scots headdress of white with a black veil, dispensed wit, advice, and gossip with a sharp tongue, and was the mother of my newly acquired beau, the Prince Ranieri di San Faustino. The prince was a charming man who liked to play the piano while I sang. He was mad about music and composed a number of things. Irving Berlin published one of his fox trots, much to Princess Jane's amazed chagrin.

Prince Ranieri had also gone to work, which shocked his family, who lived in the tradition that it was worse than dishonor for a member of the Roman nobility to engage in gainful occupation. However, the prince must have inherited his tendency to be useful from his American mother.

The Princess Jane was very gracious about our interest in one another. She came to me late one night and said that, on thinking it over, we were really a charming couple and that I could save him for himself by taking him with me into the musical world where he belonged. A kind of inverted make-an-honest-man-of-my-son! And all this without really serious intent on the part of either of us, since to me—and to him too—it was only a Venetian interlude inspired by a moon, the inevitable break-off with George, and a common interest in music.

The newspapers featured a story "She Jilted a Biddle to Marry a Prince," which I saw when I came home that fall, but the prince and I parted with complete understanding—he to marry his girl, and I to join Biddle for a brief amnesty at the home of the John Storrs in Touraine. Storrs was a sensitive fine artist, she a patient hostess who spoke wonderful French. The Storrs took in paying guests and mixed their artistry with Boston aristocracy. One Back Bay grande dame there made the visit doubly pleasant by insisting that no English be spoken and we practice our French exclusively, which she proceeded to do with the most incredible lisp. She had a gossipy old face and audibly loathed Americans, painters, women, and me. She wore long gloves and the most atrocious jewelry in all sizes and colors—brass, glass, gold, and otherwise, with enormous earrings that seemed to pull her ears off. Purely social people always feel that the greatest snobs with the most insincere affectations are the artists: of course artistic folk always feel that the shoe fits the other foot. The Boston lady hated artists, but I could match her, hatred for hatred, and did.

That visit to the Storrs in Touraine was a pleasant ending to my vacation, in spite of the Siren of Beacon Hill. I didn't want to leave Europe. Just at the moment for my return, I rebelled. I felt that to go back to the *Music Box Revue* for another year would be disastrous for me. Even if I had to borrow the money to do it, I wanted to stay on and study. I cabled Sam Harris to release me from my contract. His return cable said that Berlin had written some songs especially for me and that, much as he understood my ambitions, he regretted he would have to hold me to my bargain. So, in a stew of contradictory emotions and ambitions, I returned home.

The second *Music Box Revue* was staged by John Murray Anderson, to whose good nature and charm no greater tribute can be paid than to say that although he called the chorus girls the "beautiful blonde idiots" or the "sappy brunettes," everybody adored him. Frank Tours, who had been musical conductor of the earlier *Revue*, was back again. When I held a high note too long he used to send little vitriolic notes backstage adorned with caricatures that were as funny as they were poisonous. My dressing room was shared by Florence O'Denishawn, who was in a perpetual state of nudity glossed over with stage paint. Oscar Shaw sang opposite me. He might have lacked the fine voice of the tenor in the earlier *Revue*, but as a man he was a great improvement over him. But more than to anything or anybody else in that second *Music Box Revue* my memory and affection turn to Fanny Brice, with whom my friendship then began.

Fanny was the loyal, lovable, and gallant wife of Nicky Arnstein who, in spite of Fanny's brave defense in the New York courts, was condemned to Sing Sing. Fanny had made her career the hard way and was used to sticking her chin out and grinning; but only those of us who worked with her night after night knew the torture she was going through. She kept the truth from her children and told them their father was in Paris. As Christmas approached, the children wrote letters to their father in "Paris," telling him what they wanted from Santa Claus. Fanny somehow managed to have all letters answered by Nicky and postmarked Paris. To climax the deception she ordered a pair of rabbits that the children had specifically requested from their father shipped from Paris. When the box arrived with its big customs seal and its many French markings, there was much excitement and happiness. Daddy had remembered. However, when the box was opened, what seemed like millions and millions of rabbits—like an endless chorus line of Rockettes—tumbled out of the crate. The journey had been long and, rabbits being rabbits, nature had taken its course. Daddy, Fanny explained to the children, had been more than generous.

Fanny used to get the most wonderful letters from Nicky in prison, which she often read to me. Once she finished a particularly beautiful message from him and sat dreaming over it. "You know," she said, "I don't know what the world thinks, but to me he's a great gent."

Fanny had a penchant for playing the horses, and I, having been brought up on thoroughbreds, was not loath to play along. There was a direct wire from Fanny's dressing room to Belmont Park. Max Hirsch, outstanding trainer and great friend of Sam Harris', used to tip us off. There were some weeks when I made more money taking Max's advice than singing Irving's songs.

The *Music Box Revue* was slated to close in Chicago after a brief tour in the spring of 1925. Before we left New York, I decided to approach the Metropolitan for another audition. I had enough money in the bank to begin studying abroad, and I felt that if I didn't do it now, it would be never. Otto Kahn was in Palm Beach, but I telephoned him and asked if he would be good enough to arrange another hearing. It was done.

I had lived in such high hopes after the first audition that what happened the second time almost crushed me. Never since, when I have on occasion sat through auditions at the Met and seen other hopeful young singers turned away with the same customary polite "Thank you" from the little audience of judges out front, have I failed to remember the agony of that day. All that was given me that afternoon, at the conclusion of my songs, was a cordial but firm "Thank you." I was dazed. I could hardly believe that this had happened to me after Gatti-Casazza's promising words on the previous occasion. I waited on a bench inside the Thirty-ninth Street entrance, and when Mr. Ziegler came out I begged for a moment in his office.

Ned Ziegler was very kind to me, firm and candid in his advice. He did not put me off with soft words and pooh-poohs. He said frankly that something had definitely happened to my voice in the year between the first and second auditions. "Your voice," he said bluntly, "has lost color, resonance, and pitch. Probably it comes from singing the same songs night after night. I don't know. But it isn't as good today as it was a year ago."

I could only nod my head at him in agreement, like a straw puppet with the strings out of control. Finally I said that I knew that fatigue and routine had done their work but it wasn't too late. I would get out of my present regime and set up another; certainly it was not too late for that. He shrugged his shoulders. "But why do that?" he said. "Why not stay in operetta? You have had a sensational success, you are a highly paid singing star on Broadway—surely that in itself is a great career."

Artur Bodanzky came into Ziegler's office and heard my lament and Ziegler's comment. He joined with him in advising that, since I had a career already in the making, it was absolutely foolish to throw it away for an opera career which he, Bodanzky, was convinced was impossible, no matter how hard I worked. His final remark was that I should probably never learn to sing on key. Years later, when I made my debut in *Louise* at the Metropolitan, Bodanzky came to my dressing room and said: "I never thought you could do it. You're only beginning your career now, and there is nothing you cannot accomplish if you wish."

I had a performance at the Music Box that night, but before I went to the theater I called Otto Kahn on the long-distance telephone and with tear-choked voice told him the result of the audition. He tried to console me, murmured something about it probably being for the best, but I would not listen. Before I hung up I told him that in spite of everything everyone had said, I was definitely leaving Broadway for Europe and study, and that I was willing to wager him one hundred dollars that within two years I should have my Metropolitan Opera contract. "Nothing," answered Kahn, "would give me greater pleasure, and even if I lose that hundred dollars, I'll be betting on you."

I finished out my contract with the Music Box, going with the show to Chicago. I was determined to get hold of all the money I could to give me some financial independence for the next few years. By a stroke of luck, an opportunity to add to my cash reserves came to hand there in Chicago. I met Lilian Rosedale Goodman, who had just written a song she wanted me to sing. That song, "Chérie, je t'aime," proved a sensational success. I took a contract for two weeks at the Palace Theater in New York, sang my fool head off on "Chérie," and, with the money I already had saved, came away with a nice tidy sum.

Now I took the decisive steps. I cut myself off from musical comedy, Broadway, and security. Irving Berlin told me I would lose my "flare" if I studied for opera, but his gloomy predictions did not worry me. Against his pessimism I could balance what Sam Goldwyn had said when I told him that if I studied seriously I might even get to the Met someday: "Listen, kid," was his answer, "the day you get to the Met, I'll be in the front row."

Well, now it was good-by, Broadway, hello, France. My bridges were burnt and the road ahead might lead to no place at all. But at least I was doing what I wanted to do, and that in itself was good.

Good-by, Broadway, Hello, France

THE STORY OF THE French Riviera has always been told as the saga of English escaping from the London fog to the dependable sun of the Mediterranean, of purposeless American expatriates, or of those who had waited too long and needed too much money with which to enjoy life. That little strip of land between Marseille and the Italian border has been lampooned or puffed up as the winter playground of jaded millionaires and the international smart set by writers. But to me, and to so many, it was much more. It was the fun place of the intellectuals and artists who possessed few of the worldly goods but had a lively corner on things of the spirit.

Not being able to afford to live on the Riviera in the heyday of its winter season, I became a Riviera-ist in the summer, when "no one" went. And because my friends and I had so much fun there out of season, we created in time a season of our own, with so much effect that the French Riviera had expanded, until the war, from a popular international winter playground into a summer resort as well. When I was awarded the ribbon of chevalier of the Legion of Honor in 1939 at my debut in *Louise* at the Metropolitan, a partial reason for the award was gratitude for the part I had played in opening up that bit of French terrain to year-round traffic.

My very first taste of the Riviera had come in the cruise made some years earlier, when I had gone up to St. Paul from Bandol and seen what a lovely life could be had for two dollars a day. When I quit Broadway, determined to make an operatic career

for myself, I thought of it at once as an ideal place for inexpensive
quiet and study. I had written Mary Garden and asked her
advice on how to proceed. She recommended her operatic coach,
Richard Barthelemy, who lived in Monte Carlo. Then, knowing
my limited finances, and because she had a generous wish to im-
plement tangibly the advice she gave, she offered the use of her
apartment in Monte Carlo which she kept only for study or for
the overflow of her family who might want to stay on the Mediterranean coast when she closed her villa.

Thus I returned to the Riviera, a bewildered young student
who slept each night in the famous Garden gold-and-green bed
with fantastic gold eagle on top and gold brocade cover, doing
my own cooking and washing amidst rococo splendor. In the
apartment below lived a mutual friend of Garden's and mine,
Doris Chapman. Doris and I used to cook our dinner and enter-
tain jointly to cut our expenses. Once when Dick Barthelmess
came and found me servantless in this elegant apartment overlooking the *opéra-bouffe* town with its neat little square below my
window, he insisted on taking us out to dinner because it jarred
his sense of propriety to have the hostess of such a grand ménage
act as chief cook and bottle washer. While we were out together
Dick saw across the restaurant beautiful Jessica Sargeant, of New
York and Boston, whom he had met on the boat trip over. He
raised his glass in salute and said, "Look, that's the girl I intend
to marry." (He did, later, and they still are, and we're devoted
friends.)

Barthelemy started working with me on *Manon,* and I devoted
myself, with absolute concentration, to the study of that opera,
various songs of the French repertoire, and the French language
itself. The usual life of Monte Carlo remained a closed book, and
it was to be a long time before I even got near the Casino. I might
have been in Paducah for all *I* saw of the slim vampirish sirens
who supposedly raked in gold over the baccarat tables. What
social life I did have was centered around the musical events of
Monte Carlo. That meant, in Monaco, that its main focus was
the Monte Carlo Opera House. The Prince of Monaco, its chief

sponsor, had his own private entrance and sat in his great box. I heard many concerts and operas there, less elegantly seated. I remember Yvette Guilbert, particularly, who sang there at sixty. She was ageless and in her person seemed to represent the whole French style. Gone were the famous long gloves which she had always worn and which Toulouse-Lautrec had immortalized. Gone was the slim princess-gowned figure. But there were still the flaming red hair and the tense, tight-strung femininity. After her performance I met her with friends on the terrace of the Café de Paris, where all Monte Carlo gathered at apéritif time. I told her what an inspiration she had been, not so much because of her voice, but because as a great *diseuse* she represented all of French style. Her reply was the typically sage, practical one of the far-sighted prudent French bourgeoise. "What a wonderful métier it is to sing my little chansonettes," she said. "It is not the voice which remains important except as it acts as an instrument for the expression of the spirit. Operatic arias are so stagey and conventional, but with my songs I search for reality."

Once Dicky Fellowes Gordon and I went to the Monte Carlo Opera to hear Fritz Kreisler play. Dicky, humorous, bitchy, and charming, too, who looks like a tall, gray-haired, and handsome Isolde and has never done much with her own beautiful voice, although she has made a career out of telling everyone else exactly how to run their life and adores it, was a friend of Kreisler's. She took me, limp with hero worship, backstage to meet him. Kreisler's gray, leonine head, his intense romanticism, his mastery of his technique so that he could discard the mere skeleton of virtuosity for the inner core of music, had always left an indelible impression on me. Out in the wings we met Kreisler's wife, the witty, pungent Harriet. She told us that her husband had gone into his dressing room to change, having taken his last bow in utter exhaustion. I said to her: "I know the maestro should be left alone now, and I don't want to disturb him, but will you tell him that I have never heard him play so well as he did this afternoon?"

His wife answered succinctly, "My God, you're so right. When that son of a bitch wants to play, he really can play."

I never think of the Monte Carlo Opera House without remembering that Mary Garden, who should have been its most
brilliant star, had found her own way of refusing that honor.
The Monte Carlo impresarios had been after her all her life to
sing there. Her villa had brought musical and social prestige to
the Riviera, and they considered that a season with her would be
made. Each year Guinsburg would send his telegram asking her
to open the season, but each year she had only one answer,
"Merde," an economical enough reply signifying in the one word
dismissal, reason, and point of view. When she did finally sing
Carmen there, I am sure that when Guinsburg came back to kiss
her hand, she probably dismissed him with the same "Merde."
But how eloquently she could say it!

I had an interlude during this winter of study that was brief
but memorable. Barthelemy, my teacher, had to attend the debut
of another pupil at the Salle Pleyel. I had an invitation to go to
St. Moritz while he was away. Not having money for the trip, a
group of friends chipped in and made up a fund to pay my expenses. It was a Hans Christian Andersen tale come true. It was
my first trip to Switzerland, and the snow-covered fairyland, the
costumes of the people, the very thinness of the air intoxicated
me so that ever afterward I would go to St. Moritz, if only for a
stopover at the Palace Hotel, where Mr. Badrutt and my friend
Billy Reardon gave us such a happy welcome.

High point of the trip was a dinner given by the Grand Duke
Dmitri for the hero of the Cresta Run, the dangerous slide where
one belly-whopped down a steep slope at a million miles an hour
for a silver cup and a moment of limited glory. Those who survived were wined and dined for their trouble. Dmitri was on his
honeymoon with beautiful Audrey Emery, fascinating American
from Cincinnati, and he made a merry host. He insisted that I
sing his favorite melody, the "Love Song" from *Rose Marie,* the
"Yoo-hoo" song he called it. He was so eager that I agreed, and
he went in search of a piano, which—incidentally—he shoved in
himself! I stood up to sing, opened my mouth, and not a sound
came out. Everyone waited expectantly. I tried again. My

thoughts rushed madly back to that other time of grief when I had lost my voice in New York. I was panic-stricken. "I can't sing, I've lost my voice," I managed to squeak. Everybody started to laugh. It seems I was only suffering from high altitude.

I repaid the Grand Duke for his hospitality in later years by singing the "Yoo-hoo" song whenever I saw him. I liked Dmitri, brother of the Grand Duchess Marie and half-brother to that dream girl, Natasha Paley, now Mrs. Jack Wilson. I realized that Dmitri was reliving his bygone years in Russia when he ordered out his sleighs for a moonlit ride up the mountainside, to the delightful accompaniment of the tinkling of bells through the snow, as he drove his guests to a festive little dinner at some little inn high in the mountains.

One night, after my return to Monte Carlo, my friends, the Louis G. Kaufmans, who were traveling through Europe in a private car, came to visit me. Ciro's, with the best manager-maître d'hôtel in Europe, Maurice, was opening that evening, and they invited me to join them, planning to go on later to the Casino. I had never played the tables and was reluctant at first, but Louis and his wife Daisy, who loved to play roulette, boohooed and insisted, so that my scruples vanished under their pressure. Louis, who was president of the Chatham-Phenix National Bank, didn't consider it ethical for a bank president to indulge in gambling and stayed away from the tables. However, his punctiliousness did not involve others who were not engaged in responsible high finance. He even encouraged it, because it was good sport to watch. When we arrived at the Casino, L.G. urged me toward the tables. "Maybe," he said, "you'll have beginner's luck." He showed me the routine (like a cagey banker, he knew how it was done, even though he never did it himself) and then lent me a thousand francs with which to play. I was off.

I had a hunch about number five. It's my lucky number, so I played it. It won. I left my money there. It won again. With my heart doing queer swan dives inside of me, and without the remotest idea about percentages, theory of play, or psychology, I simply sat there and repeated five until, in utter nervous exhaustion, I had won 43,000 francs, including the original thousand-franc loan, which I repaid to L.G. with 10 per cent interest (a far better rate than the Chatham-Phenix paid, too)!

Forty-three thousand francs! For doing nothing! I was so overcome with the daftness of it that I lost my perspective. Later, when Fefe Ferry opened the Summer Casino in Monte Carlo and wanted me to sing, I had the effrontery to ask two thousand dollars for two songs. Fefe gagged at my price. "Look," I answered, "think of all those people sitting in there making money for doing nothing. At least I'll sing."

The forty-three thousand francs changed the color of my life. My winter period of study with Barthelemy was nearly over. What was the best thing to do with the capital in hand? At the cabled suggestion of Condé Nast, I decided to remain on the Riviera, where my money would go further than anywhere else. He suggested that I go to Mr. Sella at the Hôtel du Cap at Antibes and he would advise me where I could find the cheapest and best place.

Clutching my ill-gotten though welcome gains, I went to see Mr. Sella. Yes, he could find a place for me. Yes, it was inexpensive, as it was out of season. And, yes, he did. I rented from him the little pink villa called "Villa de Cèdres" that stood on the grounds of the famous Hôtel du Cap itself, across the way from the house of Sir Hugo de Bath, husband of Lillie Langtry. I got it with a cook named Marie, who made such wonderful ice cream that guests used to serenade her each time she served it at luncheon. I wrote Ruth Goldbeck (now widowed by Walter Goldbeck's death) to come down and share the villa and expenses with me, and when she accepted, our little ménage was complete.

What a wonderful life we had! You were in paradise—with the rocks from which you could dive, the most magnificent swimming in the world, no semblance of luxury, and even the heat that doomed the Riviera as a summer resort an additional bonus. If you didn't want to swim, you could fish off the rocks instead of plunging in yourself. You could rent a car for a nickel and travel along the Grande Corniche, high above the sea, with the snow-covered Maritime Alps towering protectingly in the background. You could stop at one of the little fishermen's wharves and order a succulent bowl of bouillabaisse for fifty cents. All the big restaurants and villas were closed for the summer, and we had the run of the gardens and rocks. No American, up to that date, had had the courage to visit the Riviera in the summer, but through force of circumstances we discovered what a land of Cockaigne it was. We started sending postcards to everybody we knew, telling them that while there was rain in the rest of Europe, here there was sun, swimming, and us. We told them that we were wandering all over the place dressed as we wanted, living as inexpensively as was necessary, in a sunny, happy world of our own. Come one, come all. Our friends took us at our word. Soon our little colony included Anita Loos and John Emerson; Donald Ogden Stewart stopped by on his honeymoon with Bea, now the Countess Tolstoy; Alec Woollcott, Harpo Marx, F. Scott Fitzgerald and his Zelda; and Charlie MacArthur, who introduced himself while we were both swimming out in the Mediterranean in front of the Little Eden Rock Restaurant.

Like all things that fatten and grow fashionable, the summer Riviera lost some of the carefree abandon as time went on and took on a kind of vulgar tourist chi-chi which made one sigh for the lean loveliness of the early days. The dignity of the established winter season would retreat with the first sign of mistral heat. Hitherto we had delighted in the informality and the spaciousness that stayed behind and had welcomed the canvas covers on the windows of the large hotels, put up to keep out the objectionable summer sun; the Casino tightly closed when M. André, the directing genius of the Casino, and Zographos, the great baccarat player, retired to the privacy of their yacht en route for Deauville; the large villas shut and shrouded. Suddenly, with the approaching thirties, there was a difference. All the hotels remained open, Antoine rushed a shop down, the *haute couture* ran showings, the quiet private homes put out "Rooms for Rent" signs, the cocktail-time terraces of the Carleton or the Martinez demanded reservations away in advance, and the streets looked like Broadway. It became gay and foolish and "having-wonderful-time"-ish, but I couldn't help resenting the change somehow. Even the French, who were making quick little fortunes out of the unexpected traffic, resented the intrusion. The French have a way of budgeting for a system of living according to set income, with never any need beyond that, and are irritated by anything that disturbs the routine.

In the second season of our stay, the Hôtel du Cap, guessing that there might be something in this summer-season stuff, kept its doors open, the first to do so. Dr. Marafioti came there with his family, and I had the added advantage of a teacher as next-door neighbor. Barthelemy would commute from Monte Carlo for my operatic coaching, and between my study with him and my scales with Marafioti, my life was strenuous and concentrated. But all of our circle of friends on the Riviera were hard workers. That is why the fun that went along with our more serious pursuits was so hilarious. If you work hard, you play hard. It made for a good, healthy, and unforgettable life.

Much of the raciness of these days came from getting through the pixy pranks devised by MacArthur and Fitzgerald. That hilarious pair wrote the most (in)famous scenario for a movie, which we made on the grounds of the Hôtel du Cap. I, with a deep sunburn, played the Princess Alluria, the wickedest woman in Europe, and Ruth Goldbeck was the farmer's daughter, suffering the usual trials, tribulations, and ecstasies of the salesman's farmer's daughter. MacArthur, just to make the pot boil more merrily, had added a touch of incest to the script and with rare political foresight chose as his "incestor" the villainous son of heaven, the Japanese Ambassador. Incestor worship, I suppose. One of the devices of the script was to write the titles on the outside walls of my pink villa and photograph them that way. But during the night the collaborators would always think up a few new unprintable titles, and I never knew, when I looked out in the morning, what new four-letter horror would be chalked up on my house to throw into a dither the tourist schoolmarms who might be passing by. I complained and scrubbed once or twice, but the new captions that then appeared were so much worse than the old that it seemed better to do with the four-letter words one knew than those one knew not of.

One night the police telephoned and asked if we could identify two Americans who claimed their names were MacArthur and Fitzgerald. What had they done? we asked. From the policeman's voice it sounded, at the least, like a mass murder. No, merely kidnaping, we were assured. It seems that the two had enticed the orchestra from the Hôtel Provençal over to the Fitzgerald villa for a nightcap. Once in the villa, they had lured them into a room, given them a bottle of whisky, and then locked the door. On the other side of the locked door, Fitzgerald and MacArthur propped themselves up with their own bottle in two easy chairs and relaxed for an evening of song.

"Play," they would bellow through the door. "Play and we'll let you out." The men inside played one song, then another. Their captors were insatiable. They kept calling their requests in threatening tones. "Play, or we'll keep you here a week." "Play this, play that—go on, play." The music grew weaker and weaker as the poor players waited for the two to tire, retire, and permit them to do likewise. The impromptu command performance lasted until dawn, when the musicians were released with a thank-you-for-a-nice-evening from the boys. But by this time the musicians didn't think it was funny. They were so indignant that they had gone to the police and demanded the arrest of the two crazy Americans. Did we know them? the police wanted to know. What a wonderful moment for all past and future revenge! It was with some reluctance that we finally admitted to a passing acquaintance with the two.

Montemezzi came that summer to see Mary Garden, who was at her villa for a late summer vacation. Going over to the Hôtel du Cap to look for his friend Marafioti, he was told the doctor was at my place. I was at that moment doing my scales, had reached high D and was sustaining it in full voice. The sound reached the waiting Montemezzi on the terrace. He walked across the grounds and came silently in on Marafioti and me. We looked

up and saw him. He greeted us with, "There's a voice to sing
Fiora." I was thrilled. Here was tangible praise indeed! When I
did make my debut singing Fiora at the Metropolitan in *The
Love of Three Kings,* with Montemezzi conducting, I was no more
excited than the day he heard me on the Riviera. If the Metropolitan was the goal, Montemezzi's praise cast a bright prophetic
light in its direction.

Moranzoni joined our musical colony that summer. Because of
his connections with the Chicago Opera, Moranzoni was a close
friend of Garden's, and I consulted him on the possibilities of
arranging an audition with the diva. I felt that by now I was
ready to be heard and advised. Moranzoni was able to arrange it,
and the day was set. When Alec Woollcott discovered that an
audition was being planned, he cornered me and confessed that
he was anxious to meet Garden himself, because *Cosmopolitan*
magazine wanted him to do an article on her. He had been
unsuccessful so far in getting through to her. Would I, at my audition, put in a word for him? I agreed to try.

I went with Moranzoni to Garden's beautiful villa. She had
such an unaffected and genuine pride in it that when I expressed
pleasure, she showed us through the house. Her taste was impeccable. Here was one prima donna who didn't clutter her home
with second-rate *objets d'art.* Everything expressed a catholic
knowledge of the arts and the instinct to throw out whatever did
not fit into her own kind of abundant, purposeful living.

She asked me with businesslike briskness to sing. I did an aria
from *La Bohème,* then an aria from *Juliet.* At her insistence, I
sang the aria from *Louise.* She listened carefully and quietly. She
dismissed *Bohème* and *Juliet* as routine soprano affairs, but settled down, after *Louise,* to a real discussion of the role. She advised me to start studying it at once and promised to arrange an
audition with Masson and Ricou, her friends who were directors
of the Opéra Comique, when I was ready.

Garden was generous and matter-of-fact in her advice and
headed straight for truth, with no polite detours. She felt that
anyone who couldn't take sincere criticism had no business trying

to be a real artist. She gave me, for the first time in my life, a feeling of serenity so far as my career was concerned. I knew that here was the most valuable thing I could have—criticism that I could believe in and take, no matter what difficulties were involved. Most artists are accused of not being able to take objective estimates. But that isn't true. Any artist will welcome criticism if he feels it comes from a master in the medium, given in friendly sincerity. One gets angry at and resentful of only those with a smattering of ignorance who use advice as a sugar-coating for malice.

Before leaving Garden's villa that day, I broached her on the subject of Woollcott, whom I described as a brilliant American writer and critic and a renowned raconteur. She had, she said curtly, never heard of him. I elaborated that he was here, on the Riviera, expressly to do a story about her for *Cosmopolitan.* "Who isn't?" she said. I pleaded Woollcott's cause, threw in Harpo Marx as an added inducement, and then said good-by.

A few days later I received a call inviting Woollcott, Harpo, Townsend Martin, Moranzoni, and myself to lunch. I dashed over to Alec with the news, and he pranced with delight. However, when the great day came and we were finally in the Presence, Alec, suddenly and surprisingly, became intimidated as I had never seen him before (nor ever after again). That debonair, rascally, voluble, bibble-babbler lost his tongue completely in a real case of stage fright. Garden, instead of being flattered by the silent worship, was merely bored. She wanted some sign of Alec's fame as a brilliant story-teller, which I had extolled extravagantly a few days earlier. From Harpo she expected nothing, since I had told her he was noted for his silence. But Alec that day was just the Little Man Who Came to Lunch—undoubtedly hoarding the full blast of his crotchety humor for a certain future dinner hour.

Mary decided to hold forth at the luncheon table herself, since no one else was doing it for her. And after luncheon, as we sat on the terrace sipping coffee, she, being a show-woman and psychologist, climaxed the afternoon with one great Garden story. Her little blue Dresden demitasse in hand, she began pacing up and down the terrace as she recalled her debut at the Opéra Comique. She was then a young American student who, through friendship with Sibyl Sanderson, had been permitted to attend every rehearsal at the Comique, where the preliminary rehearsals were being held for a new opera called *Louise*. Mary, eager and ambitious, had studied every word and gesture as she sat out in the empty stalls, listening.

On the night of the third or fourth performance Mary, who was seated in some obscure corner of the theater, became aware of a long and tedious intermission after the second act. Soon an ominous restlessness spread through the house. People coughed, programs shuffled, everyone took up the cry, "What can be the matter?" Suddenly Albert Carré, the director of the Comique, was seen dashing through the theater, looking for an American girl called Mary Garden. He finally singled her out and without explanation dragged her backstage.

"You have to go on as Louise," he said. "I've been told you've learned the role." The soprano, he hastened to explain, had laryngitis. They hurriedly rushed Mary out of her prim tailored suit and prepared her for the third act.

When the curtain went up—she told us, as she walked up and down her terrace, the little blue cup in hand, reliving that moment—and she stood there listening to the overture, she turned and faced the backdrop curtain where the scene of Paris is painted with all the little lights that go on as evening falls on the city, and said to herself, "Mary Garden, this is your moment. Tomorrow Paris will be at your feet!" Then she turned around, faced her audience, and started the great aria, "Depuis le jour." At the conclusion that Paris audience cheered itself hoarse.

Shivers ran up and down our backs. That young American girl had guessed right. From that moment Paris had indeed been at her feet as the greatest interpreter of French opera of our day. Alec was pop-eyed with admiration. He began to bubble over like a schoolboy caught in an enthusiasm he could not control.

"My God," he said, "what a story, what a beginning!"

Garden turned and looked at him directly with a fixed stare

and said in a charming and insidious way: "But *that,* my dear Mr. Woollcott, is a story which you cannot use in *Cosmopolitan* or any other magazine."

As we motored back to Antibes, Alec regained his tongue and said, "Well, regardless of my apparent lack of success, there is the most charming and eloquent bitch I have ever met."

One day as we all sat on the terrace of the little pink villa, we heard a soaring tenor voice, definite and vibrant in its tonal quality even in the banal "O sole mio." Alec Woollcott leaped up and shouted, "God, a tenor! I'm sick of having only one soprano for 'Sweet Adeline.' There's just the voice we need. I'm going to find it." He followed the trail of sound to the hotel and over to a stepladder where a big, handsome house painter was putting a new coat of paint on the shutters.

Alec pulled the bewildered workman off his ladder and over to our living room. There we got him to sing again, with Marafioti to hear. "He's terrific," we shouted at one another, while the big clownish fellow shuffled his feet in befuddlement. Then, although he hardly understood what we were saying, we persuaded the reluctant painter to give up his house-painting and study singing —we would make up the purse.

Marafioti, who was planning to leave shortly for America, could not take on our protégé. Well, then we'd send him to Milan. "Milano, Milano," we shouted at the man. He looked as if he didn't know what had struck him. This was too much. A purse— Milano—give up a nice job like house painter? We were the crazy Americans. It took us a few days, but we packed him up, bundled him off, and waited for another Caruso to develop.

Alec was put in charge of receiving reports from our protégé. Unfortunately they got worse and worse. He had taken the routine of the studio as long as he could, then broke out by putting in all his time in the cafés singing, making love, and swaggering. His teacher had persuaded him he was a great find, and the dazed house painter now announced boldly that he was the world's top tenor. Finally a report came from the police in Milan, who wrote to Alec that our protégé had been jailed for keeping Milan awake all one night by serenading the townspeople through the streets with naughty songs. Alec found this quite touching and decided perhaps he ought to bring the singer to America to serenade in like fashion the weekly session of the Thanatopsis Poker Club. Alec managed to get him out of jail, but the last we heard the man had remained in Milan as a singing waiter. From then on Patron Woollcott was convinced that all singers were a little bit off.

Our little season on the Riviera that year was officially closed with the farewell dinner we gave for Alec Woollcott and my beau from Paris, Chato Elizaga. Chato, whose name was really Lorenzo but was nicknamed Chato for his little short nose, was a nephew of the Mexican president, Diaz. He was the gayest and most eloquent beau in all Paris. He called me Madame Pompadour but didn't go into the reasons why. I found myself quite seriously engaged to Chato and even went so far as to get my trousseau ready. We both were sure it was true love. But again I weighed career against marriage and decided that the music I wanted was not the wedding march. So when Chato was off on an automobile trip, I went to see his sympathetic mother late one night and told her to tell Chato that I'd decided to follow my career, that I had loved him very much but was sorry, I wanted to sing. Next morning I sailed for America.

But here on the Riviera, Chato was still my funny, gay, and dashing beau. He and Alec were returning to Paris the next day, so we decided to give them a farewell Dutch Treat dinner under the stars on the dirt terrace of the now marble-paved and famous Edén Rock. The gala dinner consisted mostly of a Mediterranean platter and Vin Rose, the light red wine of the country. We had had such a happy summer and we had so much toasting to do that we got quite warm and mellow on our parting salutes. Probably the most original toast of all was proposed by Zelda Fitzgerald. She and Scott always seemed to me straight out of *The Beautiful and Damned* and never more than when she stood on the table and said, "I have been so touched by all these kind words. But what are words? Nobody has offered our departing heroes any gifts to take with them. I'll start it off." Whereupon she stepped out of her black lace panties and threw them towards the two guests of honor, for the lucky one to catch. Alec, dear prim soul, was too shocked to make more than a pretense of reaching, and Chato naturally caught the prize. Chato saluted Zelda with a wave of the panties and said that since he was a hero he could thank her only in a heroic way, by jumping from the highest rock, with the panties clasped close to his breast to protect him from harm. Then, being man to suit foolish action to word, he jumped from the rock with all his clothes on and the little black panties against his bosom. We all dashed down the rocks after him, and soon everybody was in the water, still fully clothed.

The effect of salt water on the alcoholic content of Vin Rose sometimes produces the familiar blur. We all edged out to the parked raft before it got us. But suddenly we noticed Alec emerge completely naked out of the shadow of an overcast moon. Apparently he had lost all his clothes in the Mediterranean plunge and now, blissfully unaware of his native state, was climbing a ladder to the shore. He walked over to where he had left his straw hat, solemnly put it on his head, lit a cigarette from the case that had been left there, and walked with great dignity up the path and to the hotel. We watched him with a kind of fascinated and dulled horror, loath to remind him of his embarrassing lack of clothes because we knew, knowing puritanical Alec, how strong his reaction would be. We didn't see him again that season. He had already departed for Paris by the time we could get the end of the story from the room clerk. Alec, we were told, had fortunately come into an empty lobby. Unaware of the picture he made with hat and sans clothes, he came up to the desk and with habitual pomposity said to the clerk in perfect although not overfluent French, "Donnez moi le clef." Then, *clef* in hand, he vanished, straw hat and all, to the upper regions and out of our ken, like one of the wee ghosties of his own inimitable tales.

My work on *Bohème* was progressing. My Italian was also coming along in fine fashion. Italian was the first foreign language I really learned to speak, and when I was to go to Italy to study, this knowledge of the language afforded the greatest surprise and delight to the Italians, who felt somehow that while all Americans troubled to learn French, few applied themselves to the language of Dante and Verdi. Incidentally, while I was living on the Riviera my French took on a Provençal accent, characteristic of that part of France, that I later had to work to lose, as I had had to work to rid myself of my American southern accent. In addition to working on *Bohème* in Italian, I started working on *Louise* in French with Barthelemy, who continued to commute from Monte Carlo.

This happy, fruitful summer on the Riviera came to an end. Armed with Garden's letter to Masson and Ricou at the Comique recommending an audition, I went to Paris. They were both very kind and enthusiastic. They told me that my voice was ready and that it had the quality the French loved, but I was still unprepared as an actress. They said a contract would be waiting for me any time I felt ready for it, but they were interested enough in my career as a whole to suggest another year of hard work. In their opinion, it would be a setback to attempt a Comique debut without the necessary acting techniques.

Mary Garden had also given me a letter to Albert Carré, artistic director of the Comique, and I went to him at once for acting lessons. Carré was an extraordinary man, once in love with Garden, with a special paternal affection for me because he said I gave my work more intense concentration than any young student he had ever had, and he liked my ambition. He and Ned Ziegler of the Metropolitan looked like brothers—thin, *élégant*, quiet-voiced, with distinguished-looking white heads. I treasure the many long letters Carré wrote explaining each role I studied with him and mapping out a definite procedure to follow for my career. All the letters were colored with that particular personal affectionate interest which seems, with few exceptions, to exist only in Europe between student and teacher or artist and impresario. Here, in America, the relationship between artist, directors, and teachers more often remains always on a cold financial level. There is little of the warmth that comes from people all working in a métier they love. The main spark exists in terms of the box office.

Albert Carré's whole approach to acting was based on the use of intelligence. He insisted that before attempting any effect from a singing phrase or a bit of stage "business," the effect must be intelligently acted out in the mind before. Acting was the continuity of a reflex from the preceding thought, and each thought must be given its own individual life. Carré started working with me on the *mise en scène* for *Louise*. He planned other operas for the future, but he felt that one had to work in one role at a time to really achieve perfection.

The return to Paris gave me an opportunity to see Sacha Guitry and Yvonne Printemps for the first time—and I thought her the most enchanting woman on the stage. I also went to the Opera one night with Sol Hurok to hear Chaliapin in Boïto's *Mefistofele,* Italianized version of Goethe's *Faust*—an intensely operatic piece, particularly suited to Chaliapin, who was at his best when he could bite his teeth into a role that called for savage forcefulness and superhuman rage or anguish. His Mefistofele was a torrent of primeval force, and he achieved quite as much effect with his spoken lines as by singing—which is the essence of a great singing actor and the foundation of all true musical drama.

Chaliapin always arrived backstage to put on his make-up long after the rest of the cast was on hand. Everyone always worried about whether he would have the time to do a proper job on the complicated make-up for Mefistofele or Boris Godounoff, but Chaliapin had been so trained in the Russian theater school that he managed to make the curtain on the dot, no matter how late he got to the theater. Hurok took me backstage to meet the great bass that night, and I was impressed with his quietly controlled, soft-spoken manner. However, we all went on a party afterward and ended up in the small hours of the morning at Chaliapin's place. I remember vividly how he sat sprawled back in a deep armchair, with his shoes off, singing Gregorian chants in full thrilling voice with no thought at all of the sleeping neighbors. But then Paris never complained of such honors.

Ruth Goldbeck, who was in Paris too, took me one day to have lunch at the studio of her friend Vladimir Golschmann. It was in a tiny street, the Val de Grâce, for the talented Golschmann was obviously as young and poor and ambitious as we were. I remembered that gay, congenial lunch when I was in Philadelphia not long ago singing in concert at the Robin Hood Dell with Golschmann as conductor. He was still ambitious for good music, enormously talented, and had remained as young and gay as I remembered him in Paris.

My studies with Carré had some amusing interruptions. One day Melchior and I gave a joint recital at the home of the Baron Rothschild. There I met the young Duc — ——, scion of an old family whose grandmother's estates at Rambouillet included the most magnificent private forest in all France. He took me to visit his own château in Dampière, where he showed me the original papers of Racine and told me about the great friendship between his grandfather and the noted French dramatist.

All my friends were delighted over my friendship with the duc and ambitious that it turn into marriage. They rallied round like dear devoted aunts. Elsa Maxwell wrote me not to give it up. Elsie De Wolfe, who had been visiting another of the duc's renowned estates—he had fourteen—sighed and said, "I have just been up to the Château de Tours, and it definitely needs a woman's touch." I wondered if perhaps they were right and it would be a fine thing, until one day the duc took me to a wide space of land near the château and said, "My great ambition is to have a private golf course here sometime." I looked at him blankly. Certainly, if this was his great ambition, why did he not gratify it?

He didn't hesitate at all in his answer. "It's just a question of money," he replied. I then realized that the meager fortune of even a prima donna wasn't enough to keep fourteen châteaus going, and that the duc should look to greener pastures, for just love wasn't enough.

I decided, because it was economical and possible to find there the solitude necessary for work, to return to the Riviera. But before

I went back I took a little jaunt into Central Europe, chaperoned by the circumspect Rudolf Kommer. Kommer picked his friends with rare instinct. He had been a tutor at the court of Franz Joseph and his friends loved him. He was the greatest match-maker in the world and had played chaperon to many before me. I was delighted with Kommer's invitation and duenna role because I was then involved with a new beau, a young American composer, and as always, not finding it fun to travel alone, I liked nothing better than to take each new romance on a trip, where, armed with Baedekers and a package of books on history and art, we could discover beauty together. Perhaps I felt that anyone who could stand the test of keeping pace with me through old churches, galleries, and palaces could hold up through anything.

We adored each other and set out with something of the George Sand-Chopin illusion. Our trio's first stop was Munich, and I saw there the careful way the Germans, who even then crowded the Deutsches Museum as if by order, studied everything, evincing their national pride and interest in the exhibitions showing the development of mechanical and natural science. We saw the operetta *Maritza,* which was then such a great success, and afterwards we sat in the Regina Hotel grille with all the artists. There was one lonely man in the crowd who sat apart from all the rest. It was Ferenc Molnár, once a great friend of Kommer's, but the two had not spoken for years. Now Molnár watched the inimitable Kommer, always contagiously funny, as the center of the group. He looked so gloomy I was glad to leave the place and that doleful look. But it seemed, from then on, we ran into Molnár everywhere. I was glad when Kommer, at my insistence, finally promised to kiss and make up.

We motored to Garmisch to visit Fritzi Massary, great German actress, and her husband, Max Pallenberg, outstanding German comic. Never will I forget the countryside, with its lovely mountains in the background and the little houses and chapels spaced half a mile apart, all out of the Grimm brothers' fairy tales. After a visit at Fritzi's enchanting place we left for Leopoldskron, Salzburg, and Reinhardt's Castle by way of Lake Starnberg. The

Salzburg Festspiel Haus, built in the old riding school, was preparing for the August festival which Reinhardt was staging. We
had coffee at the famous Tomaselli Kaffee Haus, and there again
found Molnár sitting all alone, looking sad as the Sorrows of
Werther. We heard that his girl friend had just left him and sighed
consolingly.

We visited Reinhardt's Castle, which had originally belonged
to the Archbishop Leopold and the King of Bavaria. Reinhardt
had purchased it in 1914 and restored it to its former splendor. It
was in the most romantic German baroque style, with a lake to
one side and beautiful gardens filled with fine old statuary. It was
here that Reinhardt staged *Le Malade Imaginaire* of Molière in
the Salle des Fêtes with Max Pallenberg in the lead. Kommer
told us of Reinhardt's neighbor, the old countess, who always
insisted on being invited to the Reinhardt festivals and then fell
asleep after twenty minutes and snored loudly through the rest
of the production. Kommer suggested that for this performance
the old countess be invited to arrive at the castle twenty minutes
before the play was to end. The invitation was sent out that way,
the countess arrived, fell asleep just as the play ended, snored as
predicted, and when she awakened, expressed her thanks and
appreciation of the play and went home—completely unaware
of the skillful timing.

That trip ended in Italy, where we did all the standard things—
saw Rome and the Coliseum by moonlight, had dinner in Sorrento, overlooking the Bay of Naples, got into an argument about
Wagner, Puccini, Rubinstein, and Hofmann while making the
hair-raising turns on the Amalfi Drive, visited the villa where
Wagner wrote much of *Tristan*—and Garbo and Stokowski wrote
another page in romantic history. My young composer and I fell
out in Naples, where, riding through the back streets with their
pink-faced houses, clotheslines full of washing, and babies everywhere, my beau saw only garbage, overcrowding, and improper
bathing conditions. "Why do they all smell so?" he wanted to
know, while I sighed over the color and the picturesqueness. I
felt he had failed me completely—there was the Bay of Naples,

Vesuvius, the museum with Pompeiian wonders. His possibilities for cultural companionship didn't impress me. He sailed for America while the band played "Tea for Two" and I waved good-by with tears streaming down my face and relief in my heart.

It was time for more work, so I returned to the Riviera. Then came an unexpected windfall. One day a check arrived in the mail for several thousand dollars for royalties on the song I had sung at the Palace when I said good-by to Broadway—Lilian Goodman's "Chérie, je t'aime." It seemed incredible to me because I usually had to work so much harder for anything I got. Feeling that this was "luck" money, I decided to buy a house with it. Ever since I had seen Garden's villa, I had wanted my own on the Riviera. One rainy afternoon I set out with Ruth Goldbeck and Walter Creighton on a house tour. There, just below the Benjamin Guinness property "Nôtre Dame de la Vie" at Mougins, was what I wanted. Bridget Guinness had really discovered this little villa for me. It was small and simple, with a wonderful jasmine-planted garden, and even in the rain and mistral I took one look at it and said, "Here's where my money goes." Set back in the hills behind Cannes, in the old Roman village surrounded by the Maritime Alps, it was a dream come true. It was called "Casa Lauretta," and as time went on and my career progressed, the villa was built up too. The guest room was added with the bonus from "One Night of Love," the terrace was enlarged with royalties from "Love Me Forever," but it has always remained simple and comfortable and my kind of house. Someday, when this war is over, I hope to go back to it again.

Settled in my little villa and deeply involved in my studies, I found myself too busy for social life. However I do remember meeting Marguerite D'Alvarez, the great Peruvian contralto, who fascinated me with her wit and her unbelievable looks. She was an enormously majestic woman built on swelling Junoesque lines who, without ordinary beauty, still gave the impression of beauty. She had a rich and salty sense of humor and wore the most incredibly old-fashioned clothes. For instance, she went swimming in bloomers with ruffles below the knees, a high-necked long-sleeved shirt and bathing turban, "against a sunburn" as she put it. She would descend into the Mediterranean with a kind of grande-dame elegance and then, in a rich musical voice, would engage in the most urbane, modern, and unpruned conversation. Montague Norman, head of the Bank of England, who was also there, would engage in a duel of witticisms with D'Alvarez, and there was nothing funnier than to watch and listen to those two. Montague, with his G.B.S. body, his long beard, and a wit of his own, would wear his straw hat while swimming, while D'Alvarez, like a Mack Sennett girl in full theatrical make-up, would swim beside him, both of them carrying on in high voice a lusty, sharp, brisk, and highly flavored literate conversation. Alec Woollcott, who was back again, wearing a yellow bathing suit that just seemed to sit below his bay window (he was called the "Yellow Peril" by Norman, who claimed the bathing suit matched his Algonquin pallor), used to sit with me listening to them. I decided to give a little dinner party for Mary Garden and D'Alvarez on the terrace of Juin ès Pins, the little seaside restaurant, because I knew that D'Alvarez had sung with the Chicago Opera while Garden was its director and thought they would be old friends. Never was friendship deadlier. I spent an evening of chills and fever as the two prima donnas threw thunderbolts at each other. D'Alvarez was enormously gay and vivacious and malicious and kept her end of the table roaring with laughter, while Mary held court at the other with her usual seriousness and directness, but later I thought that though D'Alvarez kept you in continual laughter, you immediately forgot much she said, but you remembered afterwards every Garden gesture and story. I also learned later the cause of animosity between the two. During that Garden-directed season of the Chicago Opera, which one wit has described as unparalleled for both magnificence and deficit (a million dollars!), Mary had brought D'Alvarez to Chicago to sing Delilah. But D'Alvarez, in descending the three little steps which tradition puts in the way of every entering Delilah, had slipped and skidded down on her backsides. Whereupon Garden was heard to exclaim in a loud voice from her directorial box, "My God, she's making her entrance into the Chicago Opera like Balaam into Jerusalem." Mary's remark went from critic to critic and D'Alvarez' career in Chicago was shortened by that apt allusion.

In the late winter of 1927 I read in the Paris *Tribune* that Otto Kahn was in Paris. I telephoned him collect at the Hôtel Ritz and asked if he was coming down to the Riviera. I explained that I wanted him to hear me sing again. He said he had no plans for a southern trip, but if I felt I had truly made great progress, he would treat me to a round-trip ticket to Paris and hear me there. I met him at the home of Edward Herman, where I sang for him. He listened quietly, then gave me the encouragement I had been hoping to hear. "There has been a remarkable improvement," he said. "I see also you are more serious than ever and more unwavering in your ambitions for opera. I am sure Mr. Gatti will want a third audition, and I shall keep my fingers crossed that this third time will work the charm."

I returned to my little villa with my head in the clouds, only to find that events had traveled even faster than I. There, waiting for me, was a summons from Mr. Gatti to come to Milan for my third audition for the Metropolitan. I and my sister Emily, who was at the villa at the time, set out for Italy and five days of preliminary study with Moranzoni in Varese. Then, on June 12, at the Teatro Lirico, before Gatti-Casazza and the Italian conductors Serafin and Bamboshek, I sang arias from *Manon*, *Bohème*, *Louise* and *Romeo and Juliet*. I knew that my whole future was suspended on this moment, and I felt the strain severely. I shall never forget the moments of waiting after the audition as I paced up and down backstage, with a group of other expectants pacing in their own corners or humming nervously. I had seen Gatti smile, but not until Bruno Zirato, formerly Caruso's secretary, more recently with Toscanini, rushed up to me with the words, "Come down, for we have good news," did I hope to win the tussle.

The next day, the 13th of June, I signed my contract for the

Metropolitan in Mr. Gatti's Milan office for seventy-five dollars a week. Mr. Gatti cautioned me that it was better to remain in Europe for one more year to sing in small opera houses for the experience, but I was too overjoyed to be analytical, too fearful of the uncertainty should I not start at the Metropolitan at once, and too broke to put off the necessity of earning some money again. I told him that if I could have the contract to start that year, I would take my chances on it. He agreed, and it was made out for the season of late 1927, with my debut scheduled for early in 1928. The contract itself was in my hands before the two-year wager with Mr. Kahn was up. Mr. Gatti also signed a contract that same day with Everett Marshall, the American baritone, who had nervously shared the previous day's auditions with me. I gave Mr. Gatti a big hug, a gardenia boutonniere, and said good-by. He looked at me with a friendly smile and said, "This time, my dear, it is not good-by, but au revoir."

How Emily and I celebrated that night! Chato had come on from Paris for the audition, and he, Emily, Zirato, and I sat under a grape arbor of a Milan outdoor restaurant and stuffed ourselves with spaghetti. Mr. Gatti had put a clause in the contract calling for more weight, because I was still skinny from the *Music Box Revue,* so I ate and ate, and we all drank chianti and sang and danced through the streets of Milan. The next day I returned to my villa on the Riviera. Bamboshek came there at Mr. Gatti's suggestion, and we started work on *Bohème* and *Romeo and Juliet.*

That fall I landed at the Port of New York, contract in pocket, and a new career on the way.

The Metropolitan

THE METROPOLITAN OPERA HOUSE has not even the distinction of being set at the core of New York's theatrical district. It sits off at the tag end of the Times Square area, in the heart of the garment belt, without the tattered romance of Broadway to color it or the stuffy dignity of Fifty-seventh Street to keep it company, and with no indication in its shabby, greenish brick exterior that here is the citadel of American opera. It is as shocking at first glance as the prewar sight of a wrinkled, grimy original from a Paris *couturier* as it is unpacked in a blare of publicity for a New York style show. Is *this* what all the fuss was about?

Across the street, 1440 Broadway spills its thousands and thousands of needle-trades workers, its hundreds of out-of-town buyers, its manufacturers of Bonnie-Wee and Stork-Ahead clothes, in a constant ebb and flow of humanity that reaches high tide at noon. On the other side, from Seventh Avenue garment workers press in swarms alongside the stage entrance, form in little clusters against the weathered posters, lean against the ugly, iron fire scapes that ring the building, and talk about the I.L.G.U. in loud assured voices as stray musicians file in for rehearsal.

Once past the lavatory-ish tiled outside lobby, the scene changes. The stairways that fan out on both sides are well proportioned. The faded gilt and red plush reflect a cozy *fin-de-siècle* elegance. Inside, the auditorium is large, regal, pleasantly chandelier-lit, and always drafty. After a while the quondam air of the place grows upon one. It never has the fine sweep of the Paris Opera House or La Scala or the Colon of Buenos Aires. But for an

American singer it has definite glory and an impressive history. It is always awesome and fosters love and indestructible loyalty in anyone who sings there. It is THE METROPOLITAN—where American singers were once the poor little match girls looking in, while American society worshiped at the feet of Italian opera and Italian opera stars. There is a power to the Metropolitan, on one side of the footlights or the other, that is inescapable. One can make sharp criticisms of the Metropolitan point of view, but the Opera House itself—ugly and grand, surrounded by a maelstrom of cloak-and-suit operators—remains the end of every American singer's dream.

Built in the mid-eighties by New York's socially elite who felt they needed an opera house to put the final artistic stamp on their newly acquired wealth, the Metropolitan reached its most grandiose era in the years before World War I. Those were the days of largesse and extravagance and Rabelaisian fable. They tell of Caruso, out to dine, who was asked by his hostess if he couldn't just hum a little tune across the dinner table. Caruso hummed—and next day sent a bill for three thousand dollars! And of Melba, who arrived at a party given by Luytens, the architect, in London, where she made more than her usually impressive entrance. "Oh, my dear Nellie," Luytens greeted her, "I've never seen you look so ravishing. All that I need to make me completely happy is to hear a few of your golden notes." "Hear them you shall," she answered, "if you decorate my new house in return." The bargain was made—and kept.

After the war the fortunes of opera fell somewhat. The rich were not so unfailing in their patronage, and opera could not make the adjustment. It could not do what the theater has to do— find support in an audience that will pay at the box office because it likes what goes on in the house. Edward Johnson, Gatti-Casazza's successor, has done a miraculous job of trying to prove that opera is not merely a social luxury but one of the arts that people will pay to hear. The subscription boxes are gone—along with *the* Mrs. Astor who always used to make her entrance at nine o'clock regardless of the earlier curtain time—and gone are the *de rigueur* white tie and tails. Now one may even see sweaters and skirts; and anyone who wants to and has the price can come and sit anywhere in the house. Both are healthy signs of progress indeed, during wartime at least. People are learning to lean back and relax and really enjoy their opera, whether from a front seat in the parlor during the Saturday-afternoon broadcasts or a red-plush one at the opera house. If you remove the social cachet of opera, take from it the dry-as-dust display, the going only to see and be seen, what you have left is a vigorous, honest enjoyment of the music itself. This popularization may not bring back the golden era, but it does bring opera closer to the hearts of the American public. I, for one, think opera should be subsidized by the Government as part of the social progress of a nation. This would take from it all class distinction and enable it to become a part of the main stream of American music.

If opera is to keep out of the red, it must turn toward the development of American artists and the furthering of American music. In spite of all the handicaps which come from the lack of a training school and its box-office responsibility to set up its casts with first-rate experienced artists, it is attempting to do this very thing. American opera has had to fall back on European artists who come here backed up by years of experience and training in the small opera auditoriums of Europe. Our own young artists cannot compete fairly with these seasoned performers. Their initiative and natural talents become shrouded over with fear and gaucherie, and few survive the ordeal. Just look back and single out the amazingly small number who have survived the trying years of secondary roles.

No one disputes that the influx of European artists has always had a most healthy and stimulating influence on American opera. But that very stimulation should have taught us how urgent was the necessity to find an outlet for developing talent here equal to the European. Until the war most European singers have come here, made their fortunes, and gone home to spend them, instead of becoming an integral part in the development of musical standards of this country, and too seldom have they taken interest in young American singers. Perhaps now the situation will change, with the whole world looking to America to emerge into leadership in all branches of art. With their own opera houses closed, the foreign contingent that rushed to get citizenship papers at the outbreak of the war and found a haven of welcome here will show a deeper gratitude and appreciation of our generous hospitality by aiding with their American dollars and musical devotion the future musical culture of this country.

What a tragedy that we have no training for young singers in theater technique and no small stage on which students can practice and lose the self-consciousness which often lasts away beyond the debut! Too bad that there is no department in our opera house to teach make-up to young artists. Every Madame Butterfly who comes out looks anything but Japanese. Chaliapin studied with Stanislavski at the Moscow Art Theater. It was part of his background. But who is there here to take an interest in opera students and teach them how to create physical character? It has always been a habit of mine to arrive two hours or more before a performance so that I can take my time putting on make-up, wig, and costume as I run through the score, thus reaching for the mood of the character in advance. I have learned, through long experience, how important these physical attributes are to the complete three-dimensional presentation of a role. But why let a singer go through trial and error on her own—why can't there be guidance and instruction to clear up the more obvious pitfalls?

In years to come all students will study with musicians, rather than with famous singers: for the future operatic art will depend more directly upon musicianship than on the knack of the pure vocalist. If opera is to hold its own with the theater and motion pictures, singer-actors will have to carry direct communication to the operatic audiences. It is difficult for any highly individual singer to teach singing because, consciously or not, the particular personality is grafted upon the student and the teacher tries to mold with his own "tricks of the trade." Too often singers permit the student to become drunk with constant singing of melody without laying the groundwork of vocal study. It makes for distortion of fresh young voices and quickly injures them. I always try to tell young students of the famous baritone who studied scales for ten years, then one day asked his teacher when he would be able to sing a song. The teacher answered, "You won't have to learn songs with me. You'll just be able to sing them once you get those scales right."

The most beautiful natural voices in the world are right here in America. Turn on your radio and listen. The valuable Metropolitan's Auditions of the Air, for example, bring many voices to the attention of the public, but one wonders what the final outcome can be without proper guidance. Although the winners may reap a few lucrative years in concerts with the name of the Metropolitan to enhance their value, the overnight thrill of becoming a Met star should not make them forget that they are still a long way from the top of the ladder that is only reached the hard way —the "climb up" step by step.

The overexaggeration, the emotional turmoil that goes on behind the footlights, carries over into the bread-and-butter lives of opera stars. With so much bamboozlement and posturing, is it any wonder there is a shortage of sincerity? In the midst of oh-darlings, and how-divines, you learn to look for the hidden knife aimed straight for your back. Almost everything goes—the backbiting, the gossip, the feuds, the intrigues, the "Foreign Wing" against the rest of the world, the closed corporation of repertoire and style!

The headlines of the past played up operatic intrigues. Today, though more rarely, they continue to electrify opera news although often grossly exaggerated. When the tenor starts slugging or the soprano does a little shadow-boxing on her own, names become headline mud. Such outbursts of self-protection, called temperament, cause a nation-wide decision that such stars are unmanageable. Which seems hardly fair if the opponents are compelled at a crucial moment to defend their artistic honor in front of a sold-out house. Personally, I have never *deliberately* taken part in intrigue or public exhibition of my strong-arm prowess. If I have led unwittingly with my chin, then I've had the intestinal fortitude to fight it out. I've enjoyed and relished the other fellow's success as much as my own. It inspires self-improvement. But I know how stimulating competition can be, and I can go after success with as much vigor as anyone. But anything that disturbs the unity, the success of a performance should be beneath the dignity of a self-respecting artist.

Thank God my career has had the adventure of being unconventional. One of the funniest and most maddening contretemps I ever got into with another artist was at the Metropolitan. My sparring partner was that eminent foreign tenor who came here in a blast of underground publicity about his vanity and instinctive lack of gallantry; a reputation that overshadowed anything anyone could ever dream up against prima donnas. All too bad, because, along with this publicity, it was admitted that he had a good voice. When I was told I had to go into *La Bohème* with him I protested loudly. I was told to go ahead and try it—after all, one could not always trust to hearsay. That advice seemed sound enough when I found that the rehearsals went off splendidly. There was a great deal of friendliness between the Polish tenor and myself, and we all loved one another too, too much. In the midst of all this sweetness and light I thought that perhaps his reputation *had* indeed been hearsay. The day of the performance, which was his American debut, he kissed my hand and I gave him, in a mellow mood, my blessing: "Best of luck," I said. "We've had wonderful rehearsals. I hope the same goes through now. Don't forget that the audience you're singing to is a Grace Moore audience. Make it your own."

What was my surprise when, standing backstage, peeping through the little peephole with my candle in hand, and awaiting the opening bars of Mimi's music, I saw him take the chair into which I was supposed to faint and push it backstage, so that I should have to do my fainting upstage! I made my entrance and tried to signal him, thinking perhaps he had gotten the stage directions muddled, but he pursued me upstage all the way to that misplaced chair until I fainted into it almost too realistically. Then when I sang the aria he sat smack in front of me so that I couldn't

see the conductor. I never knew what bit of deviltry was coming
next! Johnson and Ziegler, who witnessed the whole business,
ducked outside to Thirty-ninth Street for some fresh air and to
avoid the possible mayhem that might occur at any moment on
the stage. They came to see me after the performance. They
agreed that the Polish tenor had been incredibly bad-mannered,
but they added, "Well, my dear, it was terrible but a great performance."

"I will never sing with him again," I said flatly. "Once of that
sort of thing is enough."

Johnson and Ziegler did not tell me until later that my contract
called for another performance with the same tenor. I tried to be
adamant. I protested, but the management persuaded me, as they
always do, that what must be must be.

By the time of the second performance of *La Bohème* the reputation of the Polish tenor had spread considerably throughout all
the backstage regions of the Metropolitan—and there was nothing
hearsay in the personal experiences that stagehands and members
of the cast could and did tell with bitter relish. Again I watched,
as I had on the first night, for my opening bars of music—this
time with fear and apprehension; but lo and behold, as I saw the
tenor stoop down to shove the chair out of position the irresistible
force met with an immovable body. The stagehands had nailed
down every stick of furniture on the set!

I had prepared the roles of Juliet, Micaela, Mimi, and Manon
in Europe. I had worked musically on that of Louise, but had not
finished the study of the *mise en scène*. It was decided that I
should make my debut with the least hazardous role of Mimi in
La Bohème on the afternoon of February 7, 1928. There was
quite a build-up beforehand, which culminated during the month
of January in my appearance, for the first time, before a motion-
picture camera for the Pathé News weekly. With me was Senz,
make-up expert and faithful wigmaker of the Metropolitan. The
newsreel men were enormously friendly and seemed pleased about
the coming debut. I invited them all to come and hear me sing at

the opera, and a Mr. Palmer, from *Collier's* magazine, who did a story for an April issue, said that there was a wonderful movie in the story of my childhood and the early days of the beginning of my career because it was so typically American. It was all exciting and heady as champagne.

Then, in mid-January, Tennessee friends invited me to lunch at the Bankers' Club. I walked into the room of the then highest restaurant in the world, on the fortieth floor of 120 Broadway, and faced eleven men, all Southerners, some the most influential men in the country, there to encourage the new "Tennessee opera star." I was the lone woman until coffee time when wives appeared. Among the guests were my father; Norman H. Davis, Under Secretary of State in the Wilson Administration; Mr. Rand of St. Louis, the biggest shoe manufacturer in the world; Dr. George E. Vincent, president of the Rockefeller Institute; and Jesse H. Jones, a Tennesseean, now of Houston, Texas, and Washington. I was swept with the sense of power of the Metropolitan—and the charm of southern gallantry. Many years later, in 1936, at a Tennessee Dinner given for me in Washington and presided over by the beloved Cordell Hull, I was presented with a scroll electing me to honorary lifetime membership in the Tennessee Society of Washington, D. C.

Bellezza called a first rehearsal on the twentieth of January at his apartment, with Edward Johnson, who was to sing Rudolph. That first rehearsal was followed by days of endless practice. Finally we had two stage rehearsals—and one orchestra rehearsal the Sunday before the debut. It was with a shocking start of unpreparedness that I came before the footlights in the vast, empty auditorium. I suddenly realized that it was the very first time I had ever walked on as a performer on any operatic stage. The report had been circulated—and is still current—that I had sung in European opera houses before my American debut, but it was not so, although I wished, as I went onto that stage for the first rehearsal, that it were.

Studio preparation is a poor substitute for the actual experience, but it was too late to turn back and take that year off in

Europe which Mr. Gatti had suggested in Milan and which I had vetoed through impatience and fear. Now I felt as if I were cramming for an examination, and I was terrified that my voice would become clouded by physical and vocal strain.

Bellezza and Edward Johnson, my Rudolph, were wonderful through it all and worked with unending patience. February sixth found my apartment full of newspapermen, but when they saw how nervous I was they were considerate enough to put off their questions until the day after the performance. Mother and Father had come from Tennessee with my brothers and my sister Emily. Emily tried hard to quiet me—she kept preparing glasses of hot milk until dawn, but I slept only four hours that night.

That nervous tension, that feeling of sick physical strain before a performance has never left me. That is why, on the day I sing, I still find it absolutely necessary to relax and remain completely alone. The only personal quarrels I have ever had have taken place just when they should not—the day I sing—and never, until it is all over, do I know what has happened. Today people who know me know better than to come near. I make those hours before a performance my own, scuffling around in dilapidated boudoir slippers and old clothes, a kind of mental preparation for the evening's elaborate opera costumes. And never does the strain let up until three or four hours after the concert or performance. That is why I can't just leave the stage quietly, with a sense of work done, and so home and to bed. After a performance I continue so high-pitched that then I want to see people, talk to them, feel movement and sound around me. I want to go out to supper and laugh with my friends as I feel the little knots of nerves along my spine unwind themselves.

The morning of the debut found me shaken and unstrung. Marafioti came and listened to a few runs and scales, then I set out for the opera house. Everyone backstage—Johnson, Scotti, Didur, and all my fellow artists and the stagehands, some who had worked with me in the *Music Box Revue*—was warm and friendly and encouraging for my success. Earl Lewis, box-office wizard at the Met, was all smiles.

Rosa Ponselle was the first person to come to the stage door and wish me luck. Later Mr. Ziegler and Mr. Gatti came to my dressing room and quietly chatted of operatic things in general. I remember clearly, as I sat trembling and putting on my make-up, that they both spoke of their great admiration for Ponselle's voice, and that Mr. Gatti said he considered his finest production to have been *Pelléas et Mélisande,* with Johnson and Bori.

Mr. and Mrs. Otto Kahn were giving a luncheon that day for my mother and father, Mr. and Mrs. Cordell Hull, Senator and Mrs. Lawrence D. Tyson, and Mr. and Mrs. Finis Garrett, all from Tennessee. Because the party was unavoidably detained and could not arrive on time for the overture, the performance was delayed at Mr. Kahn's request, one of the few instances in Metropolitan history that a curtain has gone up late. Afterward I heard the story that the curtain had been held because I was throwing a fit of temperament. What an overplayed word! I have a temper —that I know. Howard Taubmann in his recent book *Music on My Beat*—one of the most amusing books on musicians I have read—says: "If there has been a more difficult singer at large than Grace Moore, the trade hasn't heard of him or her." Well, Mr. Taubmann, what constitutes temperament with me? It has more often been a case of exaggerated conscientiousness. That day I was too frightened, too dry of throat and petrified to do anything more than sit, like a condemned man, with my heart pounding mercilessly, as I waited for the call, "Miss Moore, Mimi's entrance."

As I stood behind the closed door of Rudolph's studio, ready to knock, with one hand hanging on jitterily to a wobbling candlestick and the other clenched tight, I prayed. Finally the knock, Rudolph's "Who is there?" and my first "Scusi," as Johnson opened the door. As I heard the first sweep of applause from the filled house, a wave of emotion broke over me and deafened me to the sound of the orchestra. Then, of all things, the archetype of feminine disasters occurred and I had to get behind a chair to pull up my slipping garters. In all the nervousness and excitement of that first act my voice only occasionally rose clear, rich and free

—but the last high C was flat, and the usual backstage organ that takes up the melody as Rudolph and Mimi exit at the end of the act had gotten lost in the excitement too, and did not play.

There was tremendous applause from the audience, as if everyone were rallying round to lift my courage, but I felt unhappy and disappointed about that high note. However, the second act was sung with spirit, and from the third act on, I began to forget the outside terrors, lost much of my self-consciousness, and voice and acting took on the real character of Mimi. As the curtain fell on the dying girl, I felt that the beauty and pathos of that scene had in some measure reached across the footlights.

We took twelve curtain calls, and Beatrice Lillie, Ethel Osborne, Miriam Hopkins, and Jane Draper threw violets to me from a right-hand box. The stage gradually filled with a large crowd of camera and newsreel men. Mother, Father, family and friends surrounded me with tears and laughter, quite oblivious of the grinding newsreel machines. There were flowers, telegrams, all the rush and clamor of a successful "first." Among the floral good wishes was one I remember particularly—a great horseshoe with a ribbon, "From your friends on the Côte d'Azur"—contributed by the tradesmen, my gardener and his wife from the South of France. Too tired and dazed to analyze that to me momentous day, I went home to my apartment for a quiet dinner with the family. The next morning I awoke to a kind of fame. The newspapers carried stories and pictures on front and inside pages. On the music pages there were criticisms, some favorable, some not. The only one that was at all constructive for a bewildered young artist was written by Samuel Chotzinoff for the New York *World*. Afterwards he told me that the rumor had it I had paid him ten thousand dollars for that good criticism! I suppose on the installment plan out of my seventy-five dollars a week! My bed was covered with telegrams from all over the world—and I suddenly realized I was an opera star!

It has never been the critics but people who have made my career—but then are not all real careers made and sustained that way? I have deep regard for constructive criticism, but unfortunately that is the rarest variety. After the heartaches, the long, conscientious labor in learning a new role or a concert repertoire, and the continuous financial grind in sustaining a career, the least the critics can do is respect one's efforts, whether or not the result is to their liking. James Huneker had the quality of compassion and respect, yet never compromised with his own innate taste and acumen. First he understood that an artist came into court with work-toiled hands; then, second, he proceeded to examine the evidence with impartial, heart-warmed judgment.

My sympathy goes out to the critics who suffer through long musical seasons of opera, symphonies, and concerts. It is enough to create a bad case of musical indigestion. Couple the weakness of the digestive organs with the lack of perfection and ideals in the commercial musical world, and one can understand why often a critic's appraisal is cantankerous and acidulous. But must there be a continual harping on the golden age of the past? Since the artist must go through his creative growth and adjustment in full view of critical opinion, the critic should offer at least the humanity of understanding. It seems to me the critic has a duty to help the artist find himself through constructive analysis rather than prolong the period of uncertainty as the artist flounders for sincere opinion and guidance. We all know that opera must eliminate many of the old standards that keep it old-fashioned. A new era must set in if opera is to be preserved and progress; and a new kind of singing actor must develop to keep it going. The critics will have to understand and fight for this future along with the artists.

I always read criticism of myself (as well as of everybody else) as much from personal interest as from curiosity to see the real effect on the public that must pay cash for the seats. Bad criticisms have finished many careers. They never mattered to mine. The public and I have been friends for a long time, come praise, go praise. For years the New York critics never quite made up their minds about me. Recently Virgil Thomson, in his unique and inimitable fashion, wrote an article in the New York Sunday *Herald Tribune,* entitled "The Case of Grace Moore," which was a tribute to the conscientiousness of my career. Many people whispered that it was confusing and disparaging. I felt it was compliment enough to be a "case" and thanked Mr. Thomson wholeheartedly.

I've had critical acclaim throughout the rest of the country and Canada; and European writers have treated me with serious and warm friendliness from my first appearances. But in New York, praise had been illiberally scattered until I sang Louise, in the opera of that name, at the Metropolitan in 1939. Then, for the first time, I was awarded good notices in bouquet form—notably the splendid account by my friend Olin Downes in the New York *Times*. I was delighted because I felt that Louise was really in my heart and skin as well as in the throat. I immediately "took heart" and prepared the title role of *Tosca* and that of Fiora of *The Love of Three Kings* with its composer Montemezzi. I made my debut in the Montemezzi work in Chicago with such brilliant confreres as Ezio Pinza, Charles Kullman and Robert Weede, and with Montemezzi himself conducting all performances there. (Later our performance in San Francisco was hailed as the greatest artistic triumph in twenty years of opera.) Ashton Stevens, whose column in the Chicago *Herald and Examiner* was an out-and-out rave, wrote me personally that "the town is still thrilling to your superb Fiora. That was singing I'll remember along with Patti's Rosina and Calvé's Carmen and Chaliapin's Boris. God bless you for it, rarest of the Singing Girls!"

In the Chicago *Tribune*, the intensely musical Cecil Smith wrote a heart-warming and constructive analysis, and Robert Lawrence of the New York *Herald Tribune*, who once lambasted me as Manon, did a turnabout-face and wrote a special article on my Tosca. I've been enormously grateful for any orchids thrown my way across the footlights or in the critical columns: for even though it is the faithful public which keeps a career alive, there is no artist who does not relish the happiness of approval, deny it as he may. In looking back over the criticisms written in the past about other opera stars in the same roles I have recreated, I consider I have not fared too badly. I rest on the premise that to be discussed at all is better than a blank wall of silent neglect.

I know that adverse criticism of her Carmen hurt Rosa Ponselle profoundly. She retired with one of the loveliest voices ever developed in America—much to my grief, for I felt that opera was losing an American champion. My feeling for Ponselle has always been one of tremendous admiration. Mary Garden instructed me to see her Carmen because it was "the best since Calvé"— high praise indeed from Garden. Since then Gladys Swarthout, whom I love dearly as a person and as a singer, has developed a Carmen that is highly individual and provocative and ranks with the best interpretations of that role. Perhaps Ponselle was personally right in retiring. When we last talked, in a little terrace restaurant high above St. Moritz, she tried to explain it to me: "I am thirty-nine years old," she said, "and have never had any fun. I worked and sacrificed all my life for this career, so I think I had better start now before it is too late." From Ponselle's point of view there is undoubtedly compensation in her retirement, but I can only regret the critics and the other intrigue that contributed to her decision.

I remember during one season working so painstakingly over my costumes for *Romeo and Juliet* with two of the greatest authorities in France; visiting museums, swatching fabrics, and then, finally, from Georges Barbier designs Lanvin executed them for me. But these costumes were so authentic, clean, and fresh and stood out so in the shabby ensemble on the stage, they shocked the sensibilities of the critics. Some of the press lambasted me the next morning for wearing them and claimed they were completely out of keeping. In a rage I wrote to Pitts Sanborn telling him exactly the history of my costumes, where I had found the material for them, and indicating, point for point, their authenticity. He thanked me for the information and, I was told from Paris, he checked my story and found it true. But he never verified it in print!

Sometimes the Sublime Brotherhood borders on the ridiculous. A California critic once wrote a concert notice on one of the best performances I ever gave around the fact that I wore an

Tosca

Grace Moore, Lucrezia Bori and Lawrence Tibbett with
George Sloan of the Metropolitan Opera Board

Grace Moore posing on the set of *Louise* with
her husband Valentin Parera and co-star Ezio Pinza

Grace Moore and Dorothy Kirsten in *La Boheme*

Grace Moore and Tullio Carmanati in *One Night of Love* , 1934

emerald necklace and was married to a charming man! And one of the funniest critical impasses in my career concerns a business friend of Alexander Ince, the Budapest publisher who recently edited the *New Theatre Magazine*. The friend, who now heads one of the most important news-picture magazines in the country, had issued a stern edict against any favors to me in its pages. "But why?" I asked Ince. "What in the world has he got against me? I don't even know the man." Ince shrugged his shoulders. "It seems," he explained, "he doesn't like you and doesn't want to give you any space *because you did something to his dog.*" That, I think, is a fine basis for critical musical judgment! Furthermore, I don't *even know the dog!* We had never met socially. I wouldn't do *that* to a dog!!

Naturally I learned many of these things slowly after my debut at the Metropolitan. And I've had many happy experiences there. So often after a performance, Désiré Defrère, the stage manager, who is a wonderful cook, would come out with us and wander into my kitchen, where he would turn out a beautiful supper that always started with steaming luscious onion soup. That true-and-tried body of men, the orchestra, are friendly comrades. The men backstage are hearty, friendly, and convivial and always refer to their foremen as *maestri*. Sometimes their conviviality leads them into temporary disaster, as happened with the backstage crew at the Chicago Opera when Farrar went there to sing Humperdinck's *Königskinder*. It was a farewell performance, and Farrar sang it in great triumph. After the curtain had gone down, the members of the personnel of the opera became involved with the backstage crew in a poker game. The opera personnel lost heavily. Finally, in lieu of money, they offered the specially trained geese of the *Königskinder* as stake, thinking they would not be needed again on stage. The electricians won, took the geese home, and we hope enjoyed them. But they had not reckoned on Farrar's popularity. Because of popular demand the opera management ordered another performance of *Königskinder*. "But, my God," thought the crew, "what about the specially trained geese?" In desperation they ordered a flock of ordinary geese and on an hour's notice tried to train them. When Farrar, not knowing of the switch, entered on the stage, the fowl started up such a honking and bru-ha-ha and flew around in all directions that the bewildered diva almost had to retreat before the cadenzas of the geese.

I have made many friends among opera personnel and have felt closest to the young American singers coming in, as I did, under fire. I have tried to point out what they would be up against and what they stood to gain. Most prima donnas acquire protégées only for the purposes of hero worship and sympathetic publicity. They give advice, but seldom money, in payment for adulation. My young accompanist once told me that many divas never permitted aspiring pianists an opportunity to play solo on concert tour for fear it would detract from the diva's prestige! The adulation and advice may be enough for others. I have always gone along on the assumption that hard cash and determined backing were more efficacious.

Of course protégées can sour on one. One of my saddest experiences concerns a young American protégée whom I brought from Europe with money raised among my friends. I had met the girl on the Riviera, where she was working with Marafioti and struggling along in hopes for a career at the Opéra Comique. Her husband was a pianist, and the two had saved a bit of money and gone to France to pursue their studies. Things had not gone well, the money had evaporated, and they were anxious to go back to America, where she could continue with Marafioti. Thomas L. Chadbourne gave me a dinner party at Cannes on his yacht with Lady Cunard as hostess. Knowing how desperate the young student was, I broke all orthodox tradition on that yachting party by wandering around the deck singing and taking up a collection. When I had added what I could afford to what the guests and generous Tom Chadbourne had contributed, we had a purse of three thousand dollars. I put the money in a bank in the girl's name, and she and her husband sailed with Marafioti that late summer.

Therefore it was something of a shock when, the next season, during a performance at the Metropolitan, she was overheard by close friends of mine in a neighboring box criticizing me with great venom. In a loud voice she kept repeating, "God, if I were up there on that stage I'd certainly show everybody what this opera is all about."

My friends did not know who she was, but she was such an obstreperous anti-claque they were curious. They inquired during the intermission and were told she was my *friend*. After the final curtain this erstwhile protégée came to my dressing room and threw her arms around me, tears in her eyes, as she praised the evening's performance. She left the dressing room as her neighbors of the box came in to say hello.

"Who is that, Grace?" they asked me. I told them. Whereupon they recounted what had happened during the performance, the outrageous things that had been said while I was singing, and the general maliciousness.

I was hurt and angry. The next day I went to Marafioti's studio, where my protégée had immediately preceded me. She was telling him how magnificent had been my voice the night before. As I came into the room she snatched at my hand and caught it in a frenzy of devotion. I held onto the hand, squeezed it as I lifted her onto a level with me, then smacked her solidly across the face. She turned livid, looked for a moment as if she was going to pull my hair, but decided against it and flounced out instead.

"Never let her in this studio again," I said to Marafioti.

He answered blandly, "I wondered when you would come to that."

On the other hand I take great pride and joy in the career of Dorothy Kirsten, that lovely-voiced soprano who was brought to me by a radio columnist at a time when she was working in a dentist's office every day and scrubbing the floors of that office three times each week for the extra overtime pay. When she sang for me in clear, flutelike tones, I listened to her and thought, "Here goes again, I'll take another chance." In a few weeks I had her on a boat speeding towards Italy, with lessons arranged for with a singing teacher recommended by Gigli. She went with a wardrobe of new clothes and extra pocket money for little trips. I wanted her to see what I had seen of Old World culture—to visit the galleries, really get to know the fine art of the country and learn the language. Among the books I gave her to take along was the inevitable, beloved *Jean Christophe*.

When Dorothy Kirsten returned from Italy because of the war, I helped launch her for a debut at the Chicago Opera, where she sang Musetta to my Mimi in *La Bohème*. She was a great success, and I felt my job was done. The rest was up to her. When she married recently I gave her, as a wedding present, complete clearance of all her debts to me. There was payment enough in knowing that another American voice had been accepted by the critical public.

But back to the year of my debut. The first thing I discovered was what terrific box-office appeal there was on a concert tour in the name "Metropolitan." When I went on my first trip under the management of Charles Wagner to Nashville, Tennessee, where I had once been a student at the Ward-Belmont College for Girls, I found thousands of people at the station, the mayor on hand with a key to the city, and a committee to usher me off to the Executive Mansion of Governor and Mrs. Horton, where I was to stay as their guest. "But," I thought as I saw the crowds, "I want a serious career. I don't want just to be a personality." I realized there was money to be made in such a concert tour, but it served to throw me even more deeply into my work. I was too much of a realist not to sense that floating along on such success might be deadly—and short-lived. I determined to extend my experience.

I finished that first season at the Metropolitan, which included a successful debut as Juliet, singing with Gigli as Romeo (Johnson with the best legs in opera looking like a real Romeo alternating) and De Luca and Tibbett, then spoke to Mr. Gatti about the future. "I'd like to return now," I said to him, "for that year of touring in European opera houses that you suggested in Milan. I think I could use that further experience."

Mr. Gatti encouraged me to sing everywhere in endless search for experience and gave me his blessing. Now, once again, I sailed for France—but this time as an opera star with a Metropolitan reputation and a taste of musical fame.

The Provincial Circuit

BEING NO MORE NOR LESS than human, the first flush of prima-
donna success produced the usual comic results. Clara Marafioti
not long ago told me how screamingly funny was my departure
for Europe that year. "I remember," she said, "going down to
your cabin to say good-by and finding Jane Draper there, waiting
for you too. You finally arrived at the head of a whole retinue of
men, not another female in sight, everyone feeling very gay after
a farewell dinner. Condé Nast headed the group, carrying a whole
orchid tree. White-haired Mrs. Harrison brought up the rear
with the jewel case, luggage-laden porters and minions following
in her wake. Jane, the Doctor, and I became hysterical watching
the ridiculous procession from the side lines." "The only thing missing," said Dr. Marafioti, "is the parrot in the cage to complete the
mise en scène for 'Enter Madame.' Then you rang the bell, and
when they asked what you wanted you said in French, 'Send the
chef up—I want to order my breakfast!' "

It sounds silly, young, and somehow 'way in the past. Those
were halcyon days, and wasn't I an opera star? Everything was
fun. Bea Lillie, Clifton Webb, and his gay and bubbling mother
Mabel were on board that trip, and we had a merry time. The
ship's doctor was a Dr. Petit, on whom Bea and I both cast covet-
ous eyes, turning the little duel into a private battle of wits—all,
of course, without Dr. Petit's knowledge. First Bea would fake
seasickness, then I would, and while the whole ship complained
because there was no Dr. Petit when wanted, we had him trotting
from my cabin to hers in desperation, while Mrs. Harrison

frowned at our antics. Dear Mrs. Harrison, only once in all our travels through Europe together did her prim, dry manner break down, when she remarked, as I dragged her through the Palace at Fontainbleau into the apartments of Maintenon and Napoleon, "Well, one had to be famous in some respect to deserve such beds, but how difficult always to live up to one's reputation after getting into them!"

I started my commuting tour of Europe in Deauville, where I sang Juliet. From there I went directly to the Opéra Comique in Paris. This was my big European debut, one which loomed almost as importantly in my mind as the Metropolitan. *La Bohème,* with which I have made my debut in twelve leading opera houses throughout the world, was chosen as my first vehicle. What a joy it has always been to sing at the Comique! The intimacy of Manon and Mimi are so closely interwoven with the personal spirit of the theater itself that these typically French heroines seem an indispensable part of the place. Because I had learned Mimi in Italian, it was decided that I should sing it in that language while the rest of the cast sang in French.

Announcement of my debut had got an unexpected press in the French and Paris-American papers, and the curtain went up on a crowded house. I could feel the atmosphere of intense interest, and though there were many of my friends in that audience, there were strangers who wondered how *l'américaine* was going to fare. The silence that greeted me as I stepped through the door to meet Rudolph gave me courage. It was a listening silence, respectful, on *my* side. It put me at my ease, and my voice felt free and completely under control. I sang better that night than ever before in my life. The applause after my first aria was tremendous, and I have never had an ovation which made me happier. After the performance a host of friends and newspaper people all rushed to my dressing room with congratulations and huzzahs. The whole hallway was lined with flowers. "It's the most successful American debut since Mary Garden," everyone kept repeating, and manager, directors, opera personnel all said, "This Opéra Comique public is a difficult one, you have done very well."

The press next day was overwhelming. After the yes-no comments of the American papers, it was good to read in the Chicago *Tribune,* Paris edition:

Not since the days when Mary Garden made her sensational debut at the Opéra Comique has any young American artist met with such instantaneous success. After her first aria, "Mi chiamano Mimi," Miss Moore literally brought the audience to its feet with lusty cheers and was called before the curtain ten times after the first act. At the conclusion of the performance, the audience put aside its dignity to manifest in no uncertain terms its complete approval of an artist who shows every sign of carrying on the splendid traditions established by Mary Garden and Geraldine Farrar.

The *Tribune's* competitor, the New York *Herald,* Paris edition, was equally fulsome in its praise:

Miss Moore's debut revealed to the public a singer of exceptional talent and of great promise. No Mimi has ever shown a softer and more melodious voice, above all so well balanced both in the high and the low register. That is where many singers often fail.

This warmth, this generosity, this kind, abundant friendship has been a consistent appraisal through my European career. It also swept me along in an even greater ambition and an even greater desire for perfection.

My second performance of *Romeo and Juliet* was at the Royal Opera House in Liége and was a great improvement over the first Juliet sung in Deauville. The artists and the Personelle of the Opera and the public were both generous, although reputed to be rather "*froid,*" and there was continued applause. But it was the criticism of Georges Thill, who had come to hear me, the sagacious criticism of one artist to another, that pleased me most of all. After the performance we went on a gay supper party with M. Gaillaird and his family and William Martin, the American tenor who had been such a splendid Romeo to my Juliet. They told stories about the artists in the various opera houses, and it was the first time I heard of horseplay among the Olympians. One story concerned a tenor who had to present the soprano with a bouquet of flowers at various intervals during the opera he was singing. Someone had attached a hidden string to the bouquet, and each time the tenor would reach for the flowers, the string would pull the flowers to the other end of the stage, where the tenor would have to rush for them. Finally the distracted man, driven too far, sat on the bouquet and offered the roses one by one to the soprano as he sang his aria.

This kind of practical joking seldom goes on in the solemnity of the big opera houses, but running into it in the provinces is refreshing and gay (providing, of course, it doesn't happen to you). The informality of the provincial houses has produced a spate of stories. One of the funniest—because it's one of the saddest and most Chaplinesque—concerns the baritone house painter who was signed by the Naples Opera Company and told to learn the role of Escamillo in *Carmen*. Being a house painter, it took him five months. The fall season arrived, and the management, deciding they would give no *Carmen* that year, instructed the baritone to learn the part of Germont senior in *Traviata* instead. The poor man worked night and day. Finally came the opening. He walked out onto the stage, handsome and dignified as Germont, and started singing, his voice soaring free and beautiful, when suddenly, through confusion, overwork, and the sad fate that always plagues the little man, he broke into the rousing strains of the Toreador song while the music of *Traviata* played on.

And where but in a provincial house could two rival baritones, who had prepared for the same role, take out their rivalry with such grand buffoonery as to permit the one who found his contract had been canceled to appear on the stage anyway the night of the performance and sing the *whole* role through along with the other baritone!

After Liége I was scheduled to sing at Rouen. Here I had what might be called my first operatic temperamental row. I still think it was not temperamental, but a justified display of temper; but label it temperamental if you will. I had arrived from Paris for a rehearsal in a very happy mood, having lunched sumptuously at

La Couronne d'Or, the renowned restaurant in Rouen, and enjoyed the soft, misty beauty of the rain-drenched French countryside on the way. I was met by the stage manager, an obvious garter-snapper. I asked him who my tenor was, and was told that so far there was none. Since this was my first Manon, I was naturally concerned about the rehearsal. But the concern was mine alone—no one else considered a rehearsal necessary.

"But I want a rehearsal—we were scheduled for one—and I want a tenor," I insisted.

At last they unearthed a sleek-headed "type" who was purported to sing tenor, and we started the rehearsal. Mon Dieu, how his voice shook and rattled! The rest of the cast was so complacent that finally the futility of continuing overwhelmed me and I lost my temper. With a few definite French words, climaxed by that jack-of-all-trades *bon mot*, M———, which oddly enough is often used in place of "Good luck!" in the French theater, I stamped off the stage. I went to my hotel, had a hot bath, and got into bed. I was called out of it by the opera manager. "Sorry," I explained, "I can't possibly sing my first Manon under such conditions," and hung up. Then I sent off a batch of telegrams to Paris announcing the fact.

My manager, the late Alexander Kahn, arrived from Paris the next morning, heard my story, and agreed that I had made the proper decision. He went off to the theater and evidently arranged to pay something for my failure to appear that night. The little saga ended with Kahn and me lunching at the famous Hôtel de la Couronne with a famous musician and his mistress, a big, fat, mascaraed dramatic soprano with fat, short, stubby white hands loaded with demi-semi-precious jewelry. In all the *je comprends's* that flowed across the table, all the *mais oui's* and *c'est dommage's,* I almost promised to sing a performance of *Manon* for nothing to make up for the embroilment—but, temperament or not, at least I avoided singing my first Manon under such inauspicious circumstances.

It was in the enchanting old opera house at Bordeaux that I did sing my first Manon—a wonderful old house, completely intact with all the original *boisserie* from the days of Louis Seize (intact, that is, until the reported bombing there not so long ago). Standing on the stage, with the cast in the court costumes of *Manon* that become so a part of the same period as the theater, I thought what a pity it was the audience didn't come in costume too.

I had flung all my money into a stupendous entourage and had arrived in Bordeaux complete with Hispano-Suiza, Albert the chauffeur, and a French maid. I found my confreres only moderately cordial with the exaggerated politeness that implies insincerity. My grand entrance was, after all, not unusual for an opera star. But there was a great change in attitude on the day of the dress rehearsal that I couldn't help noticing. Such a bowing and scraping and throwing of bouquets! "What has caused this sudden affection, these unexpected *beaux gestes?*" I wondered. "But," I thought, shrugging my shoulders, "what the hell! If they want to put it on thick, who am I to complain?"

However, after the performance, when I was out to supper at the famous Chapon Fin with Georges Thill, who had driven down to hear me, I told him about the quick-change attitude on the part of the opera personnel and asked if he knew any explanation. He laughed. "I can tell you," he said, "now that it's all over. Your French maid, Marie, noticed the reserve of the management and artists towards you, an unknown American, and resented it. She schemed for some way to break through the ice. Finally she whispered into the manager's ear that he ought to treat you with every special consideration because you were the mistress of the richest man in the world."

"What!" I shrieked at Georges.

He nodded his head. "She gilded the lily even further. She said your lover was a certain elderly oil magnate who was known to dole out dimes to his caddies but to whom France had every reason to be most grateful."

I hardly knew whether to be mortified or hysterical. Georges took the why-not view—the pragmatic French view. "After all," he said, "the manager of this theater manages others throughout France. Why not play the story to the hilt? For one thing, even

without your affluent 'friend' you have proven that you can stand
on your own."

Georges was apparently right. The next day the manager said to
me, "Even without the influence of your *bon ami* you can sing in
any of my houses in France."

Georges Thill was an extraordinary man who knew a great
deal about music, women, and the world. He was the reigning
tenor in France and something of a matinee idol. I liked him tre-
mendously, but I had a devil of a time trying to get him to change
his manner of dressing. He dressed in the fashion of a small-
town dude—I suppose today one would call it "sharp." He was at
the other end of the fashion slide from George Biddle of the strawberry tweeds: but neither man had *it* when it came to clothes.
One of the joys I take in Val, my husband, is that he knows how
to dress simply and with unerring taste. Women seldom admit it,
but they take as much pride in a man's clothes as everyone freely
admits a man takes in a woman's.

While in Bordeaux I again saw M. Sicar, manager and pro-
prietor of the Chapon Fin where I lived. I knew M. Sicar from
other visits, when I had been shown through the miles of underground wine caves owned by him. Indeed I once took enough
time in Bordeaux to go through all the famous caves of the region,
learning about wines from the master makers. I love wines and
through my schooling with M. Sicar became so proficient in my
knowledge of them that once on the *Ile de France* in a wine-
tasting contest against a group of long-bearded Frenchmen, who
had sipped in their wine with their mothers' milk, I managed to
get third prize. I remember that Chevalier got second, and we
both lost to a rosette-lapelled French boy who had probably been
incubated on Romanie St. Vivant. The night I sang Manon in
Bordeaux, I found my dressing room filled with cases of vintage
wines from the region's famous vineyards instead of the usual
floral designs and tricolor bouquets.

I returned to Paris and the Comique for my debut there in
Manon. I was carefully prepared by Albert Carré and rehearsed
assiduously from morning until night with the members of the

cast. I was fortunate to get Michiletti as Des Grieux, for he was an excellent artist. The day of the performance there was a tremendous crowd outside, two and three deep, waiting for hours to get in. This in the days before I had ever made a movie. I always received the peanut-gallery audience in my dressing room, and one night as I walked out the stage door into a hubbub of friendly greetings, I heard one American voice say, "Great stuff, kid—great show."

I always compared this stage-door crowd, queued up for hours and sustained by long staves of bread, wine, and cheese, with the crowds that flocked to see me after the movie success. Coming to the Comique as an unknown—unknown, that is, except through the press—my first success there was kindled from the warmth of the audience itself. But after I went back to sing, surrounded by Hollywood fame, I always knew that while half the audience was there because it wanted to hear me sing, the other half had showed up out of curiosity in a name and a personality.

The first Manon at the Comique went off splendidly. Emma Calvé, looking incredibly young, was there and said, after the scene of the Cour la Reine, that only a lyric soprano who had learned the art of complete vocal relaxation in the Marafioti technique could sing so easily that last sustained high D.

I sailed back to New York for my second season with the Metropolitan, when I sang Micaela in Carmen, Juliet several times, and Mimi in Bohème. I returned to Europe immediately afterward to continue my tours of provincial houses—going to Monte Carlo and the Cannes operas and back to the Opéra Comique. I had always wanted to sing on the Riviera, for I felt almost like a native Riviera-ist. La Bohème was sung in Cannes before the ex-king Emmanuel of Portugal, who came backstage afterward to congratulate me, sending an enormous bouquet of flowers in his wake. That season a native Frenchwoman named Lily Pons sang at the Cannes Opera House too. From connoisseurs I had heard reports of her beautiful voice, but it was not until America discovered her that Lily Pons won the sensational recognition she deserved. It was in America that Lily and I became friends. She is warm, gay, a good comrade, and she and André Kostelanetz are charming hosts in their lovely Connecticut home.

I returned to Paris for the Comique performances—and again, as always, felt myself a different person the moment I reached that charmed city. Nowhere else in the world do I feel so free, natural, and at home as I do in Paris. Perhaps because it is the other side of the coin from Jellico, Tennessee, but I need merely to walk through the streets to get a release from all tension, a clearheadedness about myself, an ebullience and *joie de vivre* that almost trails in the air.

One of the choice spots in that beloved city was the restaurant in Montmartre called Chez Nini, right below that tasteless but famous conglomeration of white stones—the Sacré Cœur, facing the square. Nini was famous for her chicken, good spirits, and hominess. She was "discovered" during the last war by Alec Woollcott and George Jean Nathan, who both turned it into a favorite hangout. Alec entertained there for a host of friends, but George Jean Nathan, being the less gregarious type, made it his favorite dinner-for-two rendezvous. Nini always served her special clients in a tiny garden back of the restaurant, where, if she really liked you, she would bring out a bottle of old Armagnac and chat about life, love, and men, about all three of which she was philosophical and well informed. Nini used to tell a wonderful story about John Charles Thomas, an habitué of the place. When he made his operatic debut at the Brussels Opera House, Nini went dressed in a dignified and elaborate white satin gown, her arms and neck bedecked with fabulous diamonds. Sitting in a box adjoining the royal family, she led the claque in ovations for Thomas.

All of this hilltop, the Butte de Montmartre, has been for me a stamping ground of good living, and I associate it particularly with Gustave Charpentier. I first met him through the kindly offices of members of the staff of the New York *Times,* who thought it would be good publicity if they took pictures of me, the new American singer in Paris who was studying the title role of *Louise* for the Comique, with Charpentier, its composer. They brought him down from Montmartre to my little apartment at the

Hôtel Astoria on the Champs Elysées, and it was a sympathetic meeting at once. He was apparently uncomfortable so far down town and suggested that we go off to Montmartre to complete the series of pictures. We went to Nini's and from there to the home of Mimi Pinson. I saw the studio with the view of the "Ville Lumière," where he wrote the music for the third act, and the other nooks and crannies of his private life which are so much a part of the opera itself. Under the trees shading the little umbrella tables and chairs of the Place du Tertre we drank a little glass of vermouth or red wine in each of these places, and he always gallantly raised his glass to the success of "his newest Louise." We were both so moved by all the excitement that we went rollicking down the Montmartre hills, singing with abandon in our fullest voices. In his artist's pork-pie hat, Byron collar, flowing tie, and short coat, he looked the living image of Louise's Julien. Old as he was, he still held onto the same Gallic gaiety that sang through his music.

No opera has ever been written that expresses so definitely the life and spirit of a city. When I think of Paris, I think of *Louise*. In *Louise* is everything that all people have loved about it. It is in the score and in the libretto too, which cannot be separated one from the other. When *Louise* opened in 1900 it caused much controversy. Charpentier was called a radical and a socialist, and some critics thundered that *Louise* taught the gospel of free love. But to Charpentier, the opera was meant to sing the freedom of personal idealism, the right to find oneself without prejudice. Louise is the one opera heroine who goes on living and taking joy in life. That is why I feel so closely part of her—her rebelliousness, her need for unfettered expression, her zest and stintless abundance. Today, when Paris lies silent, like a pile of sticks and stones, in alien hands, I prefer to think of it in terms of the human light and laughter and the human need for liberty of *Louise*.

It has always been a satisfaction to me that I studied every phrase of *Louise* with Charpentier. He gave me the score to study, and after hearing me sing it for the first time, in his studio, he paid me the compliment of saying I was one of the few people he had ever heard who could color the music with the meaning of the word. That was in part because I loved the Paris about which I was singing.

Charpentier and I formed a happy and devoted friendship. I used to worry about him financially. It seems that, needing money desperately, he had taken a large advance from his publishers in lieu of future royalties and had never participated adequately in the tremendous success of *Louise*. I couldn't understand why this man who had composed the most famous native opera of his day should have to live in Montmartre in a tiny apartment reached by four long flights to the very top floor. He told me that often when he tried to work at night the noise of the rats in the attic above him disturbed him too much. What little money he made went towards the upkeep of his wife, who had been in an insane asylum for years. It was the great sorrow of his life. It interfered with his work and prevented him from ever topping *Louise*. But like every philosophical Frenchman, he was an incurable romanticist, and even in his late seventies there was always a charming young girl on his arm as he walked down the streets of Montmartre. Their affection for him must have been a kind of compassionate sympathy because he was so much in need of companionship and order in his life.

One night I went with Heifetz to a simple little French restaurant, whose name I have forgotten, located on the side of a hill just above Nini's. It had a delightful terrace (so common in Europe, so rare in the United States) from which, on this evening, Jascha Heifetz gave one of the inspired recitals of his career. He had borrowed a violin from the itinerant violinist who wandered from restaurant to restaurant in Montmartre playing for the diners for a few sous *pourboire*. It was no Stradivarius, but Jascha played on it with more abandon and emotion than I had ever heard before. And slowly, as he played, the lights of Paris twinkled on, one by one, like the backdrop Charpentier had created for the third act of *Louise*. As Jascha continued to play, studio windows opened on all sides, heads leaned out, from all sides of the *quartier* people gathered like phantom figures in front of the terrace, to watch and hear. All Paris somehow seemed to be tangled in Jascha's web, and even the Seine below, shining like pewter in the night, flowed to his melody. Jascha continued, a Pied Piper above the city, wandering through the airs from *Louise,* some Brahms melodies, the "Caprice Viennois," all in a purely melodic strain. Suddenly he looked up and saw the peering faces all around him. He was bewildered, as if he had been shaken back to reality. In a spell of stage fright, he sat down in confusion like a gauche little boy.

One night Linda Porter, who had persuaded Mary Pickford to cut her hair, said that everyone in the world had short hair but me and it was high time I conformed. She and Cole gave a dinner party at the Restaurant Laurent, had everyone bring scissors, and ordered Antoine to appear with his head cutter and the inevitable white bib. To a piano accompaniment in the best Cole Porter style, everyone took a whack at my hair, and by the time Antoine arrived most of it lay around the chair. Thus I joined the bobbed-hair generation.

Because I loved Paris and had found such happiness and success there, I decided to rent a house. The irrepressible Charles MacArthur had a mild psychological hand in the matter, although it was the long way round. He had come to Paris with his brother and decided to look me up. The night he arrived I was giving a serious musicale for many of the musicians of the Comique in my apartment at the Astoria. Came a knock at the door. There stood a man in a black-and-white-checked suit, Stetson hat, high yellow button shoes, who opened his coat and flashed a big tin badge at me. "I'm the house detective," he said. "I wanted to see if the Americans were behaving themselves. But the manager has asked, since you make so much noise, will you please vacate in an hour."

I was outraged, I argued, and my guests—among them the *soignée* Gloria Swanson, who was the rage of Paris—became so frightened they silently stole away. When I looked around the room it was empty. I slammed the door on the "detective," told him I would not leave the hotel, and demanded an apology at once. The detective backed away, mumbled something and disappeared. I remained in my room fuming. Later that night I heard the most horrendous groaning in the room next to mine. I decided I'd play tit for tat on the manager. I called down and insisted that something be done about the people next door. The manager came up, listened, heard the fearful noises, and opened the room. Out walked Charlie, followed by the "detective"—his brother Arthur!

I decided that what I needed was a house! Furthermore, singers always need houses. Apartments are too confining, and other tenants always complain of the "noise" of music. Thus every bank balance I have ever had has gone into a house, and I will buy one at the drop of a hat. I found and rented a fourteenth-century *pavillon* in Neuilly-sur-Seine with a little bridge that connected it with the apartment house in front. It had probably once been the maids' quarters, but I reveled in its original architecture and charm. Hidden on the Rue St. James, it was surrounded by such neighbors as Daisy Fellowes, Lillie Havemeyer, and Captain Molyneux. My own *pied à terre* in Paris! This was success.

My whole experience in Paris was so completely satisfying and emotionally rewarding. With what happy pride I recall that there is still today in the vestibule of the Opéra Comique a marble plaque with my name engraved on it, in the distinguished company of renowned French artists and the other American, Mary Garden. The plaque was presented to me as a kind of thank-you for the assistance I gave in raising money for Le Maison de Retrait de Pont aux Dames, the organization for indigent retired artists of the ensemble. Albert Carré, who was then president of the Concours de Conservatoire à Paris, asked me to head the committee for the collection of money, which I agreed to do. The French have always looked out for their old artists, and it is one of the things I admire most about them. How kindly they treat their Sarah Bernhardts, their Mistinguetts, their Cécile Sorels—long after their peak they are cheered and respected, as if they continued in their prime. And so it is with the ladies of the ensemble who reach a less glorified old age. They may not be cheered, but they are cared for.

I had already returned to America when the marble plaque was put into place. Carré wrote me an amusing letter about the proceedings. The president of the Beaux Arts presided and pompously speechified that I was being placed in immortality along with the others, of whom Carré himself was one. "So you see," wrote Carré, "I can think of nothing more pleasant than spending immortality in your company."

I cannot write or think of the Opéra Comique without Mary Garden shaping the background. Garden has had a tremendous influence on my life, my career, my ambitions. Pictures of her come back at random. She was so lovely, so flaming, so much a woman—warm and soft and tender as a woman should be. When I returned to Paris in 1937 to make the film *Louise,* Mary had been engaged as a European talent scout for Metro-Goldwyn-Mayer. Val and I would go often to her flat on the Rue du Bac for long, laughing chats. The lovely salon was shaded by chestnut trees that bent close to the casement windows, and the light would dapple the myriad mementos of Mary's great career. It was "her" room—her whole life. In one corner was a souvenir painting of Mary as Salome, in another a canvas of her as Mélisande, over there a picture of her in a divine modern dress designed for her by Molyneux. Curiously there was never any great art created with Mary as subject, but somehow it didn't matter in that Paris salon. She used to say, with a sad, wry shake of the head, "It is incredible, as I sit here and think of all my past life as the creator of Mélisande, re-creator of Salome, Thaïs, and so many others, that today I am an agent for a motion-picture company on the hunt for singing movie stars."

She said to me during rehearsals for *Louise* that I was the only person who worked with her who did not try to imitate her. She was always frightened that the people who worked with her would be so busy giving poor imitations that they would stifle any imaginative creative approach to themselves.

Anyone who has not seen Mary Garden as Mélisande has missed something rare. Mary's Mélisande was an exquisite portrayal. Although she was given to gestures, typical of her training in the French school, they were never extravagant, because they sprang from an inward understanding of the character. Most opera stars are so busy being themselves, they never reach down to the heart of the person portrayed. Not so Mary—she knew her Mélisande as she knew Fiora of *The Love of Three Kings*. Mary called Fiora a magnificent liar and the most complicated woman in the operatic repertoire. "Neither Fiora nor Mélisande ever tells the truth," explained Mary to me. "That is part of their magic, and this weakness is the touchstone in the creation of either role." Mary told me that she was never separated artistically from Debussy for the four years when she studied with him, and she absorbed directly from him every note he wrote. "That is why," she said, "his music is in me until I die."

She said that young singers today would never be able to realize the fullness of their abilities, because opera managers now have the confounded habit of changing casts for every single performance. She always had a tenor and a baritone who sang the same opera with her, and a mutual artistic as well as human understanding developed. Thus they could grow into their roles together and mellow and mature through this understanding.

Mary called *L'Aiglon* the greatest opera since *Pelléas et Mélisande* or *The Love of Three Kings*. "I would have given," she said, "the rest of my life to have created it." However she was honest enough to say that Heldy, with her emaciated passion, was perfect for the role and superb in it. Mary pointed out one theatrical trick of Heldy's in *L'Aiglon*—in the mirror-breaking scene she faced the audience with the mirror and hurled it so everyone could see and hear the crash, unlike Bernhardt, who had turned her back and held up a mirror previously shattered. Heldy felt that the illusion of hearing something break was stronger than seeing it.

Mary always loved Louise as I did. To both of us she spelled freedom, frankness, femininity. Even to have had my Louise compared with hers, as the critics did when I sang it in Paris, was the pinnacle of praise. Mary was the first American to sing the role of this completely French heroine with acclaim. I was the last —for my Louise at the Comique in 1939 was sung on the eve of war and was the final performance of it before the end. Over a span of ten years—I made my debut in *Louise* at the Comique in 1929 with William Martin as the tenor and Bourdin, who had been Pelléas to Garden's Mélisande, as the baritone—*Louise* has been the heart and soul of French opera to me. And somehow when I think of Mary Garden, now in Aberdeen doing what war work she can, I remember that early morning when Charpentier, Val, the *Louise* directors, and I had gone to a little motion-picture theater in Montmartre to hear the sound track of the film *Louise* run off. As we sat listening, our eyes fixed on a blank, gray screen, we heard through the music the sounds of marching feet as France's army formed for the mobilization. Against the rising strain of "Depuis le jour"—that aria that brought all Paris to Mary Garden's feet—I remember the counterpoint of heavy boots going *clack-clack-clack* on Montmartre's ancient cobblestones.

Sing a Song of Hollywood, A Pocket Full of Wry

To ANYONE WHO HAS NEVER BEEN THERE, Hollywood is the never-never land—out of reach, out of mind. The very name spells fantasy—and its inhabitants are supershadows, beautiful, long-lashed, unbelievable. Seldom does an ordinary mortal take the magic journey across the border line. The closest most of us come is through the "movie" magazines, read under the hair drier, or through the breathless minutiae of the small-townish columns devoted to the comings and goings of these folk who *must* be true because their doings get into print. (If you see it in the *Sun,* it's so!) Indeed, the whole atmosphere of awe towards Hollywood is small-townish: did you *really* see Garbo plain, did you *truly* sit next to Cary Grant—oh me, oh my!

Mine was the typical approach to Hollywood when I first went there in 1930. I was all eyes, all ears, all Jellico, Tennessee, delighted with the promise of a glimpse at fairyland and hopeful for a nibble at the gingerbread house. But beneath the excitement was a solid wish. I wanted to help carve a niche for good music in the then-developing field of sound pictures. I did eventually—and Hollywood in turn did much for me; but my experiences there took topsy-turvy turns of fanfare, flop, flight, furor, frenzy, and finis. When I came back from it just a fair success after my first try, it almost wrecked my concert and opera career because I wasn't worth as much to the music managers as before. When I returned from it a sensational success, after my second trip in 1934, it almost wrecked my concert career again because now, being a film star, the music critics felt I had sold my soul for footage

But in spite of it all I have a very tender feeling for Hollywood. As my Spanish husband says, never two without three. As I say, in the American language of Mencken, it takes three strikes to make an out. I've had two motion-picture careers, with two varied results. What, I wonder, would a third produce?

Anyone who has had the success that I have had—let us call it a one-picture success—gains a great deal from Hollywood. One of the most wonderful things about the films, a wonder that never ceases to amaze and thrill me, is that no matter where you go you are never a stranger. After long years of stage and opera work in which I had been a star and found success, I learned through the run of *One Night of Love* that fame in the usual sense has nothing to do with the universal familiarity you gain through the screen. Hollywood made my face, my voice, my name completely recognizable here, in Europe, throughout the world. I'm not the cold, chiseled type by nature. I am as susceptible to human vanity as anyone. I plead guilty to secret delight in the simple act of recognition. It is such a concrete reaction. You walk down a street, and on account of a singing shadow on a screen, people turn, look, know you. That electric current of recognition is quite removed from one's own final personal satisfaction, but where is the girl who even in high school doesn't thrill, when she walks down the corridor, to hear a back whisper, "That's Susie. You know, she had the lead in the play."

Along with the excitement, Hollywood brought me its own special brand of grief. Like the joy, the jams you run into are widespread too. Anyone who pioneers in films runs into trouble. I did. My studio did. Music and musical tradition were a new language to Hollywood. The sheer mechanical problem of working with a full orchestra and voices trained to the far reaches of the opera—to say nothing of taking a score and adapting it to the needs of a film's run—was out of the range of Hollywood's experience at that time. The wear and tear on the voice that comes from recording, not only with orchestra but again and again to get complete synchronization, is physically and mentally harrowing. Mistakes had to be made and *were* made all around.

Furthermore, the impact of a Hollywood career on a singing career is startling, unpredictable, two-edged. The movies undoubtedly bring people into the concert hall to see and hear you "in person" who would never ordinarily go to either concert or opera. But the movies also establish a pattern which these same new concert-goers insist you maintain. I am not quarreling with the result. I like it. I like the fact that because of my movie career people come to hear me who might never otherwise do so. The critics may object to the "popularization," but music isn't for critics alone, it's for people—and the more the better.

John McCormack said to me, after the success of *One Night of Love*, "If you wanted to make all the money in the world, all you would have to do is go on a world tour singing just three songs, 'One Fine Day,' from *Madame Butterfly*, 'The Old Refrain,' and 'Ciribiribin.' " And how true that was, sometimes to my sorrow! No matter how hard I worked on my repertoire, those three songs were all for which people seemed to wait. "Ciribiribin" became a sort of signature, and although I took satisfaction from the audible pleasure of the audience when it heard me start, after repeated requests, on the first notes of that gay, tuneful melody, still it haunted and sometimes soured me.

People "in the know" have grown quite cynical and offhand today about a Hollywood contract. "Don't go," returned habitués warn the eager eastern novice (is it a slight twinge of anguish over competition?). "Sure, you make a lot of money, but what does it get you? You spend it all anyway. It's a wasteland. There's a premium on mediocrity. You never escape," et cetera, ad infinitum, ad income-tax citations.

The attitude, when I was given my first contract, was vastly different. Then everyone said that Hollywood was the land of the bonanza. It was Opportunity with a bright-light capital O. It was romance and giddy glamour and supershowmanship, where everything was colossal, heaven was run by silver-spangled angels draped by Adrian, and the devil took the meek.

Not to be outdone by the tales of the fan magazines, I went West in 1930 like the Queen of Sheba, riding in my own private railroad car complete with orchids, banana trees, and Bea Lillie. Before I left there in 1931 I had acquired two houses, a ranch and a beach "shack," for a thousand a month; two secretaries: a multilingual Russian—lovely Moura Lobec Bernstene, a friend from Paris—for foreign correspondence, and a pure-bred American for local mail; and two chauffeurs: Albert, who brought the Hispano-Suiza over but couldn't speak English or find his way around, and a local one to sit up front and give Albert sign-language directions. This was going to make good beauty-parlor reading—*or else*. When I returned East after a year of it, it was *or else*, with my hopes out of joint and my exaggerated illusions gone. In between were fun, chaos, and a score of good friends who have remained close to me ever since.

It all started with a bit of accidental hand-holding—with L. B. Mayer, or L.B., as I later learned, along with everybody else, to call him. I met him in the corridor of the Metropolitan one night when Lawrence Tibbett was singing *Pagliacci*. I didn't know Mr. Mayer from Adam. I took it he didn't know me from Eve. Mrs. Tibbett introduced us, since we were all to be in the same party, and down the aisle we went. Mr. Mayer happened to sit next to me. As the evening went on I noticed from the corner of my eye (that trusty corner from which one sees what one should see) that Mr. Mayer was watching me more than the stage. The evening went on even further, and suddenly I realized that Mr. Mayer and I were holding hands. Curiously, I didn't think it strange. We both seemed to be swept up in the musical spell of the opera. Furthermore I had somehow connected Mr. Mayer with Hollywood. And Hollywood!—you know how that is. I continued holding hands. At the end of the opera the silence was broken by Mr. Mayer's low-voiced query: "Could you be at the Metro Studios in New York tomorrow at noon?" The specificness of the question surprised me. I didn't know what Mr. Mayer had to do with Metro. I knew those studios only as a place where my friend, J. Robert Rubin, was supposed to run things.

"No," I answered Mr. Mayer cavalierly, "I can't make it at noon. How about five?"

The date was fixed. I came. There was a conference, and at the end I was asked to make a test, singing an aria from *La Bohème*. That test is undoubtedly the funniest bit of film extant. When it was run off and I saw myself on the screen for the first time, I didn't know whether to laugh or weep. I was pitilessly revealed as a very plump round-faced girl, with the bewildered look of the catch-all in a custard-pie comedy. There was only one bright spark. The voice was clear and brilliantly recorded. Mr. Mayer trusted the voice, skipped the way I looked, and suggested a contract. He did so over the prostrate forms of both Bob Rubin and Nick Schenck, who thought the test showed me up as pretty hopeless. Secretly agreeing with the latter verdict, I signed— promising to reduce to the point where I had only one chin and a modicum of curves.

A Hollywood contract! I rushed immediately to a beauty parlor that specialized in a Viennese facial treatment and went after my figure until all the unwanted avoirdupois disappeared and my pre-opera silhouette returned. Now I had lovely hungry hollows in my cheeks, one firm chin, and a discernible waistline, all according to contract.

That contract was a triumph of personal stamina. I made it without the assistance of legal advice for my side, whereas M.G.M. surrounded itself with enough legal talent to pack the Supreme Court, yet I managed to put in a few clauses that must have thrown the legal battery for a loophole. For one, I insisted on a private railroad car in which to travel from New York to Hollywood. Why I asked for it—or why I got it—remains a mystery of the turbulent past. That bit of barnstorming extravaganza seemed appropriate then in the life of a movie star. I think L.B. agreed to it only because he thought I was a new breed of animal for whom a private car was standard circus equipment.

Then I introduced my voice teacher, Dr. Marafioti, to Mr. Mayer, who, upon hearing that Marafioti was negotiating with Gloria Swanson to go to Hollywood under contract to her company, and realizing from all that I had told him of Marafioti's work that he could utilize his talents to great advantage in those early trying days of the talking pictures, offered him a year's contract with M.G.M. at a figure never even approached by any other voice expert.

Dr. Marafioti and his family preceded me to Hollywood by several weeks for the express purpose of training John Gilbert's speaking voice, which had proven so disappointing in his first sound film. After Marafioti's first contract expired, it was renewed for another year. He is still in Hollywood, having served as voice and speech teacher to most of Hollywood's outstanding stars. And during all the subsequent time I was in Hollywood, he remained my voice teacher and closest friend.

When I myself was ready to leave the East, I found to my horror I was the only one to go into that private car. The thought of traveling from coast to coast in solitary splendor appalled me. In a panic I invited everyone I knew to go West with me. Fortunately Bea Lillie, who had just signed a contract with Twentieth Century, could take me up on the rolling-stock generosity put out by M.G.M. In addition my brother Jim had three fraternity brothers who were intending to hitch-hike to California that summer. They agreed to join us only after I bribed them with a promise of jobs as extras in my picture. (P.S. Somehow that was managed too. Those were the bonanza days indeed.)

The coast-to-coast trek began. Midway I had to fulfill a concert engagement, and our car was switched during the night at the depot of the city in which I was to sing. I was awakened at what seemed an unearthly hour by the porter, who told me that the governor of the state was there to greet me, complete with delegation.

From long experience and earlier woe, I knew how necessary it was for me to keep absolutely quiet on any day I was supposed to sing. What to do? I sent regrets, but with malice aforethought said that Lady Peel of London would make a brilliant substitute. I awakened Bea, who was good enough sport, although sleepy and outraged, to accept the governor's roses and set off at the head of the entourage to the official breakfast of welcome. Poor Bea! The rest of that day she was put through the grilling kind of sight-seeing tour which only a proud governor could devise, from magnificent institutions of correction to "on your left the state sewage plant." She returned to the quiet of our private car at six o'clock with blood lust in her eye and a fine thirst for revenge. To sharpen the edge on that thirst, I was completely fresh, full-voiced, and ready for the concert. Lady Peel was too much the lady to try an undercut. Hers is, as everyone knows, the rapier technique.

When I walked onto the stage that night I saw that the governor was still on hand extending hospitality from his official box to the irrepressible, vengeful Miss Lillie. I went through my program of songs and then through a string of encores, but the audience was warm and wanted more. Suddenly I became whimsical. Bea had been so nice to me. The concert had gone well. I'd sing a song for my little English cousin. I signaled my accompanist to do one which I had never before sung in public, "Come Down to Kew in Lilac Time." Off I trilled, soaring away, when I happened to look up at the gubernatorial box. There was Bea Lillie, that inimitable mimic, mocking my every gesture, singing silently in a hilarious parody of me on the stage, flinging her arms around, throwing her head back, puffing out her chest like a pouter pigeon. Since no one can take off with as much rascally skill as Miss Lillie, I stopped short and watched her, my voice breaking midway, as my mouth hung open; and the audience, following my gaze, joined in the frenzy of laughter I could no longer control.

When I recovered my voice I spoke to the astonished audience. "Let me present Miss Beatrice Lillie," I said, pointing to the box where she was carrying on. "She has been substituting for me all day and can't get out of the habit. How would you like to have her continue her act on the stage?"

They did—she did—and it was a terrific success. The daft concert went on endlessly, with Bea and me taking turns showing off, and not until the stationmaster telephoned in a dither to say our private car was ready to roll did we leave with a kiss and a wave at that friendly governor and his friendly constituents.

By the time we arrived in Hollywood we were a couple of girls who had done very well, what with horseshoes of orchids, banana trees, crates full of oranges, and other tender souvenirs. Being careful girls, we left nothing behind and arrived in full force. Unloading us from that car created a minor traffic jam, not unlike Washington Market at five A.M. When we were finally untangled, we found ourselves surrounded by studio representatives. Loot and all, they piled us into a limousine and under police escort, all sirens blowing, whisked us through the streets to the ranch house which the studio had rented. So we came West. You couldn't say we sneaked up in the night. But if we came in like lions, we left —well, not exactly like lambs.

My introduction to the movie press followed short on my arrival. I met them all at an intimate little garden party of more than a hundred people given by the studio at the ranch house they had provided, which turned out to be a Graustarkian's dream of a dude ranch. The press came and looked askance. In spite of the orchids and the private car, I certainly looked, in a plain sport dress, unlike a family-album Metropolitan diva. They were judging by the standards set by the ravishing Farrar, the captivating Mary Garden. Here I was. Not glamorous by the movie-capital slide rule, nor an old-time beauty either. I was given a very dubious eye. The one kindly glance thrown from the direction of the Fourth Estate came from Louella Parsons. With Louella and her irrepressible Irish husband, Dr. Martin, I formed a friendship which still exists. She was as generous to me with her sagacious advice in private as in public print. Fortunately I had sense enough to know that Louella knew Hollywood better than anyone else, and I was grateful to find in her a trustworthy counselor. For the rest, you could see I was no great shakes. But they made the most of the party, swimming, egg-rolling, and rollicking about until gradually all faded away in a 90-proof mist.

They do things in Hollywood by rote. After the press party came the usual stock of publicity shots. Howard Strickland, in charge of the M.G.M. handout division, did a very gallant job in trying to launch me. I balked a bit at cheesecake, but I got far along enough in the art of legwork to pose in crisp functional tennis shorts with not one but a dozen rackets of all the championship makes—although I didn't know a love set from a lob. Next came a photograph taken with me poised neatly for a clean plunge on a high springboard at the edge of a pool—although the chlorine-doctored water of the pool frightened and upset me. Later, in a spasm of conscience, I actually learned how to play tennis and managed somehow to overcome my fear of pool water, all this to justify Mr. Strickland with St. Peter, but at first the lack of relation of the publicity stories to fact left me dazzled by its ingenuity.

In spite of the press party and publicity build-up, I should have felt at home on the M.G.M. lot with Dr. Marafioti on hand, with L.B. maintaining his belief in my eventual success, and with Irving Thalberg extending a welcome hand—and incidentally, *not* keeping me waiting outside his door for three weeks, although that supposedly lordly trick of his was used as the gambit of a recent play about Hollywood. But it was a strange, strange world. The story chosen for my first film was based on the life of Jenny Lind. Sydney Franklin was assigned to direct it and coach me in the art of film acting. About that art he said: "The thought is the thing. They say Garbo is not a great actress, but she can think so deeply before a camera that the thought is transmitted to the minds of the audience before any action reaches them. That is the complete art of the cinema and calls for absolute relaxation."

Unfortunately Franklin found himself held up by one major difficulty in the story of Lind. She had had no sex life. At least not the kind that makes movie monkey business. The Swedish Nightingale, in spite of front-office efforts, had led an exemplary domestic existence, serene and without disturbance. News somehow leaked out that the studio was trying to work up some shenanigans around the Lind sedateness, whereupon it was swamped with letters from the "Society for Jenny Lind" which threatened to burn the studio should any shadow be cast upon the beloved memory. The studio backed down on sex, finally made the picture with the character part of P. T. Barnum for Wallace Beery, which he did magnificently, and Reginald Denny, the persistent hero who never tired of trying to thaw out Jenny's heart, and gave it, of all things, the title *A Lady's Morals,* in hopes thus to catch the afternoon bijou crowd.

Only slightly worse than the horrendous title was my acting. One would have to travel far to find such comparable cardboard effects. Here in me was lodged the great Hollywood fallacy. A name, Grace Moore, had been bought along with the voice that went with it: suddenly name and voice were stuck in front of a camera and told to go ahead. No one considered that there was a necessary transition to be made from opera stage to grinding cameras: because I had done well in another medium back East, it was assumed I would carry over the same skill here. Used to the exaggerated technique, the expansiveness which must go across great space to the topmost tier of the topmost gallery in opera, I was unprepared for the adjustment of the movies, in which the whole audience literally sits in the front row. Basic training exists today for incoming stars. It was unheard of 'way back then. The theory of the expert-in-one-trade, expert-in-all removed the front office from the responsibility of doing anything about its importations except weep and wail at the box office.

Like the man who has quietly specialized on the love life of the aborigines only to find himself a best seller with a women's-club lecture contract, or the swimming champion who plows across the Hellespont right into a stage career; or the pretty playwright who turns into a prettier politico overnight: I, who had all my life run into the weird setup of being a star with little basic training for anything but singing, had to stand up in Hollywood as a movie actress in comparison with all the other really good people without any preliminary workout. Tenacity, unflinching ambition, and wishful working had gotten me through my other difficulties. The first screening of *A Lady's Morals* convinced me that the same ingredients would have to be thrown into the breach here too.

The picture opened at the Capitol Theater in New York, broke no box-office records either high or low, but in spite of me and the title, was so dignified and appealing that when it reached its

European market the reaction was good enough for M.G.M. to feel that a French version might be profitable. Carrie Jacobs Bond had written a beautiful song for it called "Lovely Hour" in memory of her dead son, and the rest of the Oscar Strauss music was charming. I was recuperating at Arrowhead Springs from my first tussle with studio megrims when a message from L.B. came through requesting that I stay over in Hollywood for the proposed French version.

"But L.B.," I protested on the telephone, "I speak so little French. Certainly not enough nor fluently enough for a movie, and what I do speak sometimes has a southern provincial accent."

"Don't worry," he reassured me with the sweeping largesse only Hollywood can display. "I'm sending the Jacques Feyders and Yves Mirande over to Arrowhead Springs to join you. You'll be ready for the French version in two weeks."

I sputtered, but to no avail. Mr. Mayer was so nonchalant about anybody's ability to accomplish the feat, he forced nonchalance in me. The tone of his voice implied that since even little Miss Temple could do a job in Esperanto, given twenty-four hours, I could certainly turn a comparatively simple language like French into fluent dialogue with all of two weeks to go. I gave up weakly and promised to apply myself with the same zeal, and one hoped with the same results, as the little Miss Temple.

The Feyders and Mirande arrived within the day and turned out to be the most amusing and delightful people. We settled down in a bungalow and proceeded to get acquainted. The French lessons went on each evening and, fortified with the courage vintage champagne gives good conversation, I soon became certain that I could parlez beautifully. Why else were we always laughing and gay with one another? Only occasionally did a black shadow cross my mind as I wondered whether during the shooting, without the champagne and the laughter, I could do as well. Mme. Feyder, the Françoise Rosay who was the sensational star of *Carnival in Flanders,* had brought only one French book along from which to carry out our studies. What was good enough, she reasoned, for the Comédie Française was good enough for Hollywood. Was not French the beautiful language of Molière? Very well. I cut my teeth those two weeks on none but the poet himself. Not even a *parapluie de ma tante* to mar the classic shape.

Needless to say I did not become a fluent French linguist within the two weeks, but M.G.M. did do the French version, and I got through it somehow without shame. Mme. Feyder was in the cast and kept a beady watchful eye on me all through the screening lest I let one *r* go unrolled. Soon holding on to my *r*'s became a minor struggle compared with the other absurdities. It was a wintertime story filmed through the heat of summer. I was dressed throughout most of it in velvets, sables, and fur hats. Artificial snow made of little prickly white chicken feathers drifted slowly down, wafted unerringly towards a cozy nesting place in my throat. I was voiceless much of the time, breathing steamily when I sang, and speaking in muffled tones. The damned chicken feathers were everywhere.

Whenever I became morbid about it, Irving Thalberg would take me to the projection room, supposedly to see rushes, then would flash that first old *La Bohème* test on the screen, saying, "Look, what a difference!" I would go back to the set somewhat encouraged. Fortunately, because the whole procedure was so fantastic, I relaxed through sheer astonishment and managed to turn in a much more natural and straightforward performance than I had given for the American screening. When the French version was released under the title of *Jenny Lind*—probably on the theory that the more adult European culture could take the facts of life unvarnished—it was well received.

The world was not exactly set afire by the Lind picture, but M.G.M., holding an option for another film, continued still hopeful and decided to team me with Lawrence Tibbett. Larry had created such a furore in *The Rogue Song*, which turned him into the most popular male singer of the day, they decided to have him do *New Moon* and co-star me. The cast, in addition, boasted Roland Young and Adolphe Menjou, who lived up to his reputation of being Hollywood's best-dressed man by coming onto the set each day in a new dressing gown. All proceedings were held up while the day's gown was discussed, with much thumbing of fabric, murmurings of "Nice goods," weighing of the pros and cons of its superiority over the one of the day before, and much guessing—"You guess—No, go on, you guess"—whether it was a home-grown design or a creation by the great Charvet of Paris for Menjou himself. Such a flutter you never saw.

Amidst all this queer bird talk, Larry and I had to carry on as irresistible creatures desperately in love throughout a menthol fog. Larry is a great character actor and one of the most gallant men in the world, and I am not averse to what is called the tender passion myself, but something would happen to us when we were thrown into one another's arms, trilling and tra-la-ing about how I love you. It seemed all too funny, and giggles would emerge instead of passionate gurgles. *New Moon* is one of those pageants of war and blood and flossy romance, whereas Larry and I belonged in a rough-and-tumble singing version of *The Guardsman*. Poor Jack Conway, who started out on the film (he's so lovable that M.G.M. thought they could turn over to him the turmoil of having two opera stars in one picture), finally took to his bed. Sam Wood, now so famous for *For Whom the Bell Tolls*, took over and finished it. He must have shared Conway's fate at the end. There was camaraderie and affection between us, but often Sam looked beaten and frenzied. Not only did he have to put up with Larry and me, we all had to put up with the sound-track difficulties. The recording was entirely primitive, and there was a great deal of experimentation as we recorded the duets. The combined strength of two voices, both above the standard Hollywood crooning level, would constantly crack the machines.

Then I began running into weight trouble. I looked something like a singing Mae West with long hair and a baker's one hundred and thirty-five pounds, which I persisted in keeping to keep my voice. Often L.B. or Thalberg would wander over to the set, look me over, then complain I was getting too plump, contrary to the contract terms which set 135 pounds as absolute tops.

"It's the lighting," I'd say meekly. But as the pounds continued to sneak up and over the fatal mark, Thalberg refused to blame the lighting. "Come up and see my scales," he'd say. I resisted as coyly as if he'd offered me a look at his etchings, and in spite of his wheedling, managed to stay away from that scale until the end of the shooting. I *knew* what I weighed.

New Moon was finished, and I was glad. Now to wait for results. I sat back and looked at Hollywood and counted the chickens I had hatched. Among them was my friendship with Larry Tibbett, which really began during the picture. It was also on the *New Moon* set that I met the present Mrs. Tibbett—the beautiful Jane. Larry had a wonderful spontaneous gaiety, and he was easy to laugh with at all the foibles and difficulties of screen production. Our friendship together has lasted throughout all these years. Not an easy achievement, because two artists, particularly interpretive artists, find it hard to remain friends when thrown into an opera milieu where jealousy and intrigue grow like weeds.

Royalty on the M.G.M. lot in those days was something to reckon with. It was no watered-down constitutional monarchy either. Queens were queens and everybody knew it. Norma Shearer was Big Queen then, who landed at her dressing-room door in the shiny, big, yellow Thalberg Rolls-Royce while the gentry bowed and scraped. But Norma, in spite of the Hollywoodian grandeur, was a very simple, hospitable woman. She and Thalberg complemented each other perfectly. They were very happy and very much in love. They entertained well and surrounded themselves with all that was rich and satisfying in their position. They had the capacity—which is more than many have—of savoring all the joy of their good fortune.

Norma's yellow Rolls-Royce was outshone only by the Italian stucco bungalow smack in the center of the lot which belonged to Marion Davies, who was adored on the M.G.M. lot—from the front office to the gateman. She was, if not the BIG Queen, at least the Queen-Come-the-Palace-Revolution. In my simple way I thought, when I first came, that any movie star could have a yellow limousine or a stucco bungalow. I soon learned that such gilded addenda came not from one's acting alone, and one could try and try but without business judgment all the yellow that one would get was in a jaundiced disposition.

Off the lot I made few friends in Hollywood. It was a strange world, and I didn't know whether one took it by sturm or drang. There were many I learned to know and love, but with the press and Hollywood at large, I was considered something of a high-hat who didn't fit in. But Bea Lillie and I managed fun on our own hilltop with our own little set. One of the most valued in it was Ida Koverman, L.B.'s secretary, who had been secretary to Herbert Hoover before she came to Hollywood. The fortunates who have had "Kay" Koverman's best wishes have found them invaluable. She mothers her little chosen group, living their lives more than her own. But my biggest moment was John Gilbert, although alas one could hardly call it romantic.

John Gilbert was one of the reasons why Hollywood was the enchanted capital for the palpitating female heart. One of the most captivating figures in all screen history, he was as much a swoon creator off screen as on. I met him first at a party given by Helen Hayes and Charles MacArthur. We talked about music, in which he had a keen and knowledgeable interest; then he asked to take me home. Far be it from me to differ from forty million other women. I was delighted. On the way, he told me about his record collection (of which I had heard much from others) and asked me to come up and listen to some of his choice *lieder*. "Fine," I said, and we proceeded to his hilltop home, where now Miriam Hopkins lives and where, when I come to visit her, I always get the Garbo suite with the golden bathtub faucets, as if to compensate for the night when I didn't.

John put on a huge batch of his records on the automatic phonograph, then disappeared. I made myself comfortable. The records kept going, and I hardly noticed that time was flying without the host himself. Suddenly he appeared. My eyes popped in amazement. Mr. Gilbert was virtually naked!

My first impulse was to get up and say, "Sir, how dare you!" But something in John's attitude held me. He was so casual about it that I suddenly felt as if I, who was supposed to be a sophisticated prima donna from New York, had to match his own unconcern or be forever labeled, heaven help me, gauche. Feeling that it would be far better to be thought naughty than naïve, I remained in my chair, and he sat down opposite, unaware of his almost-nakedness or my acute embarrassment. But the embarrassment slowly vanished as John, completely serious, picked up his glass of wine and took up the conversation precisely where he had left off when he went out of the room earlier. You could see that conversation was conversation to Mr. Gilbert, clothes on or off. Obviously he had gone in swimming. Now he felt like talking again, so here he was—talking. Suddenly, having talked himself out, he leaned his head back on the couch and went fast asleep. I actually tiptoed out for fear I should disturb him, such was his power to wake concern in a woman's heart. His chauffeur was outside waiting, taking it as a customary procedure that I found my way out alone. Apparently house rules! Next day in my dressing room appeared twelve dozen American Beauty roses with a card inscribed, "Why didn't you nudge me?"

So ended my big moment. After that Jack Gilbert and I were friends, and although we saw one another many times, we never referred to our first meeting. A few years later, when he met my husband, he twitted me about picking someone who looked enough like him to be his brother. Jack Gilbert had intelligence and culture, but his great love of life found too little outlet in Hollywood. Playing romantic scenes to beautiful women on the screen was not enough. He was adventuresome and wanted greater odds. His one serious romance with Garbo was stifled in the manufactured surroundings of the town. She was an extraordinarily simple, childlike woman, he said, with a most distorted personality, hard to get at and painfully reserved. Their love affair needed simplicity and the fresh air of the real world. Otherwise it would die the usual Hollywood death.

Miriam Hopkins bought the gloomy John Gilbert house and put the stamp of her own gaiety on it. Every time I visit there now I am impressed with the effect personality has on such apparently

insensate objects as concrete foundation blocks and plaster of
Paris. Miriam has fixed it so she can leap straight from her bed
into the swimming pool *au naturel*. She has brought color, light,
and an incessant chatter. Miriam is the only woman in the world
who can—and does—outtalk me. That means she outtalks everybody else. She is the most uninhibited person in Hollywood, with a
devastating magnolia charm. She has held onto her southern
accent but couples it with a superb nonregional sophistication.
She is also the lucky possessor of a most enchanting child, her
adopted son Michael, to whom she is completely devoted and who
is equally fond of her. When Michael came to New York not long
ago he put into a beautiful nutshell why East is East and West is
West and never the twain shall meet. "New York houses," he said,
"are very queer. They don't have swimming pools." Out of the
mouths of babes!

Ruth Chatterton was the first lady of the screen in the early
thirties, a brilliant actress, a companionable and utterly fascinating person, and we became real friends. Today theater audiences
are regaled with Ruth's lovely speaking voice, colored as in music.
Under her rather meek, quiet, subtle charm there lurked a potent
lure which was irresistible. When you walked into her drawing
room at five o'clock, where she presided over ladylike tea, you
were suddenly intensely aware that here was one of the most
alluring women you'd ever met.

At my house and at Ruth's there was a constant mingling of
stars and musicians. Every night would end up in music. I remember a version of *Carmen* we did one New Year's dawn that
would lay them in the aisles at Minsky's. Dick Barthelmess was
the Bull, Ronald Colman the Toreador, and I a very sunburned
Carmen. Iturbi at the piano played that essentially French
music with Spanish gusto that it had never known before. The
curtain came down when the Bull decided to be difficult and hide
under the couch. The stress and strain of both Bull and Toreador
lifted the couch with a great heave that brought it down full on
the Toreador's head and almost knocked him unconscious. That
may have been the blow that battered the Colman memory and

made him turn in such a stunning performance in *Random Harvest*.

My Hollywood career came to an abrupt end after *New Moon*. Although the picture became something of a box-office success because of its popular melodies and superb score, it was by no means a personal triumph. Over at Twentieth Century, Bea Lillie was hitting new lows to equal mine. They had taken this top satirical mimic and tried to turn her into Gaby Deslys with a swish. They dressed her in plumes that towered right through the roof, stuck her into spangled shorts (prophetic of the Hattie Carnegie ones to emerge some years later), made her flounce and folderol until she was anything but Bea Lillie in that picture. So, agreeing that it had been a great if not glorious adventure all around, Bea and I took our flop together and decided to go home. Good-by Hollywood, we said, and turned our faces east.

My education took a new turn when I arrived home. A Hollywood bounce, I soon learned, was a diva's nose dive. My picture failure cut disastrous inroads into my career. It removed the golden sheen from my Metropolitan debut and, what was more far-reaching, although not quite so immediately tangible, it took me out of an established category. If I had continued solely with concert and operatic work, I should have had a tag. I should have been a "serious young artist," easy to identify and label, "Please put all notices on the music page." Now—what was I? Serious artist? Well, what was I doing in Hollywood? Movie star? Hardly! Not fitting neatly, a square peg in a square hole, is a bargaining tragedy. On the next concert tour I got only half the price offered before I had gone into pictures. Although the name "Grace Moore" itself was better known, no stature had been added to it. I found myself with the heartbreaking job of having to make good all over again.

I tried to put Hollywood out of my system. Neurasthenic over my failure there and suddenly terror-stricken over the black shadow it seemed to cast on my future career, I decided to go to Europe and carry out the doctor's orders for a complete change. It was. For it was on that trip I met my husband.

Love=Is=a=Beautiful=Thing
Department

NEYSA MCMEIN ONCE SAID TO ME, "What are you interested in outside of singing?"

"Love," I answered.

And who isn't? No life is complete without it. The public usually exaggerates the scope and variety of a prima donna's amours—but then you can hardly blame it, for so does the prima donna herself. All the melodramatic trappings of the libretto have a terrific effect on real life, and the tendency is strong to carry over the emotional fortissimo. But the unvarnished truth about my love life is that it has always been perfectly normal, happy, and enormously successful.

Everyone expects, in a book of memoirs like this, that there will be a great parade of episodes. But I think that the more extensive a tale you spread of your love life, the duller it gets. I know only this: that whatever happened to me, however brief, had a remarkable way of coloring my life. Names, places, phone numbers—all these are inconsequential. It is the colors that one accumulates quite as a normal process that count. As one grows older, the "love" you may have found in this one or that fades away, leaving only the variation of tone on one's adult palette.

I have been fortunate in never thinking I loved a man for whom I didn't have the greatest sympathy and adoration otherwise. Thus nothing has ever come or gone that didn't leave a friendship behind. Unlike a great many women, I really like men. I don't think they're "heels," and I don't think, as the female Jeremiahs say, that a woman is a fool to trust them. But then men have been good to me, good friends. Perhaps it is because I have been fortunate enough to have known only the most attractive men. At least I always thought so. It may spring from my hero-worship complex. I cherish people who are important, well informed, literate. I reach out towards the experiences of others and find them much more fascinating than any I may have had myself. As I listen I become impressed; as I become impressed I feel emotional sympathy: soon, because I am an incorrigible romanticist, I am in love.

A charming Frenchman once said to me, "The most difficult thing in love is beautiful silence." That reminded me of a scene on the Riviera, when a contingent of females in the sun-bathing nook at Ethel Osborne's started talking about love. A famous blonde comedienne of the stage, who hadn't had too much luck holding her men, was bemoaning the fact right out there in the open. "Why is it?" she asked. "I'm charming. I have a beautiful body and a sense of humor." "Well, darling," I couldn't help but reply, "you're probably witty at the wrong moment."

My greatest good fortune has always been that the men I have loved have been so full of vigor, wit, and experience that sitting back quietly has been the better part of fun. The Frenchman, who was as full of maxims about love as La Rochefoucauld, taught me one other bit of a Frenchman's philosophy: "Frenchwomen," he said, "are willing to forgive a man's infidelity as long as they know his heart remains theirs, because in that way they can be sure he will always come back to them."

A woman in the public eye never knows whether she is loved as the woman or the star. For a long time I could not reconcile marriage with a career because the men who thought they loved me wanted me to retire at once, marry, and play lady of leisure. In a few instances, where the beaux were enormously rich (and there were three of the richest men in the world), it would have been profitable indeed. But much as I like comfort, wealth is hardly reason for marriage. Jewelry, one of the tangibles, has never meant much to me in itself. An armful of bracelets is only a show window for someone. I have been given diamonds and little unimportant bijoux, and once a fabulous emerald necklace packed in a box of flowers, because the man who sent it had seen it in a window and thought it reminded him of me. A quixotic, lovable and expensive gesture—and because I was fond of him, I liked the necklace. But though I may have it insured for a greater amount, I do not prize it more than a pair of thirty-five-cent old-gold madonna earrings from Mexico which I wear all the time. I'm always asked about them in the ladies' room of the Club 21 or the Colony—my favorite dining places—or Sherman Billingsley's unique Stork Club, where both the clients and the personnel behave like ladies and gentlemen. But to go back to the earrings: I invariably reply, "Why, they are rare antiques from the collection of Empress Carlotta!"

I have always felt that much of the happiness in my marriage comes from the accumulation of experience and tastes harvested from all my friends. From this one an interest in art, from that one some literary insights I might not otherwise have had, from the other a nodding acquaintance with political trends and terminology. When I married Valentin Parera, I married a man of modest means who could share this background of experience and add to it.

Alec Woollcott always said that a marriage could not be a success unless the two people both have a sense of humor—or haven't. Val and I not only laugh and cry at the same things, we're bored with the same things too. And we avoided the disaster that happens to so many professional marriages because we met when the careers of both had already taken direction. Val left a career in a bank to become the Valentino of Spain, a star and a director for the U.F.A. and well known on the Continent. Strangely enough he had even been on the Metro lot at the same time I was there, but we had never met. He had been brought over from Spain to direct and act in Spanish versions of American pictures. In so many early marriages between ambitious people, everything happens too soon; and the independence of thought and action, which career-pursuit demands, conflicts with love and domesticity. Result: frustration, professional jealousy, marriage or career suffering for one or the other. Val and I met when both our professional lives had been established—yet the best of personal living still lay ahead.

Fate seems to have had a great deal to do with Val and me. When I sailed for a vacation in May 1931, completely exhausted from concerts, opera, and my Hollywood experience, I left under doctor's orders. But it was not only fatigue which drained my energy and hope. I had reached a high point of confusion in my personal life, and I felt discouraged and lonely. I had just come through a peculiarly trying situation which involved a musically gifted and sensitive man who threw me in a dither with astrology, psychoanalysis, and a wife who still loved him.

I arranged for sailings on the *Paris* that spring, canceled them because I thought I was too tired to travel, then took the *Ile de France* instead. Val too had had sailings on the *Paris* which he canceled for the same trip on the *Ile* that I was making.

Constance Hope, a present big-time publicity expert who was then my secretary, sailed with me. As I wearily mounted the gangplank I turned and said to her, "This career stuff is all right, but I hope something happens on this trip to take me away from just living for myself."

"If I were you I shouldn't worry," she answered encouragingly. "Something always happens to you."

I waved good-by to Jane Draper and a few other close friends on the pier and then went onto the upper deck just to sit. Constance joined me, and we started playing some kind of lap game of mumbledy-peg that had been given us as a go-away gift. Suddenly the game fell to the deck and scattered around us. A tall dark handsome man who had been leaning against the railing turned from his brooding and courteously offered to help. Constance, recognizing the accent, said something to him in Spanish. I knew not one word of that language and could only look back at him when he looked at me. He picked up the game for us and left. I turned to Hope and said, "That's the man I'm going to marry." Cross my heart and hope to die! It had all the fatalism of a gypsy's forecast—"go on a trip and meet a tall dark man"—and forever after seemed inevitable.

I can afford to be sentimental about the one great romance of my life. Sentiment is always accepted and wept over a little bit if the ending is sad. But give it a happy ending that goes on for years, and at once it's the fashion to be cynical. As F.P.A. used to say, a murrain on that! Come fashion, go fashion, I shall continue sentimental about Val and me because that's the way I feel and that's the way it has been from the beginning. From the first he has never thought of himself except through my happiness. If he had been rich in money he would have lavished costly possessions on me. Being rich in spirit and understanding, he has brought me more wonderful gifts instead: the joy of living outside of oneself and for someone else—the ability to share gracefully and thereby add grace to life—the companionship in fun, in a new recipe, or a hilltop view, or travel, or work that ends forever the ghastly business of being "completely self-sufficient."

Being a romantic as well as a sentimentalist, I also cherish the details of our marriage. Everything about it seems like a story one reads and wishes would really happen: shipboard romance, marriage on the Riviera, honeymoon in a castle (borrowed) in Venice, a magic memory of Spain. Somerset Maugham once said that romantic melodrama comes closer to reality than pared-down fiction, and that is why so many writers are untrue to life. My pursuits not being primarily literary, I'm not frightened of including those things that editors are always telling authors to eliminate from a manuscript in order to "tighten it up."

When the *Ile* had been out one day I became seasick for the first time in my life, and kept to my cabin. The French Line was noted for its gallantry. As long as I had to remain in bed, Mr. Villa, the purser, sent a box of chocolates or flowers or some remembrance to the cabin each morning—along with a daily copy of the ship's paper. In it I saw each day some reference to a man named Parera who was apparently having a huge social success. "Good heavens," I said petulantly to Constance, "do you think it is our young man from the top deck? If so he sounds like a professional Beau Brummell."

Since I had almost recovered from the seasickness when the

me came for the ship's concert, Villa asked me to sing and
extended the invitation of Commander Blancart to supper afterwards. Yes, I agreed, but I made one request: would the commander invite Mr. Parera, too, to be my escort? A shameless
avowal, I suppose, that, like any woman, I was intrigued by
popularity.

Later, Constance, who had been strolling on deck, returned to
the cabin with a confession. She had met the dark man again, she
told me, and invited him to supper in the name of Grace Moore.
He had declined, saying he had a previous engagement, then
added, "By the way, what has happened to the little blonde with
you?" Constance had smiled and answered, "Oh, that's Grace
Moore." At which, according to Constance, he had said in Spanish, "Oh my God, I got her name mixed up with another prima
donna on the boat. In that case I am free for supper."

So, with both of us working on that supper date from different
angles, it was arranged. At the concert I sang to the back row (as
one properly should) because he was sitting there. And at the
table, where I sat on the right of the commander with Señor
Parera next to me, I managed to make a few necessary perfunc-
tory remarks to M. Blancart and then turned at once to Val. We
talked throughout supper and later went to the top deck and saw
the dawn come in, still talking. I must add that three quarters of
the conversation was in middling French, which we could both
understand, the rest in Val's poor English, my non-existent
Spanish, and sign language. Later, Somerset Maugham was to
say to us, at Edward Molyneux's on the Riviera after our
marriage, that he understood we were supremely happy because
neither one spoke any known language.

Val knew very little about me, I knew as little about him, we
both agreed that night that neither had ever wanted to marry before, but there was no doubt about the future. Neither wanted to
leave the other again. We decided that dawn, before we said
good night, that we would be married soon.

"I know," he said, "that you are romantic, but marriage is a
profoundly serious thing. I am sure."

"I am sure too," I answered, and so it was.

The *Ile* was due at Le Havre the following day. The last day aboard ship was spent in merrymaking and good wishes. All our friends were agape at what they called the suddenness. We tried to explain that it really wasn't sudden—it was as it should have been; but there were many head-shakes and murmurs of "No rhyme or reason to it." A dinner party was quickly arranged by the late Paul Kochanski and his wife, Jascha Heifetz (who always seems to be traveling as much as I do), and Samuel Chotzinoff, who was on his way to Europe for the summer to coach me in concert repertoire. It was a touching emotional party inspired partly by the fact that we hadn't let down the tradition of at least one boat romance on every trip. All my friends were enchanted with Val, and I was enchanted with everybody.

The French version of *A Lady's Morals*, bearing the title *Jenny Lind,* had just been launched, and I was met at Le Havre by film colleagues and newspapermen who were promptly told about the romance. Then all were brought along for supper at my little pavilion in Neuilly. Flowers started arriving, from film people, a bouquet from the Thalbergs then in Paris, from artists at the Comique. It was all so gay and happy and carefree.

Val left the next day for Spain, where he would make his own announcement to his family and clear up various affairs. We had decided to be married at once in the villa at Cannes. I hated to see him go off to Spain—I was afraid the whole affair would vanish in mist. We arranged that he should telephone me the very next midnight and tell me how things were going. Shortly afterwards I was to sing at the fabulous party Elsa Maxwell gave at Baron Guinsburg's house in the Bois. Wearing a beautiful costume designed for me by the Spanish painter Nestor, I sang the gavotte from *Manon,* then, like Cinderella, dashed from the house to my little pavilion to huddle by the telephone for the promised call. Sitting there all alone in a magnificent court robe of green satin with a plumed hat and a great collection of borrowed emeralds, I waited for the phone to ring like a trembling high-school senior in love for the first time.

Finally the telephone and Val's voice: "Birth certificate, military-service papers, family consent all arranged, good-bys have been said, I love you with my life, taking train tomorrow." Then I really knew it was true.

The next morning I sent a *pneumatique* to the manager of the Opéra Comique and broke the news that I couldn't fulfill my engagement—it was springtime in Paris, I had fallen in love, and *excusez moi, mais je m'en fiche.* Val arrived from Spain, and we were off for Cannes.

Val had never been to the Riviera in the spring, so I had the joy of pointing out how much lovelier it was then than in the wintertime. And how happy I was to show him the little villa on the hilltop as we drove up the winding road, and so fearful that perhaps he would not like it! We posted the banns in City Hall, waited the traditional two weeks until July 15, and when the day arrived set off for the City Hall. Marriages are open-door events there, so Riviera society sat with our butcher, baker, and candle-stick-maker while the mayor of Cannes married us in a simple French ceremony.

Although it was my first marriage, I had none of the conventional trappings of the bride. I wore a simple white dress made by Molyneux, a little plumed hat, and carried a bouquet of garden flowers with real orange blossoms tucked in the middle. Metro-Goldwyn-Mayer sent newsreel men to take pictures, and we posed for them under an arch made by the gardener overnight. Telegrams arrived by the score—one from my family wishing me well but somewhat disturbed over my alliance with a "foreigner." There was·a reception later in the garden of the Martinez Hotel with the main toast offered by Edmund Goulding, who followed it with a bagful of rice. Gloria Swanson met the unpredictable Michael Farmer, who was later to become one of her husbands, at the reception, and from the way those two immediately caught fire I felt that perhaps we would end up with a double wedding that very day. Val and I drove off for Italy in a shower of rice and old shoes, with the usual corny just-married signs on the car in French, English, and Spanish and the Hollywood touch of a car with newsreel cameramen aloft trailing us as they ground out more pictures.

Constance and Bill Gower had just come to the end of their own honeymoon in the fourteenth-century Venetian castle, "The Brandolini," on the Grand Canal, where Wagner wrote the second act of *Tristan and Isolde,* and they were giving it to us as a loan for ours. Venice on a honeymoon! Could anything have been finer? To cap everything, we arrived in Venice the night of the "Redentore," the great religious festival when all Venice takes over the canals in a magnificent torch-lit procession that turns the world into music. Waiting for us in front of our castle was a flower-bedecked gondola, lantern-lit and with a little table in the middle filled with cold meats, fruit, and salad. Two gondoliers, all in white with red sashes, steered us down the canal, and we drifted along with the crowd. Val and I were so moved and excited by the spectacle that we joined in the singing of the traditional Italian songs in top voice. When we finally returned to our rooms at the Palazzo Brandolini, we had made so many friends we were called to our little balcony by serenaders down below. Then, as we threw flowers to them in salute, they sang "Ciribiri-bin," its gay melody flooding the morning. It was the first time I had ever heard that song, and I loved it at once.

When we left Venice we joined Samuel Chotzinoff, who had been witness at our wedding, in Milan. From there all three of us set off for the Bayreuth Festival, to be conducted by Toscanini. "Chotzy," who was music critic for the New York *World,* was covering the festival, and the tickets for three seats which he had managed to snare were treasures beyond price. Mrs. Toscanini had found rooms for us in the private home of a friend which had been turned into a temporary boardinghouse. There were people at Bayreuth from every corner of Europe, and international society, which made a fetish of these festivals, mingled with music lovers, who had spent all their vacation money to come, in the gardens in front of the festival house.

Toscanini had been seriously affected by arthritis and conducted under great stress, but the *Tristan and Isolde* opening the festival was unforgettable. It is against tradition to applaud at Bayreuth until the end of the performance, when I have seen audiences go into an almost religious hysteria. But Val was so carried away at that first performance that in the emotional excitement he quite forgot the Bayreuth code and stood up at the end of the second act, calling, "Bravo, bravo!" Poor Val, he almost fainted when the whole audience hissed him into silence. He contained himself after that and managed to maintain the Bayreuth discipline during the transcendent performances of *Tannhäuser* and *Parsifal*.

I had met the Toscanini family in Milan in 1927, when I had renewed a friendship begun earlier on the Lido with Wally Toscanini di Castlebarco. Now in Bayreuth, the Maestro and Mrs. Toscanini invited us to lunch. Like a trio of fans, we feasted our eyes on the beautiful Toscanini profile close up and hung on his every word. He was very gay that day and extremely charming as he regaled us with stories of his career, while Carla busied herself making the *café espresso* in the little Italian coffeepot that is always part of the Toscanini ménage wherever they go. At the table next to us sat Madame Winifred Wagner and her two young daughters, and we all remarked that even though they already had the overstuffed proportions of Wagnerian sopranos, the girls gorged themselves recklessly with enormous quantities of rich German pastry.

That Bayreuth trip began the long close friendship and trusted association between Chotzinoff and the Maestro, and served to illuminate for Val and me the mutual devotion to music which was to be one of the greatest bonds of our happiness.

Before we left Bayreuth we all visited the Wagner homestead and ran into the irrepressible Melchior and his wife, looking handsome indeed and very picture-postcardy in the Tyrolean shorts, leather jackets, and Tyrolese hats, propped at just the right angle, which they affected.

Back in Cannes, Val and I set up house and began to taste the life of the Riviera together. We often visited the Maxine Elliott villa, one of the greatest gathering places on the coast. She dominated the long luncheon table, plump and splendid and still possessed of remnants of the amazing beauty of her earlier portraits, with charmingly caustic comments on her life and times, which had been filled to the brim with romance, royalty, and roistering. "Jimmy" Sheean, her nephew-in-law, has written that she had a great penchant for royalty, but I always thought she took all personages with a grain of salt and all personalities with reservation. Lloyd George was there that summer, and one day Winston Churchill sat at our luncheon table. Without actively listening to the political discussions, one's mind picked them up blotter fashion. Gaiety and sparkle came from Michael Arlen, Charlotte and Jon Boissevain, the Eric Loders, and Vincent Sheean. I've always told Sheean that he should have been a tenor instead of a writer, his voice being best at three in the morning. Diana, his wife, is the only one of Maxine Elliott's vast clan who carries on the tradition of great Elliott beauty. When we first knew Maxine she had grown to such magnitude that the slide that went from the swimming pool into the Mediterranean was the most commodious in the world because the architects had made it wide enough to care for Maxine's ample proportions.

Larry and Jane Tibbett came on their honeymoon to the Riviera, where Larry was also working on *Emperor Jones,* and Val and I decided to give them a dinner party. Jane told how they had stopped off in Paris on the way south and gone to some dimly lit club in Montmartre for supper. When the orchestra started to play, Larry, in a kind of skittish happiness, sang along with it. The others in the place, who apparently had not seen *The Rogue Song* and did not know him, applauded and asked for more. He demurred, suddenly embarrassed. Whereupon a collection was taken up to induce him to do an encore, and a kindly gentleman at the next table leaned over and said, "You ought to study, young man, you can make opera if you try."

Gladys and Frank Chapman, the unique and brilliantly talented Valentina and her husband, George Schlee, had come on from Venice to visit us. We were a happy and affectionate group then, and no matter which way the wind blows we still are. So we invited all our friends to the Tibbett dinner, including another famous baritone, Titta Ruffo, whom my husband had known in Spain, where he and Caruso were esteemed as the two great voices of that generation. Ruffo was one of the many sons of a blacksmith brought up in poverty. Through the kindly intervention of some rich patrons who noticed his love for music, his voice had been trained—but as a bass. He made his debut as such and was a dismal failure. In despair he ran away to the mountains, forsaking the civilized world forever. There he met an older married woman with whom he fell desperately in love. She was musically trained and probably a born teacher, for she taught him how to read and write and redirected his voice into the baritone range. Then she, abandoning husband and child, had gone with him to the city, where he started on his sensationally successful career as a baritone. When she died, she asked Ruffo if he would take care of the child she had abandoned earlier. He did, by marrying her and living happily ever after.

Ruffo had retired several years earlier, but the night of our dinner party, when we were playing some *flamenco* records, Titta started to hum along with Angellilo. Presently he was singing these Spanish songs in a voice of wondrous beauty, only slightly dimmed by age. Soon he and Tibbett began vying with one another, and at Ruffo's insistence Tibbett sang the prologue from *Pagliacci*. After he had finished, Ruffo applauded and complimented Larry and began the prologue on his own. Tibbett, who was just coming into the full fine use of his vocal powers and had sung the *Pagliacci* magnificently, listened with humble admiration to Ruffo, who even with his time-impaired voice sang with all the command and maturity, the finish and style which had made him so famous and which Tibbett knew took years to perfect.

That evening ended crazily. Tibbett became so exhilarated by the music and conviviality that he decided to walk some of the way to their rooms at the Hôtel du Cap. The hotel was about ten miles from our villa, and we heard him start off singing at the top of his voice. Jane promised to follow soon and pick him up in the car. Presently she left, drove the full ten miles, and failed to see him. She returned frantically to see if he had come back to our place, but we hadn't seen him. In a panic, fearing that he had fallen into the Mediterranean, we all went on a searching party. But while we looked, he continued to walk, weary and no longer exhilarated, the full ten miles to the hotel, where he promptly went to bed. We found him there and demanded to know where he had been. It was a simple enough story: when Jane had passed him in the car he had been behind a tree for purely utilitarian purposes.

Frances Alda met Larry and Jane Tibbett at a dinner a few years ago in New York and was somewhat curious as to their reception of her after the unjustifiable sarcasm directed against Tibbett in her book. The Tibbetts were polite, charming, and completely noncommittal. Finally Alda could no longer contain herself. "Mrs. Tibbett," she said with the Old World courtesy for which she is noted, "I'm surprised you speak to me after what I wrote about your husband in my book." Jane looked up and in her most socially adept manner (pretty adept it is, too) said, "But I haven't read your book, Madame Alda."

Noel Coward and Bea Lillie too came to visit us, and one night we all decided to make a real Riviera evening of it. We drove along the Corniche and found a little restaurant where we stuffed ourselves with bouillabaisse. Then we drove over to the Casino at Juan-les-Pins, to try our luck. Bea developed some trouble holding her bouillabaisse in its proper place, and during one of the tense moments of the game she hiccupped violently. The croupier, thinking she had called "Banco," pushed the pile of chips her way, and Bea came off with a very neat profit on a simple case of heartburn.

Towards the end of the summer Val and I decided to visit Spain, so that I could meet his family. I had never been there before, nor had I yet met any relative of Val's, so the trip had a double purpose. I discovered that the Parera family were numerous, happy, and beautiful in a typically Spanish way. They were all devoted to one another, especially Val to his mother, whom he resembled, and I was prepared to feel like the interloper and in-law, but though I discovered that they, like my own family, had wagered the marriage wouldn't last six months, they were completely courteous, without resentment, and overwhelmingly hospitable.

Val had prepared me with a dozen well-chosen Spanish words which he taught me to pronounce with exquisite perfection. They were my first words, and their use upset the entire household. The family was so delighted with the compliment I had paid them in learning Spanish overnight, they all started talking to me at once. But my twelve words were all gone, and I stood by in helpless confusion, exhausted of understandable speech. My silence and my woebegone expression must have seemed very ludicrous—because everyone burst into hearty laughter and thought the joke a good one not only on me, but on them. After that, everywhere I went in Spain, I encountered this hearty humor, this willingness to laugh in a friendly spirit at self and friends, which is so like our own American sense of humor. My husband numbered among his friends many of the Spanish intelligentsia. I met the poet Garcia Lorca, whose lyric words have been the inspiration of many a composer. He was killed during the Spanish revolution, and Val was heartbroken over the loss of his friend, one of Spain's greatest modern poets.

The little celebrity I had gained through being a Metropolitan Opera star and having acted in a few films was completely dimmed by Val's popularity in his own country. There was no question, he was the idol of Spain. Wherever we lunched or dined, autograph fans would surround him, and we were always followed through the streets by swarms of flashing-eyed giggling young boys and girls. Val had only recently made the film *La Bodega,* based on the famous story by Blasco Ibañez, which had swept Spain and all Spanish-speaking countries, and he was the best-loved film actor of the day.

It was a wonderful experience not being Grace Moore. Now I was Señora de Parera. The career, the hopes, the ambitions of Grace Moore mattered very little here; but there was a fascination and completeness in being Mrs. Parera that delighted and made me, for the first time in my life, deeply and wholly happy.

I adored the country too. There was a grandeur, an abandon, and a spiritual brooding that seemed to lie over the landscape and that made it unlike any other place. We had motored from the Riviera straight to Barcelona, where the great Spanish Fair was at its height. France was then preparing her historic colonial exposition and viewed with some alarm the unsurpassable beauty of Spain's exposition to which tourists were flocking from all parts of the globe. The Fair, sadly enough, was totally out of proportion to Spain's national wealth and caused a terrific deficit which did Primo Rivera no political good. But in spite of the financial havoc it raised, it remains a memorable event, especially now when we can ponder with hindsight on what was then to come. It was so lavish, with great artificial waterfalls, magnificent indirect lighting, and exact replicas in size of some of the most renowned *cortijos* of the country. It was a pageant of the splendor of the old and a review of all that was being done then in the modern Spain. One can only hope today that there will be a rebirth soon of the majestic and noble spirit that the Spanish Fair revealed.

Zaragoza—bloody battleground! Reading the dispatches during the Civil War, I could think only of the lovely fertile red earth, the Picasso-ish little towns and the white seaside city of Sitges, near Barcelona, where we went for a swim. And Madrid— beautiful, civilized, urbane Madrid—better to think of it as I first knew it and as it shall be again. The Prado Museum, where I spent all my mornings—an amazing place begun in 1785 and finished under King Ferdinand VII in 1830, filled with an astounding collection of paintings that give a unique idea of the history of Spanish painting and of the greatest of its masters: Velásquez. There were tortured, somber El Grecos, filled with the spirit of Spanish mysticism that still hangs over the land. I saw canvases, drawings, prints by Goya, who has been called the first of the moderns. Sanchez Canton, once writing of the works of the later Goya, said: "What prescience! They betray that they are among the distinct precursors of Cézanne, though the latter may never have seen these pictures of the last period." The Prado even boasted a magnificent group of Venetian paintings (to which Spanish painting seems much indebted), including some of the best and last works of Titian. When one read of bombs over Madrid, was it any wonder one felt it was the destruction of the world?

All of Val's friends in Madrid were eager to show off their beloved city to us. At one of the dinners given us in a private dining room at a famous Madrileano restaurant, I was given a sharp insight into what one might call the inherent sensitivity and dignity of the Spaniard. A famous gypsy guitarist and a *flamenco* singer had been invited in to play and sing. At the first sound of the guitar the whole party was electrified into silence, except for one fellow who so far forgot his manners as to continue his verbal lovemaking to the señorita at his side. With great dignity the gypsies arose, bowed quietly and courteously, and left the room. No amount of persuasion could bring them back. There was no anger on either side. Everyone felt that the artists were right and the whole thing was unfortunate. Artistry demanded complete and undivided attention. If all were not prepared to give it, it were better forgotten. Everywhere we heard Spanish music. That music above all others is so typical of a people— so full of magic, or, as the Spaniards say, *duende* or *brujo*. The greatest instrument for expressing it is the guitar, or the *flamenco* songs that in their guttural quality seem to come up from the hard Spanish earth.

The sensation of Madrid at the time was the young gypsy dancer, Carmen Amaya. So popular was she that you had to buy tickets one month in advance for the Teatro de la Zarzuela where she was dancing. Val used all the influence he could muster, but even with it, we had to stand in the rear of the theater while this little Amaya, with blue-black, long, snaky hair, tiny poetic hands, and a face and body full of fire and music and grace, took her audience by storm. I have never heard such ovations for anyone in any theater. They openly worshiped this frail spirit who was as tense and highly strung and immediate as an E string. She was like a passionate flame, ageless as she had been at twelve, when she had been discovered dancing in the streets of Seville during the Easter festival by Ruth Chatterton, George Brent, Ronald Colman, and Rex Smith, red-headed Irishman then at the head of the Associated Press in Spain. Enchanted with this magic child, and wishing to share her with everyone around, they had bought two hundred bottles of red wine for the crowd while Amaya danced until even she could dance no more. That was the beginning. Today that street dancer of Seville is the sensation of America and the tempestuous expression of the Spanish spirit.

Val wanted me to see Toledo, home of El Greco. "There are two Toledos," he said, "one under the light of the moon and one at sunrise. We must see both." The first night we set out in full moonlight for the Hotel Castilla, and I shall never forget our walk through those narrow mysterious streets, torn with long, piercing shadows, sharp and deadly as the famous sword blades made there by daylight. The next morning we saw the city at sunrise—so different, silent and heroic even when the streets were filled with people, but still as disquieting and mysterious as El Greco had painted it.

I became quite accustomed to the Spanish dinner hour (midnight, after the theater) and seemed to thrive on the late hours and on the rich and intensely national cuisine. One night we set out from Madrid for La Granja, the summer resort high in the Guadarrama Mountains, where the King had his summer palace and from which we could see the lights of Segovia and the moonlit monastery. We had dinner at midnight at the home of friends which ended with a chocolate-mousse pudding dessert I shall never forget. It took me an hour of wheedling, plus a song, to get the recipe from the hostess. After dinner we motored over to Segovia and we sat in the dark shadows under the archway of the monastery while in the center of the courtyard, under the light of the full moon which directed its rays like a reverent spotlight, sat Andrés Segovia, the famed guitarist, who played Mozart,

Bach, and Granados. It made an indelible memory. We were an invisible, silent audience, and the emotion of the music and the moonlight was all the more intense because it was such an intimate and solitary thing.

I had been invited to sing at the San Sebastian summer American Embassy at a dinner that Ambassador and Mrs. Laughlin were giving for Alcalá Zamora, first president of the Spanish republic. I had practiced a little song called "Paño Murciano," by Joaquin Nin, which was derived from a melody native to Zamora's province. By the time we got to San Sebastian I felt that I was letter-perfect in it. The concert was given on the steps of the main hallway of the Embassy and consisted of French and American songs, as well as my little Spanish one. When I came to it, I looked down at the President and in well-rehearsed Spanish told him that I was singing in his language for the first time and should there be any mistakes would he please forgive me. Zamora nodded his head graciously, and the piano introduction began. I started the song without a tremor, but after the first two or three bars, every Spanish word left my mind. Not daring to call halt, I improvised with some queer sounds that bore only a facsimile resemblance to the original. I thought I caught a gleam of laughter in the President's eye, but he applauded gallantly. I was shame-faced when I later faced Alcalá Zamora, but with that elastic, friendly Spanish humor he told me my song was charming indeed, although he could not fathom from which part of Spain my Spanish came! It had, he said, a quality all its own.

I had an opportunity while in San Sebastian to see a real bullfight, given for a Red Cross benefit. The only bullfight I had ever seen before had been an amateurish one put on in Frejus, the old Roman city on the Riviera on the way to Toulon, which ended in a riot when Charlie MacArthur and Scott Fitzgerald leaped into the ring to try their hand at the bullfighting (a "Laughter in the Afternoon" parody of Hemingway). The real bullfight was a terrifying experience, set in the midst of a great arena flooded with afternoon sunshine and possessed by a howling, colorful crowd. Val, who had been an amateur matador in his youthful days, tried to explain that, regardless of non-Spanish prejudice, a bullfight was the fairest sport in the world—a man's intelligence pitted against the primitive force of a beast. In spite of Val's rationale, I pulled my hat down over my eyes and re- fused to look while the picadors went through their preliminary show. But I must admit that when El Estudiante, the reigning star of the day, came into the ring, one forgot the pointless danger and became transported, as did that whole crowd, with his grace and beauty; and when he knelt before the bull and en- gaged in what seemed to be a little private discourse with the motionless animal, who stood there seemingly impaled on the man's glance, I went as wild as anyone with excitement.

Dinner that night in the Restaurant Canuto in the old part of the city was like a scene from the second act of *Carmen*. El Estudiante and Villalta, another star of the arena that day whose cape had hung in front of my box during the *corrida* because I was Señora de Parera, the wife of his old friend, arrived with their own entourages, and the devotees of the ring crowded the restaurant and gaped at the great ones. There was dancing and singing by gypsy artists who came in to celebrate the "victory," and I gave only a sneaking thought to the gloom of the other side, down at the bull pen.

Now the vacation, the wedding trip, was over. Back in New York another Metropolitan season awaited, more concerts, work again. But I was returning with a great sense of completeness: career, while important, was not all. I was Mrs. Valentin Parera too. Never did either of us have any thought of one or the other abandoning his work. Too much had gone into it, it was too much part of our very lives. Instead my marriage gave me a confidence in the future I had never had before. I wanted to sing more than ever. I wanted to sing my fool head off. I really felt like singing because I had something to sing about.

Celluloid Fame

NOT LONG AFTER OUR RETURN from Europe I decided to do an operetta, *The Dubarry*. There were a number of things that led to it. I seemed to have gained a three-dimensional view of my work and felt that I was at a standstill at the Metropolitan. I still caught repercussions from the movie-making, I found the lack of rehearsals irksome and felt restless and without scope. Even though I had been a top musical-comedy star years before, I sensed a need for a more basic approach to acting. I wanted to develop the movement and finesse that should go with any successful operatic singing. My lack of stage training was glossed over by a natural spontaneity and an innate ability for projection, but I thirsted for more. So when Leo Michel brought Tillie Leblang and her husband with an operetta they wanted me to do, I saw in it a solution to my problem.

The operetta had been a success in Germany and England, the music was delightful, the stage experience to be gained seemed invaluable. Furthermore, the European tradition of developing opera stars through the medium of the operetta established a precedent in my mind. Jeritza had come up that way and so had Flagstad, whose voice became a powerful, Wagnerian instrument only after she had begun singing those more heroic roles.

I marched over to Gatti-Casazza armed with all my reasons and asked for a year's leave of absence. That gloomy paterfamilias thought this a strange request, but with his usual friendly understanding gave me leave when he saw my determination.

The Dubarry opened in Boston, where it was a great success.

We could have stayed there for six months, but such is the lure of Broadway, we gave up the profitable realities in hand to try for the Main Stem. We crowded ourselves into the Cohan Theater—a great mistake, since the costumes and sets were too magnificent and overpowering for the intimacy of that particular house—and got off to a tremendous opening night. The popularity didn't last, but in that first-night audience was Harry Cohn, who told me later he would never have offered me a movie contract if he hadn't seen me in *The Dubarry.*

The Dubarry was a complete change. Never having gone in for leg art (in spite of the claim of one of the Met's older and more acid prima donnas that I was given my contract there not for my voice but for the appreciation the Opera's benefactors had of my legs!), I now found myself doing an act in a thin, lacy negligee with underpinnings pretty well displayed. The music was lovely and the song, "I Give My Heart," became a sentimental hit, but I sang it during a rowdy brothel scene. Altogether the transition from the opera to the lighthearted music and gay bawdiness of *The Dubarry* took me directly into a medium with mass appeal. It made the producers realize I was a singing actress instead of merely a singer and paved my way back to pictures.

The Dubarry was a happy experience all around, the gay backstage amity of the cast lasting right through to the end. However, as closing date approached and as always when a run is nearing the finish, everyone was disappointed, nervous, and on the *qui vive.* Just about that time Gracie Allen, the radio comedian, had started a nation-wide "search" for her brother. The sound of Gracie's querulous Dulcy voice asking for news of her long-lost blasted brother seemed to be everywhere, no matter when you spun the dial. One night, very near the last *Dubarry* performance, I was waiting for Percy Warren's cue when something snapped and, as they say in the trade, everything went black. Percy, who was the Count Dubarry of the play, had a line, "What are you looking for?" which he threw me as I came on the stage. That night as he spoke I stood abstracted and tired in the entrance. "What are you looking for, I asked?" came Count Dubarry's persistent question, trying to force my cue. Without thinking I answered, "Why, Gracie Allen's brother." The curtain came down in a fine frenzy of laughing hysteria and stayed there for fifteen minutes until the mirth died down on both sides of the stage.

I ventured even farther afield when, after *The Dubarry,* I did my first four-a-day, starting at Loew's in Washington, where I stayed two weeks, and then at the Capitol in New York City for another two weeks. Never once, during that month, did I sing "down," and many said that I gave better musical perform- ances than I ever had before. When I opened in Washington it was to what the newspapers the next morning called the "greatest gathering of diplomats since the inauguration," and repeatedly, four times each day, I treated my audience as if they were a con- cert audience come to hear the music they loved. Then, and always, I never felt that a $4.40 top was a necessary ingredient of musical appreciation.

Following the vaudeville engagement, I was asked to come to the Hollywood Bowl to sing. My feelings about a Hollywood comeback were mixed. I had had my baptism but was certain I could carve out some success if given a second chance. Financially, I needed another hypodermic, since most of my accumulated savings had gone, as had everyone's, in the crash. So I determined to make this trip West, the first since my previous picture venture, another movie try. I dieted all that summer, bought new clothes, and saved the most knockout dress of all for my Bowl appearance. The silken bait took.

At a party after the concert given by Jessica and Dick Bar- thelmess, Irving Thalberg, who had been at the Bowl that night, drew me aside for a long talk, the sum of which was that "some- thing has definitely happened to you and your voice." He said nothing about the movies, but he sounded pleased and interested. Next day I saw by the notices that the critics had been good to me, and I felt a new enthusiasm start in the picture capital. Two or three producers telephoned and buttered me up with kind words and praise but put nothing definite in the offing. When the flattery was finished I still held onto a mere "want to keep you in mind." But soon after, at a dinner given by Edmund Goulding, I was called over by Elsie Janis, who always shares her friends and fortune, and told that the gentleman she was chatting with, a Mr. Harry Cohn, wanted to meet me. I had never heard of him, nor of Columbia Pictures, and when he abruptly said, "How would you like to make a picture over at Columbia? Why don't you come to see me tomorrow at eleven?" I promptly forgot all about it. The next morning, for once, I overslept. But Mr. Cohn hadn't forgotten, and in answer to his call asking "where in hell" I was, I broke a record getting over to see him. We had a friendly talk out of which emerged the simple fact that although he wanted to do a picture with me, he had no definite ideas. He offered me a contract and the promise to come through with a story.

It seemed a long chance. I was frightened of walking into the same disaster as before, where story difficulties had been a trap. I had one dominating ambition at that moment. I wanted to do *The Merry Widow* at M.G.M. I had heard that Thalberg was going to do it with Maurice Chevalier, but as yet had no widow. I begged extra time for a decision from Harry Cohn and dashed over to the Metro lot to see Thalberg. How I wanted to do that picture! I used every art of persuasion I knew to convince Thalberg that I was his "widow." He was so kind but so firm. "We're probably going to sign another singer," he admitted. Finally Thalberg told me bluntly that Lubitch didn't want me, didn't believe in me, was sold on another girl.

"I'll do it for nothing," I cried. "The role was made for me—the music for my voice. Cohn is waiting to sign me and has given me until four-thirty this afternoon to make up my mind. I'll stay here until then and let you think over my free offer."

I waited at M.G.M. until four-fifteen, when I finally had to admit that there wasn't a chance. Thalberg tried to ease the blow by offering an option for a future picture. I shook my head. Well, they should have believed me. *The Merry Widow* was a flop. Disconsolately I went over to the Columbia Studios and signed what was to be the most fortunate contract of my career.

Val and I settled down in a little apartment where I helped our maid, the faithful Erma, with the cooking. Over at the studio the search for a story went on. Cohn had gotten hold of something by Dorothy Speare that he thought might do, since it was the story of a musical career, but it didn't all ring true. I went into a huddle with the writers, offering suggestions about my own experiences in opera, and finally we came out with something I felt could be believed. Little scenes like the one showing the books on the stomach to exercise the diaphragm—which actually happened to me in a studio in Milan—gave the story a verisimilitude which any music student would recognize. Of course truth wasn't carbon-copied. But the spirit of struggle and gaiety was there.

Shooting had started when, after only ten days, I was called into Sam Briskin's office. Briskin was very direct. The gist of his complaint was that he was very unenthusiastic so far, thought Cohn had made a mistake, and suggested unceremoniously that maybe it would be better to buy off my contract.

I was stunned. While I too had inner qualms about the picture, I still felt there were possibilities. Furthermore I knew that being released from a contract after only ten days would have permanent repercussions. I was making a comeback and I wanted my chance. I was determined to fight.

"You can't buy it off for any amount of money," I said flatly to Briskin.

The argument was taken to my friend, the late Max Winslow, an executive on the Columbia lot who had been Irving Berlin's partner in the *Music Box Revue* days and was fortunately one of my boosters. I took my stand firmly.

"You'll buy back this contract," I warned, "only over my dead body. I intend to do whatever I can to make this picture a success; you've got to do what you can."

Briskin was as resolved to get rid of me as I was to stay. In one of my wild gestures of helpless rage and defiance (I was fighting, after all, for the very life of my career), I flung out and shattered the office window. I startled the people on the lot down below, but more importantly, I startled Mr. Briskin, and since Mr. Cohn was not eager to call off the contract, Briskin agreed to stay out of my way for the duration.

Trouble continued about *One Night of Love,* but never after we really got started did my genuine response to the picture waver. When I wanted to sing "Ciribiribin," which cost thirty-five hundred dollars, there was an upheaval, happily this time with all windows intact. And when Cohn saw how much the Puccini music cost, he was ready to give up. I remembered the discussion over "Butterfly" when, after the sensational preview of the picture, we were invited by Gloria Swanson to her house to celebrate the evening. Harry Cohn arrived a little later than the rest and, coming over jubilantly to where Dr. Marafioti and Maurice Chevalier were talking, said: "Well, Doctor, what do you think was the best musical number?"

" 'Butterfly,' " answered Marafioti without hesitation.

"No," said Cohn flatly. "It was 'Carmen.' "

"I'm sorry to disagree with you," Marafioti said politely, "but in my opinion it was 'Butterfly.' "

Chevalier, listening to the two, became peeved and said, in his inimitable pursed-lip accent: "Mr. Co-an, if ze doctor say it was 'Butterfly,' he ought to know. He prepared ze music."

Whereupon Cohn answered: "But the doctor doesn't know that I paid thousands of dollars for the rights to 'Butterfly' and not one cent for 'Carmen.' "

I had to insist firmly that they put Carminati in the picture when they wanted Menjou. I thought that Carminati, because he was Italian, was better suited to the part of an Italian maestro. Naturally there was constant interference from the front office. We were all under tension. It was also a new world for Columbia Studios. Fortunately the people I actually worked with were wonderful. I learned to depend on Victor Schertzinger, the conductor, and on Val and Marafioti for advice. Also Joe Walker, the cameraman, and the whole crew of workmen on the set not only developed an enthusiasm for the picture itself, but a sympathy for me. They knew that every time I was summoned to the office to see the bosses, I took it on the chin. They gave me a feeling of what is known in some circles as working-class solidarity.

There is incidentally a great deal of fakery about the so-called *rapprochement* between star and crew. For instance, tradition is that at the end of each picture all internecine strife be forgotten while the star distributes presents to director, crew, general personnel. Every afternoon at four or five, when the little wagon drives up with pop, cake, and ice cream, the star shows her good fellowship by treating the house. But many a star with a reputation for popularity among the cinema great is disliked on the home set—in spite of lollipops and presents. The crews on the set represent humanity and appreciation. If they like you, they create a wonderful warmth and sympathy around you. Among the happiest trophies brought back from Hollywood is the scroll presented to me by the crew at the end of *One Night of Love*. I hang it—in memory—alongside the scrolls presented to me by the crews of *Jenny Lind* and other films I later worked on.

Before the picture was finished, even Harry Cohn, who had been carried along by my enthusiasm, almost lost confidence. The stories of the front-office rows began to simmer through the Hollywood gossip columns, and without investigating, the reporters had made mud of my reputation by the end of the picture. The musical complexities were extreme, with three companies experimenting with the sound all through the shooting. It was the first time the combination of a full symphonic orchestra and an operatic voice had been used, and they were trying for perfect results. By the time the picture was finished we were all worn out. Only Val believed in it. Everyone else could only say, "Thank God it's finished."

When the picture was previewed in Glendale and received a small ovation, Harry Cohn looked around in surprise. "Maybe," he said when the lights went up, "we have something here, but I'm not sure yet." Even after the Santa Barbara preview, attended by many musicians who showed definite excitement, he was still skeptical. Hesitant but hopeful, he felt that perhaps he dared try for a Hollywood preview, with all the usual fanfare.

That Hollywood showing of *One Night of Love* was probably the most hectic night of my whole life. When the purely professional and representative Hollywood audience rose at the end of the picture and cheered, Harry Cohn, my husband, and I, sitting together in the last row, cried with excitement. In the fervor of the moment Cohn, reaching down to kiss me, fumbled and kissed Val instead! (Every shred of Hollywood gossip is so gnawed and nibbled by the press that even *that* trifling detail made the columns and later forced Cohn, in mock despair, to cry, "My God, this will ruin my reputation as a he-man.") There were happy tears shared with friends. There were congratulations and prophecies that night. Gloria Swanson said to Val, "Who can dare make a musical film after this one?" People called it a new kind of picture, using good music so that people would love it. It forecast, they said, a popularization of the classic repertory. As Irving Thalberg approached me at the head of the aisle I couldn't resist a malicious dig. "I bet this will top *The Merry Widow*," I said. He answered cagily, "Try and top it yourself."

So here, overnight, I was a movie success: a species of success unlike any other in the world. Everything started rolling at a thundering pace, bringing an exhilaration and a feverish happiness that shook me. I came to New York for the opening at the Music Hall, accepting a date to sing with Rudy Vallee across the street in the N.B.C. studios that same night in nonchalant competition with my own picture. Val had to remain in Hollywood on some of his own work, so Maurice Chevalier and Condé Nast squired me to the theater. There were some minutes before the broadcast, so I asked Condé to drive me around Radio City. My name was up in a star's heaven of electric bulbs. Five times we circled the theater while I feasted my eyes on the bright white-lighted signs.

Condé was a kind and wise man. "Well, Gracie," he said to me then, "I always knew it would happen. But from now on the worst is to come. Now you have to sit on top of the world and hold on. Take everything this brings and love it, assimilate it for all it means, but you're going to have to separate the rose from the sting and sometimes it's not easy." He shook his head with a kind of sadness. "Your job is just beginning."

Condé Nast was always good to me, as he was good to so many. He was giving a great party for me that night, a party about which *Time* magazine in its usual crew-cut style said: "After the première in Manhattan, Publisher·Condé Nast gave a fabulous Grace Moore party to which most of the Somebodies in town gladly went." One of the Somebodies was Charles MacArthur, back at his old tricks. He locked me in the men's room while Condé and his guests frantically searched for the star who was supposed to be on the receiving line. Finally Herbert Swope discovered the MacArthur hiding place and, hurling himself against the door, managed to achieve a rescue. I exited from that men's room in a state of acute embarrassment which was in no way lessened by MacArthur's wicked giggle that flagrantly implied what-all.

Before the party I had gone back to my hotel apartment rooms to telephone my husband. Chevalier came back with me and waited while I put through the call. Finally Val came on the phone and I told him of the evening and how I had missed him in the midst of its gaiety and success. Chevalier looked melancholy when I finally hung up.

"You know," he said, "I've been all over the world, had all the beautiful women I've ever wanted, but I never knew what it is to be *in love* with anyone until now. No one ever talked to *me* the way you talked to Val. You put a wall around the two of you, and I felt very much alone." Poor Chevalier, he did look desolate that minute with his pushed-out underlip, but I was woman enough to know that his nostalgia and melancholia did not concern me. I have thought about this blithe Frenchman often in the past few years and wondered about the stories which put him on the political black list. But like all his friends, I can only hope the tales are not true.

One Night of Love catapulted me into a new world. I suddenly discovered I was listed second among box-office stars that year, voted one of the "ten most beautiful women in the world" (I never did figure how *they* arrived at that astounding conclusion or who *they* were), awarded a fellowship and gold medal by the Society of Arts and Sciences for furthering the cause of good music in the films. Everywhere my face was known. I was sitting on top of the world and frightened to death. The grueling struggle through the filming of the picture, the necessity that it turn out well or else, had been exhausting. Now, before I had time to catch my breath and sense the simple reaction that I was not a failure, I was swamped with sensational success. Editorial writers departed from purely political or philosophical spheres to comment on the changes *One Night of Love* could bring not only to the movies but to music. They said that a new era in music for the masses had arrived. Because of the picture, Fortune Gallo said he was able to sell out all operas whose music had found their way into the movie. When I went to England to sing, an editorial in the London *Times* pointed out that Covent Garden was reaping profits from the film's popularity handsome enough to balance the budget. The picture caught on so vigorously everywhere that there were forty theaters in a city like Berlin alone showing it at one time.

If I had been just a movie star, all this would have been comparatively simple. But now each time I set foot on stage, I had to make good all over again. Standing with only a piano for background, before an audience which preconceived me on a romantic Italian balcony, was more often a bleak letdown for the people out front. Without microphone, minus ballyhoo, I had to fight against the story personality of the screen heroine. Every word I said had to fit the script, each gesture be tied in with the picture. I wanted to meet all demands, but I knew it was impossible. I was making unintentional, unavoidable mistakes with the press and multitudes of people. I was spent by the tumultuous receptions that preceded every appearance, worn out before I appeared on the concert stage. A movie star could meet the press, meet her public, and that was that. But I had all this—and singing too!

Many difficulties resulted because the front-office rows had been so widespread through the columns that it was assumed without question that I was a difficult, unmanageable, and temperamental woman. This prejudged attitude upset me at first, and I felt helpless before it, but finally I became more philosophical and reasoned that if fighting persistently for what one believed in was temperament, let them make the most of it.

The confusion between concert and movie career added one final misadventure. Before going out to Hollywood to the Bowl, I had made a contract with the Columbia Concerts Bureau. My career had fallen off so at the time, they booked me to sing with three others in what was called the Metropolitan Opera Quartet. After the opening of *One Night of Love*, when there was such wild excitement about the picture, I begged for permission to buy off this contract and do my own concert tour. It was my big financial chance. My agents persisted that I hold to the Columbia Concerts arrangement. I gave in and set out to fulfill this former contract. The quartet included tenor Edward Johnson, now Metropolitan head, Rose Bampton, then a contralto, who now has blossomed out into a lovely dramatic soprano, and Richard Bonelli. I was the girl who sang the high notes. We were booked for four engagements each week, with long, wearisome train jumps in between.

Everywhere we went *One Night of Love* was playing to great crowds. The inevitable happened. Each time I came out to sing my one solo contribution of the evening called for on the program, the audience held me until I had sung virtually all of the movie. I realized after one week that I was in for it. The good sport of the quartet was Edward Johnson, who understood what was happening and apparently had heard of this new invention, the movies, and the power it held over the public. The others, while not expressing themselves overtly, showed a natural resentment. And why not? I knew how they must feel. I knew that it was galling to have one member of a skilled and highly talented group singled out for particular notice. But there was nothing I could do. A movie celebrity breeds a special interest, and while today some of the luster has been rubbed off through the personal-appearance tours that caught on in the middle thirties, a movie star "in person" was still something of a novelty on that dismal catastrophic tour.

That my associates of the quartet should have been upset is understandable. But why did the gentlemen of the press feel resentment? They called these ovations "hogging the scene." They seemed unacquainted with—or above—the effect of the motion picture on the desires and tastes of the public. Instead of realizing how helpless was a mere singer in the face of movie publicity, they objected to the new audiences that were crowding into the concert halls, they accused me of sensationalism.

Harassed by this atmosphere of resentment which surrounded me while singing constantly, not only the program music, but the inevitable, fatiguing encores, I broke down in Omaha and asked to be relieved of my contract. The manager was frantic. "If she doesn't go on I'm ruined. Why do you think I sold out this house? On account of a movie star with a voice, that's why!" At the last minute I rose with a temperature of 103, but so deeply was I enmeshed in ill will that, because of the uncertainty as to whether or not I *would* sing, there was even more resentment when I *did*. After the concert I was put on a stretcher and taken to the train, headed for New York. Newspapermen at all stops were on hand to see whether I had collapsed or walked out. So ended, in bitterness and heartache, the first great triumph after my Hollywood success.

If I had been left alone to pursue the tour I wanted, I should have built an entirely different career with completely different perspectives. I could have met all demands. My whole contact with press and public would have been different. But my opportunity never came again.

I wanted to leave Hollywood after *One Night of Love*. I had accomplished my ambition. I had scored a success and put opera music on the screen. Now the studio wanted to top this achievement and searched feverishly for another story. Val and I settled back again, this time by suggestion of the studio in the standard Hollywood palace, a mixture of Italian and Spanish Roxy rococo. It consisted of long flights of staircase that spiraled upward. You faced an endless climb to get anywhere. Beyond the age to enjoy rocketing down the banisters, and pretty tired on my feet after a long day at the studio, I decided to forego all this grandeur and the hell with keeping up front. There was enough elegant stuff and nonsense going on at the studio anyway, and what I wanted was a complete change.

So Val and I bought a trailer, the first that started the vogue among the stars, and decided to live the life of gypsies. Our first nomadic venture came the week end after our purchase, when we set out on a tour of Coronado Beach. Val rode up front in a little Ford, I huddled behind in the trailer, trying to clasp all our household belongings to my bosom to prevent their crashing to the floor. We kept driving along endlessly until two or three in the morning. "Please, Val," I wailed from behind, exhausted from bouncing around, "I can't go any farther. Why don't we just park?"

"But I don't know where we are," my husband admitted ruefully.

"Oh, the devil,"—I was too tired to care—"let's just park."

Val drove in off the road and parked. Came the dawn and a rude awakening. "Listen, you," two policemen were shouting, "whatcha doin' here? Cancha see it's private property?"

We poked our heads out of the trailer. There we were, nicely encamped on some lush greenery that led gracefully up to a big estate. We retreated in panic and pushed the little Ford home. We gave up our abortive wandering and rented a lot near Malibu Beach for $75 a year, parked our trailer there, and proceeded to live in it, commuting to and fro. My husband built a terrace on it, with a green artificial rug which fooled all the dogs on the beach. If we couldn't be gypsies, we'd be fake-rustic anyway.

Soon word got around about this new simple life and, lo, we had neighbors. Miriam Hopkins and Anatole Litvak, then married, were the first to settle next door, but their trailer was notches above ours in elegance. After that all the incoming trailers got progressively more swank and life turned grander and grander. We ended up by dining on the beach off barbecued steak served by butlers in tails and white tie, and one night Lewis and Kendall Milestone arrived with full orchestra to play a modest moonlight serenade.

It was one of the happiest summers of my life. Val and I had many friends, and since both of us love to be with people, we found our own little corner of Hollywood enchanting. One of our boon cronies was—and still is—Kay Francis, who, if anything, has grown more beautiful through the years. When Kay and I get together, it means late nights of fun and gossip or a houseful of mutual friends, for Kay's hospitality is famous. She's shrewd, she's wise, she's completely adult, completely lovable. She doesn't sing, she doesn't dance, she hasn't the experience and training that the legitimate stage might have given her, and she has always frankly said that Hollywood was her road to financial security. Yet with it all she's intensely sincere. She's done the best she can with her screen work, and by it has won a great following as well as the financial security. Never one for swank, she has put her money into safe investments, has foregone fancy real-estate plunges and the usual Hollywood splendor, and has lived with all the simplicity and grace that is the hallmark of her charm. Not long ago she volunteered to the U.S.O. for overseas duty. Without the singing and dancing to bolster her, she, and the other stars with her, did a marvelous job of morale work in their tour of the battle fronts. When she returned, she was so shaken by her experiences she found it unbearable to sit through a little dinner party I had arranged for her first night home. Our Land of Plenty was more than she could take after what she had been through.

When I visited Hollywood late in 1941, Kay gave me what I think was the last big glamour party before Pearl Harbor. According to a story in Louella Parsons' column, Kay had announced this as a small sit-down dinner of my twelve most intimate friends. I arrived to find a houseful of Hollywood's elite crowded into Kay's little place and a profusion of tables decorated with orchids, gardenias, and *leis* from Hawaii. When I rose to thank Kay, I looked at Louella across the way and said, "According to Miss

Parsons' report, Kay was having twelve of my most intimate friends. It seems to have been one of Louella's inaccuracies but a charming one. She had led me to believe I had only a dozen friends in Hollywood, but I have ninety-five."

"Touché," said Parsons.

One of Louella Parsons' newspaper colleagues is Hedda Hopper, who used to sell oranges by radio but has graduated into a first-class columnist with a knack for etching in acid and coating in sugar, as well, every facet of Hollywood life. Hedda has always made crazy hats a part of her natural chic, and her courage in wearing them has given impetus to such original milliners as John-Frederics to create them and all of us to wear them.

Jessica and Dick Barthelmess, the Lewis Milestones, Norma and Irving Thalberg, and Sam and Frances Goldwyn were constant visitors at our trailer mecca. I had known Sam Goldwyn since 1921, when we used to ride together in Central Park. Sam was my champion from the first. He came to the opening in Ohio of *Up in the Clouds* and encouraged me after it with kind words. "You're going to be a great star, Grace," he said, then added, because Sam is never one to pass up a bet, even in a compliment, "That other kid in the show, the comedian, he's going to be a success too—you know, Skeets Gallagher." Since then there has never been a debut of mine or any important event that Sam has failed to send a telegram for good luck.

I was finally called by the studio and told they had a story. Good, I could go back to work. I found the story was a cloudy gem. I now was cast in a gangster picture with Leo Carillo, who while he may not have had a heart of gold, still loved music. He listened to records of my singing from an ornate golden bathtub, and presumably was softened. Since most of the first act of *La Bohème*, which I sang with handsome Michael Bartlett, was included in the movie, I didn't consider it a total washout, but the music was certainly yanked into that movie with a heavy hand. The studio was trying to do right by me. They were so delighted over the success of *One Night of Love* that now they decreed that everything I was to be starred in must be stupendous, colossal. When the quartet from *Rigoletto* was slated for the film, four seemed a measly number to the front office. This must be big stuff, they said: terrific! box-office! I found myself singing with a "quartet" of forty. Harry Cohn said, "When I do something big—it's really big!"

I did a few other pictures, one with Cary Grant, the handsomest star in Hollywood, in which I sang "Minnie the Moocher." It took me two days to get up the courage to "swing it," and with Cary at the piano I found it great fun when I really got going. Of course later when I stood in a concert hall and heard from the balcony the cry, "Come on, Grace, give us, 'Minnie the Moocher,' " I realized how these separate lives impinge on one another. Keep them apart as you might in your own mind and understanding, your public can't and won't.

The beginning of the end in Hollywood was *The King Steps Out,* a story based on the life of Elizabeth of Austria, and featuring the maestro Joseph von Sternberg. Because it had an enchanting score by Fritz Kreisler, especially the lovely "Stars in Her Eyes," I was eager to do it, but I was terrified of meeting the self-convinced genius, Von Sternberg. Harry Cohn brought me over to the lot and locked Von Sternberg and me in his room. What technique is this? I thought. It was part of a whole build-up. Von Sternberg began by modestly declaring he was the greatest director in Hollywood. As to personalities, he said, if I hated him at first, I would certainly end up by loving him; everyone did. There was a final climax. "I know," declaimed the Great One, "exactly what to do with the music. I saw the première in Vienna. I know what to do with you. I am just the one to bring you and the music together."

I asked that the door be unlocked and, holding my breath after this Svengali-Trilby display, agreed to go into the picture. But in spite of the back-room oratory, Von Sternberg apparently didn't know what to do with the music or me. I found myself standing by a big piano most of the time, like a lump of a log, singing. The great action scene came when I had to milk a cow, singing at the same time, and I wondered if Von Sternberg had ever analyzed the difficulties of hitting high B's and high C's while trying to hit a milk pail too. With a fine understanding of vocal cords, Mr. Von Sternberg also surrounded us with barnyard smells, no doubt to add to the realism; but they also tickled the throat. It was funny at first, a nightmare at the end.

Also if Mr. Von Sternberg was wrong about bringing me and the music together, he was wrong in assuming that if I hated him to begin with I would love him at the end. I disliked him to begin with and I disliked him even more when it was over. I got so tired of seeing him in his velvet coat and velvet beret, sliding his personal microphone around, carrying on, declaiming, stamping his foot, shooting off constant sparks of what he perhaps wishfully assumed was genius. He was the Hollywood director of the comic strips down to the last yes man.

I had to get away from Hollywood after that picture. Movie reporters who had gotten wind of the cow incident stopped me as I traveled across country at the usual places like Albuquerque and Kansas City and asked what it was all about. I told them I had served my term in Hollywood, that after all, milking was something a bit out of my line, especially when synchronized with singing.

The story spread so widely among my friends that when I went to Europe for a vacation they sent me, instead of the usual flowers and books, gifts of livestock, including a little pink pig (if I only had him now, in these days of rationing!). At the pier to see me off was a movie-star cow, predecessor of the famous Elsie, all glamorously made up by Elizabeth Arden. I must say that cow was more thoroughly trained for the movies than I was and could do all the tricks except sing. Maybe she loved Von Sternberg. Elsa Maxwell, who sailed with us, was so amused by the story that she announced a barnyard party to get back to the earth. Her back-to-earth barnyard party later took place amidst all the quaint Marie Antoinette simplicity of the Starlight Room of the Waldorf-Astoria.

When the picture was released, all that was left of the cow was the hind end. Imagine—only the swish of a tail after a million dollars' worth of publicity! Although my contract still had three pictures to run, with a guarantee that would have netted me nearly half a million dollars, I had no desire to go on. I made two more films, and bought off the contract for a very modest sum.

A Cook's Concert Tour

LIKE THE QUEEN IN THE STORY who ate too many tarts, I had had my fill of canned goodies. I wanted to get away from Hollywood and close to people again. Val and I had set off on a vacation in the spring of 1936 to have our look at a world that was soon to be no more. While abroad my manager advised me to embark on a European concert tour for which, by cable and wire, there had been great demand. *One Night of Love* had been a Continental sensation, and a tremendous audience had been built up everywhere. It seemed a golden opportunity. I felt I needed the vital spark that comes only from the quickened response of a living audience. I agreed to the tour, had Edward Molyneux make some simple clothes for me to bely the Hollywood legend of feathers and spangles, and set off with Val.

La Bohème in Budapest was first on the schedule, and we arrived in this dream city on the Danube early in May. Gilbert Miller, that fabulous impresario who used to pop up all over Europe in his little plane with the casual regularity of a farmer on the milk run, flew in from London to greet us at the Budapest station. With him was Alexander Ince, then publisher of a kind of Central European *Vogue* and himself a bit of a Hungarian Grover Whalen. He was official glad-hander to all incoming artists, and knowing Ince was equivalent to being presented with a wax skeleton key to the city.

We found our rooms at the Dunapalota Hotel filled with the press, on hand to interview the first "movie star" ever to come to Central Europe to sing opera. They were an unusual representa-

tion of newspaper folk. They all spoke English with only one exception, who spoke beautiful French. They were interested in
and knowledgeable about music. And they asked no questions
about the color of my pajamas, the extent of my love life, or my
opinion on marriage, which was the stock routine between press
and Hollywood stars elsewhere. It all seemed extremely civilized
and highly urbane and boded well for my concert in Budapest.

Val and I had time to wander around the city, then so beautiful with magnificent chestnut trees sprouting their candelabra
everywhere. Near the hotel was a large terrace where all the fash-
ionables would gather for their daily apéritif of Barask, the
famous native liqueur. The women would sit there for hours on
end, sipping their little drinks while they knitted and embroidered,
for all the world like a scene out of an old-fashioned tapestry of
ladies in a drawing room that had a tree growing in its middle.
We saw that three-sheet posters announcing the opera were all
over the city, with all names written backward according to Hungarian custom. I was Moore Grace; Charles Kullman, leading
tenor of the Vienna State Opera who had come down to sing
Rudolph, was Kullman Charles.

Budapest is a city of terraces. Our hotel faced the Royal Palace,
across the other side of the Old Portrait Bridge and the Church
of Coronation. At night little lights outlined the façades of these
buildings and made the whole city drop away like the pieces in a
child's kaleidoscope. Exploring the town meant searching out its
restaurants, some of the most wonderful in the world. We had
dinner at the Kis-Royal, favorite with the Prince of Wales whenever he came through Budapest. It was noted for its chocolate
Crêpes—and justly so, we decided, when we had made off with
dozens of them ourselves, after a magnificent beginning of paprika
chicken done in sour cream.

The performance of *La Bohème* was not scheduled for the
Opera House of Budapest, although the Opera House scale of
prices prevailed, because, as I later learned, they could crowd
more people into a larger, although less distinguished, hall. The
drop curtain of this hall was a tin-roller arrangement that fell

down abruptly to announce boldly and implacably one of the leading tooth-paste creams of Hungary. And although Admiral Horthy and his family presided in the Royal Box, and the audience, dressed in the latest Paris fashions, behaved beautifully and with great enthusiasm, still it was incongruous as the devil when the cast, in nostalgic *Bohème* costumes, took its calls before this blatantly modern curtain.

There was a loud knock on my dressing-room door between the second and third acts. Because I find it quite difficult to receive people before that third act, I nearly always refuse to answer any dressing-room summons, but I was given no alternative on this night because, before I could say, "Who is there?" or investigate, the door was thrown open abruptly and two news photographers entered, without so much as a by-your-leave, in the tow of a very small, white-gowned, scintillating blonde.

The photographers started to pose the little blonde and me for photographs. In the hurly-burly of the moment I did not catch her name, but I refused, begging that they would take any and all photographs after the third act. Evidently this was quite a *faux pas,* because they all started talking and arguing in top-voice Hungarian, and the blonde, throwing me a deadly look, flew out of the dressing room. Just as she was going through the door a great basket of flowers, dislodged by the excitement and the slam-banging from its pedestal, toppled over and watered her from head to foot. She looked like a little drenched garden hen. I later learned that my commotional friend was a great star in Central Europe with many comrades among the press. When she said that I had insulted her backstage, I am afraid they believed her, since I had no chance to explain. But she *did* look funny.

After the performance, with a little band of friends, among them Howard Sturgis (who had come from Vienna, where he was then living), we set out to see the night life of Budapest. We had been told that in order to see the Danube blue, one had to see it at sunrise. Our first glimpses of it earlier that day had revealed it brown as the East River, and I secretly felt that sunrise was hardly enchantment enough to turn its color. But since it had been called the Beautiful Blue Danube, we were perfectly willing to keep going until dawn to see why.

Gilbert Miller guided us to the supper place where Magyary, the most famous gypsy violinist in the world, placed his Stradivarius under one of his three chins and played heavenly music. Ziegfeld once offered Magyary three thousand dollars a week to bring his violin to America, but being King of the Gypsies, he preferred his Hungarian kingdom. At his recent death the famous Stradivarius was inherited by his son, who will carry on the tradition of the reckless abandoned gypsy music that means so much to Hungarians. It was this same gypsy music that made me so spirited that night that I jumped up and joined the heady whirl of the gypsy dancers who were giving us a private performance.

The most famous night club in Budapest was "Arizona's," presided over by an American woman from Arizona. We were her special guests after hours, when she seriously sang favorite French songs with a terrific American accent, and her beautiful show girls threw oranges and flowers to us as they revolved around a platform high above our heads. The splash of goo on our supper table and on the men's white shirt fronts and the women's dresses didn't matter. It was all such a good show—American roughhouse, Hungarian style, a kind of paprika hot-dog dish.

The sun was just rising as we came to the door of our hotel apartment. We rushed to the window which overlooked the Danube and threw it wide. But alas, even with Aurora's so-called rosy fingers to touch it off, the Danube was still gray and muddy and quiet as a stagnant pool. Best not to look at all, we decided, and henceforth when we sang of the Beautiful Blue Danube, to keep eyes and memory shut, as the composer must have done.

Vienna was not on the concert itinerary, but we were able to visit there on the way from Budapest. Charles and Lisa Kullman met us and took us first to the darkened out-of-season Vienna State Opera, just across the street from the Hotel Bristol, where we were staying. We went through the stage door and then onto the stage facing the empty auditorium. More ornate than the Opéra Comique and less grand within than the Metropolitan, it had a peculiar, personal charm all its own. As we wandered around the stage I could sense the warmth and the aura of accumulated happiness that clung to it like a fine perfume through many years of great opera. Walking away from the building (imposing and grandiose on the outside), that same warmth and happiness seemed suffused in the air. Vienna, on the brink of despair, still held to the tradition of gaiety that had become part of her legend. The spontaneity and dash we had felt in Budapest now seemed like an overflow from Vienna, as if Vienna had so much of this *élan* she could let the cup brim over to her neighbors across the (muddy) Danube.

We visited the famous riding stables from which came the much-publicized horses Jeritza had brought with her to America when she became the bride of Winfield Sheehan. These were later starred in a Sheehan film. Afterwards we said prayers in the beautiful Stefan Kirche. Then we lunched on the terraces of the famous Grand Hotel and walked through its elegant promenades, those same promenades where Schuschnigg was to pace endlessly, up and down, up and down, until the report circulated that he had gone insane. We strolled through the stiff, formal gardens of the Schönbrunn Palace, filled with memories of the days of Elizabeth and Franz Joseph. Howard Sturgis took us to luncheon at the beautiful house of the Baron and Baroness Eugen Rothschild, who played an integral part in the musical life of Vienna. Kitty Rothschild was happy only when her salon in Paris or Vienna was filled with musicians, chatting, coffee-ing, and making music too. Kitty later told the story at a luncheon in Paris, which she gave for me and John Gunther, of a dangerous guessing game played at her Vienna home the following Christmas Eve dinner. Her guests each wrote on slips of paper what they thought would be the outcome of Hitler and the Nazi regime. It was a game of political prophecy played in an atmosphere of security as they sat around the lovely dining-room table. Just for fun, the slips of paper were put in the safe-deposit vault of Kitty's bedroom and bets placed on the winner. When Hitler invaded Vienna and the Rothschilds fled to Paris, they remembered those incriminating papers. By some of the tricks known only in an Eric Ambler spy story, they were able to send a friend, disguised as a Nazi sympathizer, into the bedroom to get the papers before the Nazi guards, at every door of the Rothschild palace, could find them.

Schuschnigg had just returned from Italy while we were in Vienna, bringing guarantees of complete support from Mussolini. Our last day we drove around to the platz where Prince Starhemberg was addressing his little personal and private army, the Heimwehr. These storm troops paraded down Vienna's main thoroughfares with Schuschnigg and Starhemberg at their head. My motion-picture camera, which had been busy those two days in Vienna, clicked into service again; I felt I just had to get this parade. I tried to battle my way through the guards that kept the public lined back, fencing off the crowd with a linked-arm formation the entire length of the street. Somehow I managed to get past the surging multitude and toward the front. As Schuschnigg approached, the policeman directly ahead of me, under whose arm I was trying to wiggle, clicked to attention and caught me in the eye with his elbow. I let out a blood-curdling scream that turned all eyes in my direction. I must have looked very funny, buttressed there against the stalwart guard, with my camera in hand. I thought I caught a glint of laughter in Schuschnigg's eye. Later I thought it was a pity he hadn't laughed—it was so close to being the last time he would have the opportunity.

When we said good-by to our friends in Vienna and cast one last look at the slender steeples of Stefan Kirche, all of us had the feeling that it would be a long, long time before we returned. The grim fate that hung over the future of the city had cast its first shadows, and parting was truly a bitter-sweet sorrow.

Now we were off to Denmark. We arrived in Copenhagen at six-thirty one morning. Even at that hour there were several hundred people and reporters and photographers on hand to greet us. As we drove from the station to the hotel in a cab, exclaiming over the beauty of the city, the driver turned and said, "Well, Miss Moore, I am happy that you, as an American, love our city, because after our king the most popular person in Denmark is the American minister, Ruth Bryan Owen."

We arrived at our flower-filled apartment at the Hotel d'Angleterre. Below us the square was flooded with sunshine, the streets filled with people off to their work on bicycles. We looked for the King among them, because the cab driver had told us that often the King went out for his morning's cycling, chatting and laughing with the workmen as he joined them in their pedaling. We could see men and women on the terrace in the sunshine, their morning coffee heaped with whipped cream, breakfasting off great juicy strawberry tarts and magnificent pastries. Across the square was the Royal Opera House, pasted with huge posters announcing the production of *La Bohème* for which I was scheduled.

We settled down to our own good hearty Danish breakfast surrounded by the press. Aided and abetted by coffee topped with foamy cream, we were all soon friendly and talkative. Like the Hungarian press, these journalists had no concern with the sensational angles supposedly part of Hollywood stardom. Instead they asked about American music, modern and past, and what the *Government* was doing to encourage the development of it. One gathered that in Denmark the Government was looked upon not as an interfering bureaucracy but as an instrument of public and social good.

I was due to make two appearances in Copenhagen, one a concert at the great Forum Concert Hall, with its glass dome and palm-lined walls which held eight thousand people and which my manager, Mr. Henson, outstanding Scandinavian concert manager and music publisher, told me had been sold out in four hours; the other a command performance of *La Bohème* at the Royal Opera, which had been sold out in forty minutes. People had slept all night in the lobby to be on hand for the opening of the box office.

The first half of the Forum program was devoted to serious music, the second half to request songs and simple American numbers. To my astonishment, the audience called for two repeats of

that unpretentious Southern song, "Ma Curly-Headed Babby."
As was true everywhere since I had become known through the
movies, there was a snapping of audience tension after the first
notes were sung when they discovered I really had a voice that
could carry without a microphone. I felt it with this Copenhagen
audience, and their sympathy and enthusiasm after each number
was marvelously ingratiating. Even the photographers, who kept
flashing and shooting throughout the concert, couldn't make me
nervous because of this solid *rapport* between me and the audience.

My dressing room was filled with packages of fruits and the
wonderful fish foods for which Copenhagen was celebrated, instead of the usual bouquets. I had told the press I loved chicken
and was writing a cook book and wanted Danish recipes. To my
intense delight I received an enormous carton holding twelve little
dressed chickens, their legs tied with pink ribbons and with roses
tucked where the necks used to be. It was the prettiest line-up
imaginable. Enclosed with them was a recipe for each chicken—
twelve in all—recipes that are still an inspiration for cooking
chickens from my own yard in Connecticut.

Ruth Bryan Owen, hearing about the box of twelve chickens,
decided that the only place they should be cooked was the American Legation. Consequently she arranged a charming dinner
party in our honor there. The butcher who had done up the
twelve gift chickens added twelve more for the extra guests, and
all were succulently prepared. When Madame Minister made a
kindly little speech of welcome to Val and me, I hardly knew
how to reply, but remembered, on the moment, a story about her
father in Jellico, Tennessee. William Jennings Bryan had come
campaigning through the South and had stopped off in Jellico as
a guest in our home because he wanted to sample Mother's famous
fried chicken. (Strange, I interpolated, that here in Denmark I
was sharing chicken with his daughter.) Bryan had taken a great
fancy to me and listened sympathetically when I told him how I
wanted to grow up to be a singer. I sang two little hymns for him
in the family parlor in my small piping eight-year-old voice. He

was going up to Williamsburg, Kentucky, a short distance away, to make another speech, and Father decided to go along and take me with him. On the stage with all the dignitaries, I sat in the place of honor—on William Jennings Bryan's knee. Then he asked if I wouldn't like to sing a song for the audience before his speech. He shoved me out to the front of the platform, and I sang the hymn, "I'll go where you want me to go, dear Lord," which Mr. Bryan later told me, in his big jovial way, had been entirely appropriate to his campaign speech and instrumental in putting it over. Before he left he promised to watch my career with a fatherly and tender interest. The story about her father delighted Ruth Owen, and we laughed over it together. The encounter in Kentucky was my first and last appearance in a world of professional politics. It has always been my theory that the less an artist has to do with the intricate world of politics—save in her own profession—the better off she is. Once at a dinner party I talked with a world-famous English comedian who had never even paid this, his adopted country—where he has made his career—the compliment of becoming a citizen. He assailed me for not join-.ing his committee to launch a Second Front. (How presumptuous it was that he, from the security of his Hollywood world, should try to assume the role of a leader.) I answered that only one artist has been able to combine politics with art, and that was Paderew-ski. But, ẑfter all, he at least went home and fought for his *own* country.

After the Forum concert a supper party was given by the Möellers, he the owner and publisher of the leading Copenhagen newspaper, she a lovely serene blonde, typically Danish-looking. Among the guests were Prince Viggo and his American-born prin-cess; Ruth Bryan Owen and various members of the diplomatic service. The supper table was set with beautiful china from the royal porcelain factories, all solid white instead of the usual blue and white sold to the general public. Mario Panza, then with the Italian Embassy, a great lover of music and favorite in Copen-hagen society, told me that the white porcelain could be sold only with the permission of the royal family, since it was their own

china. How I wanted a set just like it for my home in Connecticut!
—all solid white, and thought I, "I'd set it on a grass-green
cloth." (My wish came true, green cloth and all!)

At the rehearsal for *La Bohème* I discovered that all the cast
were Danish, and I was delighted at the chance to rehearse because hearing Rudolph sung in Danish was like listening to Chinese. The contrast it made to my Italian Mimi was so ludicrous
I was glad I had not come on to it unprepared at the command
performance itself. All the cast were splendid, and Madam Kraft,
the Musetta, then fifty-three, had a mezzo voice of beautiful
quality, plus an intuitive and sensitive acting sense. I must add
that the staging of the opera was better and more authentic than
at either the Metropolitan or the Comique.

After the second act of the performance, still wearing my costume and black wig wrapped in tulle, I was taken to the royal
box to be presented to their majesties, the first time in ten years, I
was told, that this had been done. As I curtsied to their majesties,
the King presented me with a bouquet of red and white roses
which he said he had gathered himself from his own greenhouse.
The Crown Prince and Princess Ingrid, who were also there and
spoke impeccable English, were cordial and hospitable. The King
was tall, dark, and handsome, like a King Fisherman of the Baltic
Sea (which he was). He told me he had read many stories about
me since my film success. And because all Danish artists who had
gone to America had received such a friendly welcome, he said,
he and his family were especially happy to be part of the warm
welcome of the Danish people to me and to present me with the
Medal of Honor. I curtsied, thanked him, backed out of the box,
and flew through the backstage passages to my dressing room to
get ready for the third act.

The Danish Royal Opera tradition permitted no curtain calls
except for guest artists, who took their bows alone. After the indispensable support given by the cast, I felt queer standing alone
in solitary splendor before the curtain while the audience rose in
a thundering ovation. Then the Opera director came on stage and
presented me with a blue-and-white vase decorated with a ship.

It was filled with red roses, and he made a little speech in Danish which I found, in later translation, said that the ship which had brought me to them would take me away, but they hoped it would also bring me back to them very soon. It was all so friendly and gracious and endearing, I felt it was a kind of magic I had to hold onto because it might never be captured again.

After *La Bohème*, the members of the cast had a supper party, and like any gathering of artists who have just done a good job together, it had the sense of completion and good spirit which one rarely finds in any other strata. We toasted one another in Danish schnapps, they sang a song which they had composed, called "Gracious Grace," with music by Helen Gaar, while I countered with a little toast I had learned in tongue-twisting Danish.

The next day Val and I hired a car and tried to see something of the neat storybook countryside. We drove to the lake and stopped at a restaurant called the White Ear, which used to belong to the Russian czar's mother. Later we had a *smörgåsbord* of forty-six hors d'œuvres at the Kollesgaard Restaurant, and I felt I should never want to eat again.

We left for Oslo in the middle of May, traveling through the most beautiful country of pine forests, lakes, little islands and waterfalls, where the air was as bracing as a plunge in a mountain stream. At Oslo we were met by our American minister, Anthony Drexel Biddle, who told us there were thousands of people surrounding the station and hotel. We walked through vast crowds to our car and set out for our hotel. I went onto the balcony and waved to them until the police decided that the demonstration had lasted long enough on both our parts and shushed the people away.

The concert was scheduled for the next night, and by this time the excitement was beginning to tell. I was having the time of my life and enjoying completely the thrill of cheering crowds, people below our balcony, the ovations in the opera houses. But I felt tired and nervous. During the concert itself, cameramen in the pit kept shooting photographs all through every number. Finally, in the middle of a Debussy song, I stopped and asked them if they would please let me continue and I should be happy to pose for them afterwards. The audience applauded, but I don't think the press boys liked it very much.

Hundreds had been turned away from the concert, and I was booked for another a few days later. Unfortunately I had to cancel it because of fatigue. I attempted to get some rest before we went on to Sweden. We did go to a reception given us after the concert at the American Legation by Tony and Margaret Biddle. Tony was then in the embryonic stage of his diplomatic career, but he and his clever wife had made a great many friends in Norway and were highly respected. Val and I also were invited to visit the royal family. They were in mourning because of the death of England's George V, who was the brother of Queen Maude, and had been unable to attend the concert. The day following it, I received a letter from the Biddles saying that their majesties would like us to come to the summer palace for tea.

It was a simple afternoon, the palace itself a palace in name only—really it was just a big pleasant house without the usual ostentatiousness and heavy splendor of a royal palace. The King and Queen, Crown Prince and Princess Martha, René Askin, my accompanist, Val and I, with one or two others, were the only ones there. It was all easy and gracious. We talked of music and politics, and they asked questions about Hollywood and Flagstad's American success, about which they seemed a bit skeptical. They wanted to know if her acclaim had been as great as the papers had reported. To them Flagstad was an artist who had sung in *La Bohème* and light operas, and they could not understand how she had suddenly blossomed out into the greatest Wagnerian singer of the day.

After tea we walked in the gardens which the Queen herself tended. The walks were all of closely packed red earth, making a fascinating pattern around the flower beds of white, blue, and red blossoms. Later they asked me to sing because they had been unable to attend the concert, and I did, the aria from *Butterfly* and two or three other little songs. The Queen told me of the time Melba sang for them the whole role from *Rigoletto* during a terrific thunderstorm. The afternoon ended when the Queen took me to her private apartment to see the photographs and water colors which were her hobby. As we were chatting, the King came in, went to his own room next door, and returned with a little box. He opened and took from it a gold bar pin mounted with the royal crown in diamonds, which he pinned on me. This presentation, in the privacy of their apartment, done with such simplicity and pleasant humor, touched me deeply. It seemed symbolical of the democratic, friendly spirit behind the Norwegian monarchy.

Recently I heard a story about the Concert Hall in Oslo which brought back my reactions to the firmly steadfast, quietly democratic Norwegian people as I remembered them. The State Opera of Berlin came to Oslo after the German invasion, to give a Wagnerian operatic performance. The public was ordered to buy out the tickets, with which dictum it complied, but when the curtain rose the only people out front were a scant two dozen Germans.

Stockholm next. En route we were stopped by crowds who presented us with flowers, fresh strawberries, and other fruits. Pleasant as the interruptions were, I felt that with a concert to sing I needed more seclusion. Therefore, for the rest of the trip, I decided to duck to the floor of our compartment as we went through the remaining stations and slip by unseen. Val told me people were searching from carriage to carriage, and I felt as if I were playing hide-and-seek as I kept under cover. Finally, at one station a man jumped to the side of the car, peeped in and saw me lying there. He let out a howl that brought everyone running. Well, there was nothing to do but get up and laugh with the crowd, which I did despite the fact that my hair was pinned up with bobbie pins and caught in a turban, so I looked even less a film star than usual.

The manager of the Stockholm concert had written that anticipation was high in that city and I should receive a royal welcome. He asked me if I had any request to make, and in jest I wrote, "I hope that the country of Jenny Lind will provide a carriage and four white horses to drive me to the hotel." I never thought further about that romantic nonsense. But when our train arrived we found a carriage waiting at the station with four black horses because, as the manager apologetically (!) explained, there were no white ones around. There were two men on the box in gaily colored livery, and the carriage was bedecked with flowers, and the horses had gay bouquets tied to their bridles. The streets were lined with dense crowds (the newspapers next day said thirty thousand people had come to welcome us), and Val and I, alone in the carriage, stood waving and throwing out our flowers to them as we drove along. We held onto each other, frightened and happy over the tumultuous greeting.

At the hotel we were told that every place on the terrace had been sold for ten dollars each and the fund contributed to the American Red Cross. The windows of our apartment opened out on a square which was filled with glee-club singers from the Stockholm colleges. They called, "Grace, Grace!" and urged me to come out and sing. There was no balcony, but there was a tiny roof jutting out from our window. With Val hanging to the tail of my tailored suit, I stood on that little roof, waved to them as they sang their song, and answered with a chorus of "One Night of Love," which they had called for. It was about ten o'clock, but they refused to go home, and I stayed as long as I could, but at the insistence of the concert manager I turned and found the sitting room filled with members of the press. I think they could have gotten the story of how I felt from my face. There were no words to describe the emotion that swept over me at this welcome in Stockholm. It was unbelievable, overpowering, and cataclysmic.

The next night at the concert the audience rose as I came on the stage—a usual courtesy extended to visiting artists. I was in good voice, although tired, and responded to the electric current of that eager audience. The people of the Scandinavian countries make a unique musical audience. There is none of the cold reserve expected from the Nordic temperament. They have the spark and fire of any Latin audience and give the artist the most direct communication of spirit. It was a spirit that helped me make that concert successful both from the public and critical viewpoints. A few days later I gave the second concert, at which King Gustav and the royal family were present. The latter half was broadcast throughout the country because I had to curtail the Swedish trip in order to fulfill an engagement at Covent Garden. I felt I was in better voice for the second concert because I had had two days of relaxation and a wonderful sightseeing trip through the ancient, feudal city, the Venice of the North. We visited the classically beautiful town hall and went to Gröttenburg to the old theater where the kings and queens used to hold private musical and theatrical performances, and where the royal family would often take part. Val and I visited the Jenny Lind Museum, where I played on her little spinet. The Jenny Lind Society had paid me the great honor of naming a room in the museum after me, which I dedicated in tribute to the American legend of the Swedish Nightingale.

We had tea on a terrace overlooking an open-air garden where a full symphony orchestra played while the audience, comfortably seated at little tables, enjoyed the music. Such a *gemütlich* way to listen! These geranium-hedged gardens were the scene of many a famous concert, one of the most triumphant sung by Lawrence Tibbett. Tibbett was presented with the King's Medal of Honor and later, when the King's emissary in London made the same presentation to me on behalf of King Gustav, he said Larry and I were the only two Americans ever to receive this decoration. Incidentally the engraving on the back of each of the Scandinavian medals carried my name as Mrs. Grace Moore. Val was the silent partner on these tours, making a great personal impression on people and friends. Thus I was very much Mrs. Parera, although, since it was a concert tour, very much Grace Moore too. The Scandinavian compromise was the nth of urbanity.

When we visited the fair ground, with its permanent constructions of little chalets showing all the products and specialties of Sweden, we bought souvenirs like mad—wonderful bottles of Orrefors glass, imaginative little soup dishes shaped like red tomatoes (which appear again and again these days on our table in Connecticut), wonderful figurines and china gadgets.

I had a brief romantic flurry two nights before the last Stockholm concert, at a dinner given by the Swedish-American Society at which Prince Carl, Sr., the King's brother, presided. Prince Carl, Jr., his son, was a very tall, dashing, and romantic blond who was my partner at dinner, and I'm afraid I paid very little attention to the eight hundred other people who were there, although I did make a speech when I was presented with a beautiful Orrefors glass vase inscribed to me from my Swedish friends. The speech made, and the brilliantly decorated ballroom set for dancing, I danced every dance with the handsome young prince, returning after each one to Val's *sotto voce* teasing and joshing. I knew the prince was engaged to a very charming woman, and I certainly was very much married, but I must admit the whole thing had a Cinderella-at-the-Ball excitement, and my Jellico, Tennessee, heart went pitapat.

The second concert was held on our last night in Stockholm. The Swedish custom of kicking you from behind onto the stage for good luck was carried out, to my ignorant astonishment of the why and wherefore, by Gertrud Wettergren, Sweden's famous mezzo-soprano. After the performance she and her husband, who was head of the Stockholm Museum, gave a supper for us and the Swedish artists in the basement of the famous Golden Pheasant Restaurant. It looked like a Gothic vaulted cave, aged in conspiratorial history. We sat for hours telling lighthearted jokes and exchanging backstage stories, as artists love to do when they get together. One was about the internationally known Swedish tenor who not only loved his song and wine, but pretty women as well (although reputed happily married). One night, at a command opera performance in which he was singing the leading tenor role, he failed to appear at curtain time. The management sent out a desperate call, and private police, going full speed on their motorcycles, were dispatched to make the rounds of the town in search of him. He was finally located in the leading sporting house of Stockholm, ensconced in a great golden chair, surrounded by the beautiful girls of the "ensemble" and singing in full voice the opera which he was at that moment supposed to be singing on the stage. The police hauled him out, doctored him with black coffee and spirits of ammonia, and sometime later had him on the opera stage, dressed to the hilt, singing with another variety of ensemble and with just as much gusto as he had shown earlier in the evening.

Pulling out of the Stockholm station meant leaving enough success and admiration to last a full lifetime. I felt I should never forget such hospitality and delightful friends, or what had happened to me there, nor ever lose my gratitude for it. Across from my Connecticut farm is the Swedish-American club from which, before the war, the native songs drifted across the countryside, awakening sharp and happy memories. And I and Lisa Johanssen, a member of my household staff who was once a pianist with leading Stockholm orchestras, never tire of talking about that clean-gleaming, civilized country of Sweden.

The next concert was scheduled for Amsterdam, where I was to have the good fortune of singing with an orchestra conducted by Mengelberg. I must admit I had grown a little tired of audiences everywhere calling for "One Night of Love" and "Ciribiribin." It took a great musician like Mengelberg to restore my slant on that little theme song.

What Mengelberg's political views may be now, I do not know. But I remember him from that concert for his musical sympathy and warmth. He had a human fallible approach to music which gave his genius an unmistakable tenderness. He had invited me to drive out to his home in the country the day before the concert to go over the requests which had come in for the program. In the tiny sitting room crowded with mementos of a great career, we two sat opening the requests and sorting them. "Ciribiribin," said one. "Ciribiribin," said another. "Ciribiribin," over and over again.

Mengelberg looked at me very seriously. "I do not understand," he said, puzzled. "What master is it that wrote this 'Ciribiribin'? I never have come across it."

Rather shamefacedly, I explained it was a little Italian folk song which I had sung in a film. Taking pencil and paper, I indicated the music to him quickly. He looked at my notations and then at me, amazed that I should even want to sing it. Then, when the requests left no doubt that it would have to be sung if the audience were to be satisfied, he shrugged his shoulders resignedly.

"But," I insisted, "in that case I won't sing it with orchestra. It is much too modest a song to sing with such an imposing array of musicians."

He agreed, but assigned a pianist from the orchestra who should accompany me in this strange artless song he had never heard about. Thus I sang it at first for that Amsterdam audience, with piano alone. The applause was terrific, the audience wanted it again. I looked at Mengelberg. He indicated that I should repeat it. But as I did, various members of the orchestra picked it up—first a violin, softly, then a flute, then a cello, until I finished my second offering of "Ciribiribin" that night with a rather disjointed but enthusiastic sinfonietta. After it was all over Mengelberg said to me, "Regardless of who wrote that little song, where it came from, or whatever qualities it may have as a musical composition, if you in singing it can make an audience so happy, sing it until you die."

The proposed trip to London's Covent Garden was one that loomed momentously in my mind. I knew many English artists and people of the social whirl, having met them in New York, in Paris, in Biarritz, and on the Riviera, and they had often suggested a London engagement. Lady Cunard, who had acted as Thomas Chadbourne's hostess at a dinner party given me on his yacht at Cannes, had said, "You must come to London to sing, I must launch you there." To everyone I had replied, "This isn't the moment for it. Later on I will."

After the launching of *One Night of Love* Geoffrey Toye, then managing director of Covent Garden, flew to Paris and offered a contract for three performances. The time seemed propitious, and I accepted.

We left Paris for England and were met at Dover by the lord mayor and mayoress and special writers from the leading London newspapers, photographers, and representatives of the Columbia Studios. We arrived on a cold dismal day, but there was nothing gloomy about the official welcome. I had been in England before, but this time was completely different. I was returning as a famous star: it made the whole world seem like a long-dreamed hope come true. We sped through the sedate and aristocratic English countryside, so different from the informal French, where even the little gardens back of the homes along the way had a combed and manicured look. Our arrival in London was breath-taking, and when I looked out the train windows and saw the movie cameras, the radio microphones, and the photographers, with flashlights popping everywhere, my first impulse was to stay on the train. The Columbia Studios officials had been telling us what to expect, but this was beyond their stories of the storm the film had created. The royal family had seen it at three private showings, even the most conservative British papers had written editorials, and fan clubs had mushroomed all over the British Isles.

We stepped off that train into a cheering multitude of thousands of people. I smiled, posed, shook hands and waved, then walked dazed but happy to a magnificent Rolls-Royce which was to take us to Claridge's. We drove through the crowded streets surrounded by a private escort of fans on their bicycles. Suddenly I had a great sensation of real fear. In the midst of the tumultuous reception in this imperial city I realized what this one picture had done,, was doing, and could further do to my life. I could only hope somehow that the fact that I was an established opera star of New York's great Metropolitan and a serious concert singer instead of an overexploited cinema star would be remembered.

The traditions of Covent Garden were hallowed and glorious. Given a fair chance, I felt that I could face them. I was glad that Geoffrey Toye and Dorothy Fleiteman, who later became Mrs. Toye, were on hand to guide me through the first confusions. I found the royal suite of Claridge's, where we were staying, filled with countless newspapermen and -women, dozens of cameras and newsreel apparatus. I tried to speak seriously of my music, but the press seemed slightly bored. They wanted to know how I kept thin, how I fell in love, whether I practiced in front of a mirror to eliminate facial grimaces when I sang, et cetera. It reminded me of Harry Cohn's comment at one of the Hollywood previews, "You know, you don't make enough faces. The people won't think you're singing." All these questions seemed to have little to do with my Covent Garden engagement, with my ambitions, or with me. I tried to answer them: I said yes I had practiced in front of a mirror so I would not distort my face before the camera, although the face, I tried to explain gravely, could not be so motionless that it would lose the illusion of sound. Yes, I dieted to keep thin. Yes, I had fallen in love and still was with my husband. I was disappointed at being given this kind of press routine, but since that was what they wanted, I played up to it and answered in kind. The irony of it is that the Covent Garden publicity staff, wishing to reap the benefits of the film's popularity, yet still eager to separate opera from movie house, had attempted to keep film feature writers away from all interviews until the debut had been made on as straight a musical basis as possible. I tried to abide by the wishes of the Covent Garden staff. But the hop-skip-jump I had to make between being Dr. Jekyll of the opera and Mr. Hyde of the films became an endless turnabout.

Toscanini arrived in London at the same time I did from Dover and slipped into town quietly behind the wave of excitement over the welcome given a Hollywood celebrity. When I saw him later at luncheon, he expressed delight and amusement over the incident. It had given him a chance to go about his business quietly.

Geoffrey Toye told me that every performance had been completely sold out. Personal friends like Kay Francis, Donald Ogden and Bea Stewart, and Dwight Winnan had all been able to get tickets for the first performance, but they said that some of the seats had gone for ten pounds, the boxes for fifty. Mary and Laddie Sandford told me they had to pay one hundred dollars each for their opening-night seats. We were giving *La Bohème,* and Bellezza of the Metropolitan, who was then in Italy, had come all the way from there to conduct.

Val and I had our first glimpse of historic Covent Garden, set in the midst of the city's public market place, at a gala performance of *The Barber of Seville* with Lily Pons. After the first act we were asked to go to the royal box to meet the Duke and Duchess of York, escorted there by Lady Plunkett, our mutual friend. The duke and duchess were both much better-looking and younger than any of their photographs had indicated, and their simplicity was completely disarming. The duke seemed specially interested in the mechanics of sound recording and asked detailed questions about the apparatus used in the film. I often think of those two unassuming gentle people who took over the responsibilities of the throne and in the midst of war have carried them off so gallantly. No wonder they have won the respect and admiration of the British Empire and ourselves.

I stayed in the apartment resting before the debut, signing autographs for the hundreds of fans who daily gathered beneath my window and sent their books up by my special little page boy. Val did in London what every woman did in prewar Paris— trotted out on a shopping spree. London was a man's town for going off the deep end: Bond Street the mecca of the male.

The day of the dress rehearsal arrived, and Geoffrey Toye took me to the theater. In the corridor as we came in we met a man whom Toye introduced as Sir Thomas Beecham. A hurried how-do-you-do was the extent of his greeting, and he brushed past us abruptly. I looked after him in surprise. The welcome I had found in other opera houses had usually been traditionally courteous and often sincerely gracious; this was the most brusque I had ever encountered.

The opera company was friendly and created a delightful, genial atmosphere. I was happy and grateful for the cast, which consisted of the tenor Brogioli, Pinza as Colline, Brownlee as Marcel, and Ruth Taylor, an Australian soprano, as Musetta. As I looked out past the footlights I saw a great many people in the

orchestra stalls. I was later told that these were artists of the
English theater who had been invited for the rehearsal. It was
somewhat distracting, for I always feel that a rehearsal should
be between the artist and the orchestra pit, with no consciousness
of playing to anyone out front. We started off well, and I was
instantly pleased with the perfect acoustics.

There was quite a hubbub after the first-act aria, and Sir
Thomas left his front row seat and rushed up the aisle. I vaguely
wondered why and was afterwards told that he had gone to telephone Lady Cunard that I could really sing. I was told many
other things later on, and there was enough substantial evidence
to warrant the gossip that swept London. But more of that to
come. A few years later when war had sent Sir Thomas Beecham
to America and the Metropolitan, Mrs. William Randolph Hearst
wanted me to sing *Louise* for her annual Milk Fund Benefit with
Sir Thomas conducting. I thought it a good way to end the gossip
started in London and give us an opportunity to really work
together. At the first rehearsal of that *Louise,* Sir Thomas kept
the whole cast waiting for thirty minutes on the Metropolitan roof
stage and then walked in blissfully unconcerned about the incon-
venience caused. I wondered whether Sir Thomas had overslept or
just enjoyed giving himself special privileges. However, when we
had our dress rehearsal there was no question about his brilliant
musical abilities. That dress rehearsal was a real performance.
Much to my chagrin the actual performance next day was slow
in tempo and fatigued. I had rehearsed through three tenors:
Kullman, Maison, who took to bed with the flu, and Jobin, who
had sung that last performance with me in Paris, and who finally
sang now at last minute's notice. I couldn't understand the story
circulated afterwards by Sir Thomas that I had refused to
rehearse when I had pleaded for rehearsals. We have grown accustomed in America to the ungraciousness of the Beecham out-
burst to our audiences from the conductor's rostrum, which seems
to me more sporting of the distinguished old gentleman than this
backyard gossiping. From listening later to the recording of
the radio broadcasts of this *Louise* and the previous one under

Ettore Panizza, there is no question in my mind that the Italian came off with conducting honors on the Charpentier score.

When I arrived at Covent Garden at six-thirty, the long queue that had been waiting for thirty-six hours was still there waiting for seats in the top balcony, where there were no reservations. They waved and wished me good luck. I answered, "Keep your fingers crossed."

The nervous strain which gripped me was not frightening. I had been through it before. The consciousness of the great music that had rung through Covent Garden and the comparison I was facing with the sacred names in operatic history only tightened my resolve. The atmosphere of friendliness backstage was heartening and reassuring. It meant much to me that I was surrounded by old friends and colleagues from the Metropolitan and a conductor with whom I had already worked on *La Bohème*. With the first "Scusi" I felt my voice ring clear and strong. There was no applause to interrupt that entrance, for which I was grateful, and I only realized how taut I was as I found it difficult to relax. There was a tenseness in audience and artist alike. After the aria there was a handful of scattered applause, which was hissed by the rest of the audience. I was confused, for it had gone well; and surprised, with a sudden feeling of failure. Rushing to meet it, I pulled myself together for the rest of the act and finished on a clear and ringing high C.

As soon as the curtain came down I dashed from the stage to my dressing room, locked the door, and burst into tears. There was a pounding on the door, and voices called to please come out quickly and take a curtain. Between tears I answered that I didn't want to take a curtain, since I was indisputably a failure. Val finally convinced me to open the door and literally pulled me out to the stage. I could hardly believe my ears as I listened to the most uproarious ovation I had ever received. I was pushed out by the others to take a curtain call alone. To the sound of bravos and surrounded by bouquets across the footlights, hats and programs tossed in the air, I stood transfixed by an overwhelming sense of relief and gratitude.

Later in my dressing room Geoffrey Toye explained that there was never any applause during a performance at Covent Garden, which he thought I had known. The opera finished with another thunderous salvo, and we took sixteen curtain calls. Edward Johnson and the late Paul Cravath, then chairman of the board of the Metropolitan, were among the first friends backstage to see me. There were messages, flowers, and telegrams from almost every artist in London, friend and stranger alike. When English speak of generous American hospitality I always counter with the hospitality I found everywhere that first London season, unequaled in my experience anywhere. Only Lady Cunard, whom I saw as we were going through the stage door, turned her back and seemed ostentatiously not to see me. I wondered about it absently, but forgot it in the moment's excitement. There was a cordon of sixty policemen from Scotland Yard trying to control the stage-door crowd, which kept calling, "Gracie, Gracie!" It amused and pleased me because that was my Tennessee name, but I felt it was a habit with the English crowd because of their popular and well-loved Gracie Fields.

Val and I were pushed into the car and drove off to a supper party being given at Claridge's by Geoffrey Toye and Betty Lawson Johnson as joint hosts. Betty, an American from the South who had married and was living in London, had made a firm place for herself in British society. She worked hard for charity and gave freely of her time and money to many an English cause. At the party I found that Puccini's son and his wife, who had traveled from Viareggio, were at our table. Young Puccini looked more like a bank president than the son of a musician, but in spite of his solid prosperous air, he knew a great deal about music. There were place cards at our table for the Prince of Wales and Mrs. Simpson, and the two came in a short time after we arrived. The prince was young-looking, relaxed, and chatted easily with everyone. I liked one thing he said to me after meeting Val. "It seems so unkind for people to speak of Mr. Parera as Grace Moore's husband when he is so much a person on his own," he observed. He called Val to him and spoke in Spanish. After a bit the prince said, "What do you think of my accent, my Spanish?" To which Val replied, "Well, sir, it is very fluent, but the accent is hardly Castilian. It is a little more on the Argentine side." The prince laughed and said, "At least you tell me the truth."

Mrs. Simpson told me how happy she was that an American girl should receive such an overwhelming ovation in London. The affection between the prince and Mrs. Simpson was immediately apparent. His eyes never left her as she visited friends at near-by tables, returning each time to him to bring their greetings. It was an honest, direct relationship, and one could not help respecting it. My loyalty to them was later to involve me in a contretemps with the American press which I, however, never regretted. Singing at a Saturday-afternoon concert in Cannes in 1937, I was told the Duke and Duchess of Windsor were occupying a box. I walked onto the stage, made my usual curtsey to them and the audience, and heard an unaccountable buzz in the audience which I overlooked. I sailed for home directly afterward, and not until I found a telegram from my Texas friend, Emily Coleman, music critic of *Newsweek,* waiting for me at Quarantine which warned me to prepare for an avalanche of newspapermen "as per Windsor story" did the slightest hint of disturbance occur to me. Emily's wire was baffling. I had sailed the day after the Cannes concert and knew nothing of a "Windsor story." Greeted in my stateroom by a bevy of ship's reporters, including Inez Robb and Dixie Tighe, who all said, "Come on, give us the low-down on the curtsey to the duchess," I was at a total loss. "I don't know what you are talking about," I replied. "Why don't you give me the details?"

Emily Coleman saw my confusion and asked if she could speak with me alone, whereupon she took me into the next room and explained that the hubbub concerned the curtsey to the duchess at the Cannes concert. Well, my curtsey was really for the Duke, but nobody backstage had told me he was unable to be present. I returned to the stateroom and told them to fire their questions. Why, they all wanted to know, had I curtsied? Indeed I was in a spot! I decided not to explain that it was always my custom to

curtsey to a concert audience and between acts of opera. Instead
I replied, "It seems to me the duchess is due the same courtesy
any other woman in her position would get. Anyway, she had
courage and the ability to make one man happy, which is more
than most women can do."

The photographers tried to make me give them a picture of a
curtsey, which I refused to do. Val said sharply that it was a rude
request, whereupon all the newspaper people walked out in a
huff. The press is supposed to be so sacrosanct, one is tacitly expected to forego all criticism. But sometimes press representatives
cannot be equaled for sheer impudence, and the power they wield
over people whose names make feature reading often becomes a
sledge hammer. They did come back about an hour later rather
sheepishly to take un-curtseying pictures, but I felt that all the resentment raised by my simple act toward a fellow American was a
hysterical tempest in a city room.

During the summer of 1938, when we dined with the duke and
duchess in their Riviera villa, she said, "I want very much to
thank you for your gallantry. I knew you were in a spot, and you
couldn't have been more generous. Always remember that I am
very grateful."

The day after the debut at Covent Garden I learned what was
eating Lady Cunard. When announcement was made of my contract to sing there, she flew into a rage and said she did not want a
movie star at Covent Garden. There was no excuse for that particular attitude, I felt. Lady Cunard had a real knowledge of the
musical world. She knew I had been an opera star for eight years
and had sung in serious concerts in America and Europe. Mutual
friends had patiently explained to her over the luncheon table that
I was an established musician long before I had gone to Hollywood. They also suggested *sotto voce* that, as an American herself,
Lady Cunard would be wise not to carry on any campaign against
me, because it would wake a counter-resentment on the part of
people who would be displeased by her lack of loyalty to a
countrywoman. My advance sale had taken Covent Garden out
of the red for the first time in twenty-five years. She was infuriated

that Geoffrey Toye was taking the responsibility and getting the credit for launching me in London, where she was so accustomed to ruling the operatic roost. If I had been a failure, she would have been courteous and consoling no doubt. The success was more than she could bear. Even when I returned the following year to give my first concert at Albert Hall to an audience of thirteen thousand, breaking all records, including the record-breaking farewell of Melba, she called the manager, Harold Holt, and said, "What do you mean, bringing that film star back to London? Don't you know she won't sell but a few seats? Do you call that an artistic venture?" Albert Hall was already sold out, and the manager answered adroitly and wisely: "Any woman who can sell out Albert Hall to thirteen thousand people is a great artist indeed." He might have added that the thirteen thousand came in competition to a performance of *La Bohème* with Elizabeth Rethberg which Lady Cunard had persuaded the management of Covent Garden to put on for the very night of my Albert Hall appearance.

There was a happy surprise connected with the last performance of that London engagement. Our friend Noel Coward showed up, having just returned from India, flying all the way so he could arrive on time. In the surprise and delight of seeing him in a stage box I did a "double-take" and missed a note. He dragged us off to his house in Kent for a perfectly charming, typically English week end. Noel, in the rural confines of his farm, where fat white sheep grazed contentedly in the meadows, or proudly presiding at the head of the luncheon table, where he dished up vegetables grown in his own gardens and cooked under his own supervision, was a different Noel from the blasé, nimble-witted, brittle young man his public knew, and whom we had taken for granted. When *In Which We Serve* was released we felt that it was inevitable, having seen in Noel a solid love of the English spirit that would call out the best in·him when the time was ripe.

Announcement was made that the King and Queen were to attend my last performance as Mimi that year. Unfortunately King George was taken ill, but I shall always be grateful for the graciousness of Queen Mary, who came to the performance alone. When the last curtain call was taken and the members of her party had retired to the rear of the box, the Queen stood there alone and smiled to me across the footlights. The whole audience stood quietly watching that silent interchange and must have felt as I did about the chivalry of this intrepid, indomitable woman.

The Cook's Concert Tour was over. I had found what Hollywood ballyhoo could do to one's world. It made for a good world, rich in enthusiasm, sympathy, and applause. It was evil for the artist when it bred resentment and misunderstanding. But good or evil, it had been a tumultuous and unbelievable experience, and I could only be profoundly glad that it had happened to me.

Louise — Au' voir

I HAD FELT the rushing sense of climax through all the time I was in Europe during 1937 and early 1938. French movie producers had considered making a film of the opera *Louise* and, I having been so identified with it in Paris, they asked me to take the name role. I was delighted and requested a leave of absence from all American activities to do it. I knew that making the film had been Charpentier's lifelong ambition. Not only because *Louise* was his hostage to fortune, his token to posterity whose scope would be enlarged through the wider audience a movie would gain for it, but also because he could make enough money, through a film, to buy the house on the Riviera which was one of his dreams. I thought Montmartre was his native soil and if he were ever to write a sequel to *Louise,* it would have to stem from roots planted in the environs of Sacré Cœur. But he wanted a house in the sunshine of the Côte d'Azur. When he came down to the Riviera for story conferences on the film, he managed to bring Montmartre with him—he was still Julien, with flowing tie, Byronic collar, artist's pork-pie hat. His only concession to the change in climate was to shift from dark trousers to light blue linen ones.

The film was made at Joinville, directly outside of Paris. Its producers were M. Weyler, who in previous years had been a famous French theatrical man and once literary agent for Anatole France, and M. Goldenberg, connected with the great house of Lazares Frères. Because there was no studio at Joinville where the opera could be recorded, we repaired to the Salle Pleyel for that part of the work. Bigot, of the Comique, conducted the symphony orchestra, and the French branch of "His Master's Voice" took care of the mechanics. Working in such a fine concert hall as the Salle Pleyel, we thought we were being given ideal conditions, but it was definitely experimental and we all had to learn to master the peculiarities of the situation. For one thing we recorded over a system that could give us a playback only over telephone wires: and the sound which seemed impeccable at the Pleyel came back less perfect when the track was run off at the inadequately wired movie houses.

With all the obstacles, I felt that I had never worked under such favorable personal conditions. Everyone, from the least touted technical man, knew each note of the music, was completely *au courant* of the story, and spoke the language of the cast. They were like members of a symphonic group. I had practiced long hours with Madame Cohen, one of the great diction teachers of France, to work up enough speed to give my French the fluency which the other members of the cast—all artists from the Comique and other leading French theaters—came by naturally. Everybody understood the problem and co-operated with me on it. I was so happy and ambitious for this film—the first opera to come to the screen—that nothing seemed too difficult.

The actual shooting was done in the Joinville studios, which seemed primitive after Hollywood if magnitude was considered, but which made a fetish of exactitude. Every glass, every lamp, every bit of *décor* was unquestionably authentic. Wherever possible each scene was a complete duplicate of reality, and shooting could be done on the actual spot, since the Paris of the opera had remained the Paris of the present. Marcel Dormoy executed the costumes from the original sketches and the same boot-man for the Opéra Comique production in 1900 was on hand to duplicate them exactly for the film. The *décor,* down to the last bibelot, was a masterpiece of reconstruction. When I sing *Louise* at the Metropolitan today, I wear these same costumes I wore for my Opéra Comique appearance and for the film.

Instead of the usual Hollywood array of cameras, sometimes as

many as twenty for the big scenes, and lights of the most modern
Flash Gordon invention, most of the picture at Joinville was shot
with one camera on a moving "dolly" and two lights. But none the
less, chief photographer Curtis Courant managed to get some of
the most beautiful shots I've ever seen on the screen. Courant,
one of the outstanding cameramen in France, is now in Hollywood in the process of being "discovered."

Georges Thill was the film's Julien, credible enough in spite of
his "bay window." France's greatest bass, André Pernet, was
superb in the role of the father. The whole cast produced an
atmosphere of understanding, harmony, and sympathy. The producers had such a civilized attitude. We never started work until
noon and never on Saturdays or Sundays. Thus one wanted to work
much longer than our usual eight hours. When it was necessary
to keep going all night in the rain sequences, it became part of the
love of doing the job. Afternoons from four to five there was time
off to go to the studio restaurant for a cup of tea and a bit of
brioche. Each night at eight, when we finished at the studio, all of
us would go off—cameramen, electricians, stars and producers—
to some *bistro* for dinner. Thus I learned that the best food in
France was to be found in these working-class restaurants where
each dish was ripened in the real flavor of Poitou or Touraine or
Auvergne.

All this was so different from life on the Hollywood set. There
joss is burned before the altar of assembly-line technique and fan
writers become high priests of the ritual of steam-roller industry.
They recount, with relish, how stars have to get up at five in the
morning, show up on the set by six, and work all hours to get a
picture finished. But fulfilling a schedule in Hollywood has no
particular merit per se, except the merit of greater profit. It is a
strain for any singer to use the voice constantly from six in the
morning until late at night. It must certainly be a strain for any
actor to sustain character on this ruthless sort of timetable.

The near-tragedy of making the film *Louise* was that right in
the middle of its production war clouds hung heaviest over
Europe, and hint of the coming storm swept through the Joinville

studios. Partial mobilization started the very morning we sat in a Montmartre theater, around the corner from Charpentier's house, listening to the sound track. We listened to the cries of Montmartre—to the music of heartbreak that even great orchestration cannot diminish in melancholy. Outside we heard the tramp of feet and the raucous voices of newsboys crying the order of mobilization. We ordered the sound track turned off as the sound outside clamored for attention. The twenty of us there that day hurried from the silent little theater to the street. What a bedlam! Boys with lunch boxes on their way to work had turned back midway to meet their women amidst tears and cries. Husbands and wives embraced on the street. Automobiles began appearing, laden with weeping children and household luggage—the first augur of the terrible refugee hordes that were to flee the horrors of invasion so short a time afterwards.

We rushed away from Montmartre to Joinville, driving through the fog and mist that had set over Paris, with great foreboding. It seemed to me then, as always, that Paris has the face of a volatile person, revealing in its shape and expression every trouble it goes through. At Joinville we called the company together, and I told them that although the American Embassy had suggested that all Americans return home, I was ready to go through with the film if they were. I knew that so many of the artists had given up other engagements to fulfill the film contract, and I had no intention of retreating on the bargain if they would stick to it.

The film went on. Day by day sound men, cameramen, story men were called to the colors. We knew that our wish to make *Louise* into a great film stood little chance of consummation. Too many things were missing, too many technical factors awry, there was too much strain. We would do what we could, but this first filming of opera had run into the impasse of war.

During these months Val and I were often week-end guests at the country house of Jean Prouvost, publisher of *Paris Soir,* the significant French daily, and our conversation turned constantly to politics. It was there that Prouvost permitted us to listen in on a direct wire to Daladier's first report of the outcome of the Munich conference and Chamberlain's declaration that it meant peace in our time. Not long after, we went to the Chamber of Deputies to hear Daladier make this same report to the parliamentary house of France. Daladier spoke in a low, ineffectual voice, with violent gestures, a man of flabby quietness. He seemed to plead that no one shatter the illusion of hope brought back from Munich, that no voices be raised, no questions asked. It was a curious, sad, frenetic time. Even canny Jean Prouvost believed so much that peace had been "brought back in a closed umbrella" that he had started a collection to purchase a French estate for Chamberlain in everlasting gratitude of the French people.

There were many skeptics, even among the guests at Prouvost's weekly shooting parties. Most uncompromising was the famous surgeon Dr. Martell, who later committed suicide to escape working under German orders. At a Sunday luncheon table discussion of the approaching appearance of Daladier in the Chamber, when there was great expression of optimism and on all our faces an almost tragic look of hope, Martell eyed us sharply and said, "But, my dear friends, the Germans haven't with such profound bitterness been preparing revenge all of these years just to let an insignificant man with an umbrella be the one to announce the peace terms."

Paul Boncour, distinguished lawyer and once Premier of France, came to visit the studios at Joinville, and we had luncheon with him. He was an intense little man with a great shock of white hair, small in stature, dressed flamboyantly in a sweeping cape and fedora hat turned up on one side, down on the other. I'm certain he thought that the tall crown of the hat added height, and he kept it on his head as much as possible. He was very cultured, intensely interested in music, and still more intensely concerned with pretty women. He had a penchant for writing love letters to beautiful ladies in the world of art and the *faubourgs* of society, letters so celebrated and so numerous that they often figured as tempests in the teapots of French salon gossip. But there was such a quiet dignity about Boncour that one was impressed. I was extremely fond of him and often dropped by his little house for tea. He always had a fire burning in the quiet sitting room and invariably insisted that I take off my shoes to warm my feet, which I did. Boncour was passionately patriotic and concerned with the welfare of France. He was so miserable and unhappy during those days about the condition of French political life. He knew that France was doomed unless a miracle occurred, and he was constantly sad because he could not be part of that miracle.

Some days before the last scenes of the film were finished, the producers decided to give an afternoon tea party at the twelfth-century Moulin de la Galette, the mill that is duplicated in the third-act scene of both the opera and the film. It stands in a garden with a little restaurant on one side atop the Montmartre hill. I discovered that the little party was to name me "Queen of Montmartre," one of the most delectable honors ever awarded me. In addition to our own studio group, there were many artists from surrounding studios, as well as representatives of artistic, political, and social Paris. Some of the long-bearded fry tried to look as if they belonged to the studios too, but something about them made me think they belonged to the Quai Voltaire. There was music at the party, and while newsreel cameras clicked and radio microphones were set up, I had to *ad lib* in French, thanking the people of Paris and Montmartre for their hospitality to an American artist there. I remember the occasion particularly because I tried so hard to tell how every artist loves France because France in turn loves her artists, remaining true to them long after the glory has vanished. With the first crack in one's career in America, public, critics, and managers turn a cold shoulder and quickly, cruelly forget everything that one has ever done. I couldn't help saying, that day in Montmartre, that like every artist in the world I had wanted to be a success in France because, once a success, one would never be forgotten there.

The last day of shooting at Joinville. As was the tradition, the biggest scene was saved for it. There were three thousand extras on the set, and the good-bys were fervent. The management and I jointly bought champagne for the entire cast, and just for our own private benefit the last feet of film were reserved for the bit where we stood on the balcony with glasses raised drinking to Paris— to the Paris of the present and the Paris that would emerge from travail. The toast was not an idle one. All of us felt the solemnity of the moment and what it meant in terms of personal destiny. Goldenberg and Weyler were Jewish, as were many of our other confreres, and for them we felt a special reaching out and fear. But for everyone the thought of war in France had a close and intimate terror. It may have been a diplomatic maneuver for its leaders, but for the people of France war was a terrible and personal catastrophe.

After the picture was finished Val and I took the express to Poland to fulfill a concert engagement, going through Berlin, where we had our Sunday New York *Times* taken from us as *verboten* reading. We arrived in Warsaw, where we were met by our ambassador, Tony Biddle, who had been on hand to greet us when he was minister in Oslo in 1936. Tony and Margaret Biddle had taken on new diplomatic importance. He was now ambassador to a country on the danger line of war. Margaret presided over the embassy with all the simple elegance characteristic of good American hospitality, and Tony had grown from merely playing host into an astute diplomat.

Unfortunately I had little time to see anything of Warsaw, except for the visit we made, in the drizzling rain, to the old part of the city, where the faded pink-and-blue houses stood as candy-box testimonials to a former czarist regime. Arrived at the concert hall, I found the streets lined with people who had come down from the mountains and stood there, in the chilly autumn drizzle, in their high fur hats, sheep-lined coats, heavy inelegant boots, looking at me fixedly without a smile, as if I were some strange apparition. It gave me quite a jolt. When I came onto the stage I noticed that the house was packed, all the boxes and pit filled with uniformed men and bejeweled and glittering women, while up in the balcony sat the silent, unsmiling peasantry. There was trifling applause as I appeared, always

disturbing for an American in a foreign country—especially during that particular time, when applause for you was also an expression of how the people of the country felt about your native
land and its diplomatic policies. But I was overwhelmed after the
"L'Amero" aria from Mozart with a tremendous burst of approval. Making my exit from the stage, I found the manager
mopping his brow.

"But I don't understand this audience," I told him. "This kind
of applause is usually saved for the end of the entire program."

"Oh," he answered, "I didn't want to tell you before the concert, but these people thought you couldn't sing without a horn.
That's how they picture a microphone—as the horn on His
Master's Voice. They're applauding you wildly out there because
they're relieved they hadn't spent their money for nothing."

There was such war tenseness immediately sensed throughout
all Warsaw that I was certain the concert tour would be canceled.
Mobilization was going apace everywhere. It seemed as if I were
perched on the edge of a volcano. No one, I felt, had any heart
for music.

"Not at all. People want and need music," my managers replied. "Your concerts are sold out. You must fulfill them."

A previous engagement had been made for me to sing *Louise*
at the Opéra Comique in Paris, and consequently I had to "post-
pone" extending the tour to Constantinople and Sofia as previously planned. But I did go ahead with the concert in Bucharest,
although getting there was a complicated affair. My accompanist
was Jewish and was not permitted to cross the German border on
the way to Rumania. But I did enough kicking about cancella-
tion of his passport to stir diplomatic turmoil all along the way
and finally got him to Bucharest.

Bucharest was as different from Warsaw in atmosphere and
attitude as Paris is from Boston. As we drove to our hotel, which
overlooked the gardens of King Carol's palace, we could almost
sense, without seeing or hearing, the dancing and singing in the
streets. It was a kind of miniature Paris, gay, cosmopolitan, venal.
In the lobby of the hotel we ran into more people from

Washington than one saw in the prewar Mayfair. There was
Senator Bob Reynolds on stopover from one of his political sight-
seeing jaunts through Europe, and many old friends from various
embassies in Washington. The air was heavy with prophecy,
chicanery, and speculation. Everyone seemed in a hot stew, and
the feeling of war, unlike the personal fear it awakened in Paris,
here produced a sense of melodramatic Mata Hari theater.

We, for some strange reason, were assigned a private body-
guard by royal order—a kind of F.B.I. man who spoke both English and French. As the sight-seeing tours continued we realized
that he was on hand to protect us from getting "gypped" in true
Rumanian fashion. The tradition of graft in tipping and buying
off red tape is accepted as a kind of "amusing" national characteristic and commodity of the country.

Val had been having passport difficulties. Some of the countries
we traveled through required a Spanish Loyalist passport, others
accepted only Franco's. It took magic or forgery to have both, but
we were anxious to avoid such tricks. We were told that a passport switch had to be made at the Hungarian and German
borders, and our "F.B.I." fellow said he could arrange visas with
Hungarian and German consuls in Bucharest to carry us through
crucial moments when our train passed across these borders. He
said he would need three hundred dollars cash advance to effect
the transaction, promising to return the rest. It seemed exorbitant,
but we gave it to him and awaited results. Next day he returned,
flushed with success, but with not a penny remaining. Val was
furious. He called one of the consuls directly and learned that he
had been happy to give us our visa for the nominal charge of
ten dollars. We were trying to reach the other consul, there were
visible signs of an approaching crisis in the life of our Rumanian
pal. He burst into tears, quickly dried them, shrugged his shoulders and sighed. "I am very sorry, but I took my girl friend out
last night. She loves champagne, and now I haven't your money
at all."

The night of the Bucharest concert I faced the most unconventional and implausible audience I had ever encountered. I decided

that all Rumanians were delightfully mad. Even after I had
started my first group of songs, people kept filing in and out of
the aisles, standing on their seats to peer through opera glasses at
me and at friends across the hall, waving frantically and joy-
ously and often audibly to one another. It was the damnedest
thing! Then, in the middle of one of the loveliest of the Debussy
songs, a pretty blonde-six-year-old walked directly onto the stage
from the audience and calmly handed me a bouquet of orchids.
I stopped the song, accepted the flowers, then asked the audience
if they minded if I started over again! There was an answering
burble—no, no, no one minded, if I didn't. The second half of
the printed program was tossed overboard at the insistent request
for the song hits of my films. The photographer wanted a whole
series of shots of the audience and me posing together. I was completely baffled. Well, when in Bucharest, do as the Bucharestians.
They were so cordial and enthusiastic, and they were so obviously
having a good time and wanting me to have a good time too, that
I gave up the struggle with tradition and took them as they were.
I had a feeling that these voluptuously beautiful women, shrouded
in fabulous jewels, and these Graustarkian-looking officers would
just as soon have the concert go on forever, it was all so pleasant,
and all I had to do was stand up there and sing the songs they
liked best.

   Finally the concert was over and Val and I went on to a supper
given by the American minister and his wife, the Franklin Mott
Gunthers. There I met the fascinating raconteuse and internationally known hostess, Marthe Bibesco, who came up, peered at me
and said, "I just want to see if you look the same as in the films."
She then sat and talked but never told me if I did or didn't, which
I'm sure she was capable of doing in no uncertain terms. Because
my stay was so brief it was decided to take me to the gypsy
quarter that very night. The little gypsy quarter, on the edge
of the town, was alive with music, and the gypsies played and
danced for us until dawn, plying us with *tzigane* food all the
while. We had to leave early in the morning, and some of our
gypsy friends decided to "play" us off. They came to the hotel

while we collected our bags, and as the train pulled out of the station they handed us bottles of wine and serenaded not only us but the whole row of heads leaning out of the train windows. I returned directly to Paris, where I was booked to sing *Louise* at the Comique, with Georges Thill, the Julien of the film, and Pernet, who had been the film's father. Mary Garden was in Paris for the performance, and I had several days in which to rehearse with her, using the Salle Debussy at the Salle Pleyel. Mary had worked a little with me on *Louise* years before, but I had never had the opportunity of going over each detail as we did now. We both worked under terrific pressure, and she would say jestingly to me when the lessons were over, "Well, I'm going home to bed to rest up for tomorrow. You're the only person I have ever met with the same intenseness in her work as I have."

It was wonderful rehearsing with Garden, because she never dictated what *she* thought should be done with a role. She permitted you to find out for yourself what the character was all about, while she sat out front as an audience of one and gave you her reactions. Her criticisms were always constructive, rather than destructive. She had a mellow approach to teaching. She imbued you with such enthusiasm and friendliness and was so uncanny in pointing up strengths as well as weaknesses that her reactions were immediately absorbed in your own interpretation, naturally and spontaneously.

When I thanked her for what she was doing she said, "You have imagination and individuality enough to go ahead and create the role on your own. But you must want, as all artists do, the one critical *friend* who understands both your nature and your ambition. Just one such critic—that is all that is necessary—but one who sees you as a human being, aware of your limitations and capabilities, and able to help you unravel them. The trouble with most artists is that they are all mixed up with too many people who advise and confuse them to cross purposes."

This was my first *Louise* of the winter season at the Comique (up until that time I hadn't yet sung it at the Metropolitan), so the three days of intensive work with Garden before the performance was like a last-minute cram session for an examination. Because of all the publicity which the French press had given the filming of *Louise,* the Comique performance took on the air of an event. It was being given under the patronage of the President of the French Republic, and all Paris flocked to the Comique that night. The Opéra Comique in those days had become somewhat as informal as the Metropolitan is now. Customarily people no longer "dressed" for it, and attendance had become casual and easygoing. But the night of this *Louise,* the old building was resplendent with beautifully dressed women, men in white ties, and all the glamour and excitement that seems traditional to opera.

We had had our dress rehearsal the day before, when M. Thill did not show up because he was indisposed and M. Pernet could not show up because he had had a quarrel with his *petite amie* and had walked the streets of Paris to forget his sorrow during most of the night and wasn't up to rehearsal when the time came. They put substitutes into the rehearsal, and I was assured that both M. Thill and M. Pernet would have recovered from their respective indispositions by curtain time the next night.

When the curtain did go up and I looked toward the little window of Julien's studio from the living room of Louise's parents, it was with a slight sense of shock that I realized they had put in a new tenor, Raoul Jobin, now of the Met. Tenors are always disappearing in *Louise.* I've learned to sing my passion across an operatic window sill to any face I see there. After the first jolt, everything went off very well. But when the door opened for the music of the father and, instead of the tall, lanky Pernet, there walked in a great big fat father whom I had never even seen across footlights before, I felt as if everything had gone haywire. I wondered what would happen trying to get through with two artists with whom I had never rehearsed—but I need not have worried. So well trained are the Comique people, they were able to take this kind of emergency in their stride, and by their very ease produced a parallel ease in me.

During rehearsal Mary had criticized the attitude of most singers during the third-act aria. She disliked the fact that almost always they stood in the middle of the stage singing the aria as a personal exclamation of song quite apart from Julien. Mary had insisted that I sing the aria close to Julien as a love song to him, and thus as a love song to Paris too. Puccini had said of this aria, the first time he heard it, that it was one of the most difficult in the operatic repertoire, jumping as it does constantly from high to low and with such dramatic sweep it is difficult to subdue it in the intimate passages. Furthermore one must open an act cold with it, although the whole opera preceding the aria leads up to it as a climax. Too bad that Charpentier did not score it in the middle of action, when the artists are still warmed with the preceding passages of music. No matter how often I have sung it, nor how much courage has been whipped up, the third-act curtain always finds me with the inevitable trembling of the knees and dryness of throat. During this particular performance, I took Mary's rehearsal advice and, coming close to Julien, sang directly to him as I felt I had never sung this music before. The whole performance had seemed especially intense, like a last desperate reach for comfort in the midst of a war scare. Now the aria was almost like a patriotic song, removed from anything synthetic or operatic. My feeling must have gone across the footlights, for at the end of it there was a tremendous burst of applause, led (as the critics pointed out next day) by Mary Garden herself. The ovation was so prolonged that at the insistence of the conductor I did the rare thing—I repeated the aria, again to enthusiastic applause. At the end of the act I turned to Mary Garden's box, in which sat Val and Paul Boncour, and I bowed to her. The audience, still clapping, turned and applauded her too. Most people knew of my attachment to Garden and of her interest in me, so this ovation was a tribute to both of us. Mary had to stand and take a bow; then, unpinning the bouquet from her chinchilla wrap, she threw it to me on the stage. I felt as if both of us were sharing an embrace from the people of Paris. Backstage afterwards we found the famous green room of the Comique filled with photographers, friends, and flowers. Mary, Val, Paul Boncour, and I were photographed together, a picture I treasure among my most precious souvenirs.

An aside on this performance and the press: There was undoubtedly a sensationalism about the evening due to all the front-page stories with headlines such as "Grace Moore Conquers Paris in Louise"; nevertheless it was a serious and well-constructed musical presentation and was so considered on the inside musical pages. Yet when I returned to America I read the report of a certain musical roving critic who wrote of that performance with unabashed heavy-handed sarcasm. What his words indicated, aside from his own personal vindictiveness, was a lack of understanding of French musical taste and an inability to take into account the rush of Gallic emotion, which swept me along too in an overwhelming wave. That *Louise* was the last given at the Opéra Comique before the invasion of France. The crack of doom was in the air that night, and the usual polite inhibitions did not hold. To me it is one of my lasting gratitudes that as an American in Paris I was part of the fervid farewell to *Louise*.

When I sailed from America for the Riviera in 1939 I was asked what the object of the trip was. "I'm going to the South of France," I answered, "for the last trip for many years. War seems inevitable."

All things had taken on a perhaps-never-again nostalgia. We sailed the blue Mediterranean waters in the yacht of our friends Jessie and Jimmy Donahue, picnicked and sang together under the spreading cedar trees on the Ile St. Marguerite. Serge Lifar danced in the moonlight on our terrace to the music of *Tristan and Isolde*. But everywhere gay abandon seemed shrouded with impending disaster. Even the birthday dinner I gave for Val on August 15 in our villa at Cannes had this same feeling of sad finality. I remember particularly that when Douglas Fairbanks rose to toast Val and me, he said: "It is wonderful to drink to two people still so happy in their original marriage. It gives us all hope. But I also want to say good-by to a world we have known and loved here and which I think I shall never be part of again." Doug, with all his buccaneer grace and vitality, is dead now. So is that world he loved so well.

Now it was the summer of 1939, and Val and I were vacationing in our home at Cannes. I had fulfilled numerous engagements throughout Europe, including one in my beloved St. Moritz en route to Geneva, when I sang to an international convention of clubwomen headed by Mrs. George Mesta. But there was a conviction of quickly passing time that was climaxed one afternoon, as we all sat under the awninged terrace of the Grand Hôtel, when news came that the sailing of the *Conte di Savoia* had been canceled. A sudden hysteria swept the entire seacoast. Countess de Montgomery, head of the magazine *Marie-Claire,* telephoned us from Paris that we had better leave at once. There was a mad scramble for train reservations, but, lo, they were unattainable. I was able to secure a place in a third-class compartment with eight other women while Val decided to set out in the car, with a back seat full of extra tins of gasoline, for Paris.

The good-by at the villa was most difficult of all. Julien, our gardener, who was in uniform, had walked all the way from his barracks in Nice, since all transportation had ceased, and arrived in time to join in the farewells. We opened a bottle of our best brandy and, with him, his wife, and son, drank to France, their personal welfare, and our early return. Quite spontaneously we threw our arms around one another and wept a little bit. Later we sent American seeds to Julien through Howard Sturgis, who was doing Quaker relief work, and when I learned that French soldiers occupied the villa I was delighted to know that the French vegetables they ate were grown from American seeds.

We heard from Julien for the last time when he wrote just before the German invasion that an American Red Cross boat had arrived and he and his little son had gone down to the dock in Cannes to meet it. They had had no milk or fresh flour for a long time and, he wrote, I would have been moved to see how the French people received these gifts from America. The whole town had gathered on the dock to greet the boat, a little band played the "Marseillaise" and the "Star-Spangled Banner," and old and young stood and waved, with tears streaming down their cheeks. Then, wrote Julien, as the boat pulled into the last dock, everyone went on their knees in thanksgiving, and many waved little American flags to the American crew.

Val and I dined recently in Colorado Springs with the Bill Gowers, old friends who had loaned us the Venetian palace for our honeymoon. (Constance Gower and I both have a passion for houses and buy them with a flick of the wrist. The only difference is that she lives in hers, or someone else does, but I work to keep mine open and empty, since most of my time is spent traveling and living in hotels.) Bill Gower has been doing a splendid job for the Red Cross in England and was in France even after the Germans had occupied Paris, commuting between Occupied and Unoccupied France on Red Cross missions. He told us that when the last Red Cross boat arrived in Cannes, Laval had given orders that nothing about it was to be printed in the newspapers. The French populace was so angered by the decree that every bakery shop along the Riviera had put up signs announcing, "You are having this bread by the grace of help from America," and in each bakeshop window two flags were crossed, the American and the French.

I reached Paris after a slow train trip from Cannes and went to the hotel, where I was to meet Val. Hours passed, and when he did not arrive, I became frantic with worry. However, he finally showed up, battered and tired, with a sad tale of woe. He had been stranded on the road, the gas had leaked, there had been a lightning storm. He had been poisoned by gas fumes, revived on the marble slab in a little butcher's shop.

That last night in Paris was completely unforgettable. There was a total blackout, the first of the war. I was sitting in my hotel room at my dressing table when the lights suddenly went out. I dashed to the window, wondering if something had gone wrong with the circuit. Paris lay beneath, black except for the silver light of a high pale moon. Then out of the blackness the whole city seemed to cry as with one voice. The blackout was so unexpected that everyone had dashed to window and street to see what was the matter. Now the voices were raised in question, and it seemed to me as if this were the voice of Paris crying in the dark. Later we went to meet Edward Molyneux, Valentina and George Schlee, and friends, and sat on the terrace of Fouquet's for dinner. We looked out on a Champs Élysées grown suddenly strange—people walking slowly and silently; the buildings clothed in sinister shadows. Afterward, in the moonlight, we found our way to the Boulevard des Italiens, where *Louise* was playing. Even in the blackout people were queued up to see it. We stayed for about twenty minutes for one more glimpse of the film—one more sound of that joyous tribute to the Ville Lumière, now so shrouded in ominous shadows of war.

Later we went to Maxim's where all was light and gay. No one seemed to realize what was happening, and the restaurant had a capacity crowd. People had flown to Paris from all over Europe, and that night many were trying desperately to cover up their fear. Perhaps they thought now they were safe in the fort, for certainly nothing could happen to France. "The Maginot Line, you know—the invincibility of the French Army," they said. Sadly enough, both would have been truly invincible if they had not been hindered in becoming so by French politics.

Today, they say, when you go to Maxim's a large sign greets you with the words: "This restaurant is reserved for Aryans." Queer addition indeed to the old-fashioned murals, the gilt and plush, and the Merry-Widow-waltz gaiety.

We were assigned tentative passage on the *Manhattan* pending the turn of events, and Val and I left by motorcar. The last thing we saw as we got into our car en route to Havre was Norma Shearer on the sidewalk in front of the Hôtel Plaza-Athénée, surrounded by her twelve trunks. She was making a search which aroused our curiosity. What would a woman select in this last frantic moment? Norma suddenly emerged with the latest French nightie and the tallest hat I'd ever seen, and blissfully said good-by to the rest of her belongings.

We stopped off at the Golden Pheasant Restaurant in Rouen for a farewell luncheon on French soil. Only six persons sat in the corners of the once crowded and gay eating place. When we left, the waiters gave us a little crockery pheasant filled with pâté de foie gras to take to America.

The boat was scheduled to sail in the late afternoon, but when it failed to do so we decided to go out and have dinner. To reach the restaurant we had chosen we had to go through the red-light district of Le Havre. While we were in the restaurant I discovered I had lost my jewelry case. I rushed out to the street and in trying to get a taxi, made such a commotion that all the windows of the *bordellos* flew open and the girls leaned out to ask if there was anything they could do. Finally one girl put a fur coat on over her kimono and drove me back to the hotel in her little French car. Fortunately, when we arrived there, I discovered that an American professor had found the jewel case and was at that moment standing at the concierge's desk with it. I threw my arms around his neck and kissed him. He was aghast at all the commotion. And I was so happy that when the girl drove me back to the restaurant, I treated her and all her friends to as much champagne as I could round up. It was plentiful and good. As we were leaving to go back to our assigned quarters in the boat, which we had been told were in the swimming pool, we heard, from every window on the street, the girls of the kimono trade lustily singing, *"Ma mère est morte."* The hysteria of the blackout and the vintage champagne sent them dancing through the street without even their kimonos on.

At the last moment about three hundred people canceled their boat reservations, having decided perhaps that there would not be any war in France after all. Thus our tentative reservations were made final and we were permitted on the boat. Although we had paid a tariff over the usual first-class prices, we took whatever accommodations we could get. Elsa Maxwell slept expensively in the captain's bed, and the captain slept outside on a couch; Val and I made shift in rooms shared with others; some had no rooms at all but bunked in the lounge or on deck.

Two days later, out at sea, we all sat around the radio and listened to Chamberlain's declaration of war.

It had come. We broadcast the British national anthem, the "Marseillaise," and the "Star-Spangled Banner." Outside the waters of the Atlantic beat against the American ship with a rising early-September threat. One couldn't help wondering whether those waters spread a wide gulf between us and the madness of Europe or whether their far-reaching distances were only a delusion of safety that would evaporate in mist.

Jusqu'au jour, Louise—au'voir.

Far Away Meadows

THE ATLANTIC WAS NOT WIDE ENOUGH, nor the waves high enough, to keep us out of war. What it did do, on this side of its waters, was knit us more closely together from the tip of Tierra del Fuego to the Alaskan Highway. In 1941 I became a small stitch in the knitting process when I set out, under the patronage of Nelson A. Rockefeller, Coordinator of Inter-American Affairs, on a tour that included many Pan-American countries.

The whole trip of twenty-two thousand miles of concert and opera in six weeks blends into a kaleidoscope of airplane hops, short-notice dashes at early dawn after one or two hours sleep, constant crowds, the warm, happy remembrance of enthusiastic receptions—and always the emotional undercurrent that there was a job of friendliness to do beyond the concert performance. I shall never forget the gay hospitality, the capacity houses everywhere, as in Santiago, Chile, where we broke the attendance records of the Prince of Wales, and the glad greeting of discovery that I knew how to speak Spanish and could talk as well as sing to our good neighbors.

Bright as neon lights in my memory are the concerts in Puerto Rico and in Trujillo City, where we found the streets decorated like a festival, and I left with the Order of Columbus of the Dominican Republic pinned proudly on my chest; Caracas, city in the mountains, reached by a winding hairpin-turn road, where every man, including the President, looks like a handsome Spanish don and every woman is a beauty, and where the hospitality of the Phelps clan was lavish and heartfelt. Then the late arrival in sinister and magic Trinidad, where I sang my concert in a wrinkled evening gown which I tried to disguise by the great bouquet of flowers presented by the presiding governor general—Trinidad, which army wives told us was the most expensive place in the world to live, army pay inadequate, and where almost all had taken extra jobs to pay for proper food for their children. And after Trinidad Belém, which rose to fame on the great tidal wave of rubber riches, now a city of past glory—its opera house a faded pink marble rococo jewel standing opposite the Grand Hotel. Then the fabulous golf game at Curitiba, Brazil, where I had to take on ten caddies as an appeasement gesture, loaded them with handbags, coats, hats, cameras, and borrowed golf clubs and filled their brown chubby hands with American dimes. Uruguay and Paraguay—a wealth of exquisite laces, Panama hats. The bouquet of one hundred orchids from the governor of one of the states of Venezuela, music everywhere, and the jungle bordering the Amazon.

Swinging over the port of Rio for a bird's-eye view before landing; the unforgettable beauty of Sugar Loaf, the Corcovado Christ dominating the whole city, the white beaches at the water's edge, and the black-and-white mosaic walks of the Copacabana, sharp and clear in the brilliant afternoon sun. The polished modern airport of Rio, with thousands cheering. The *Tosca* debut before a brilliant international audience, and the thrilling elation of success as my colleagues Frederick Jagel and Alexander Sved, both of the Metropolitan, took bows with me. Then *Manon*, with its malicious bad lighting and featherweight conducting—boos at the stage door by the rival claque of a disappointed prima donna, unable even with their boos to turn away the American triumph. Meeting and listening to the music of Mignonne and Villa-Lobos, two of Brazil's great composers, imaginative music, pregnant, intensely individual. Photographic memory of that great statesman, Dr. Oswaldo Aranha, Brazil's Foreign Minister, who with President Vargas and his famous senhora, brings honor to Brazil not only politically but as a real champion of unity between North and South America. The award from President Vargas, "Sign of the Southern Cross," Brazil's highest medal of honor, which I was told I was the only American woman ever to receive. The charity concert organized by Senhora Vargas, where Walt Disney and I raised six thousand dollars in a small theater seating a few hundred people. Brazil —filled with warmth and life and civilized enchantment.

Then the great rolling Argentine. Buenos Aires, where I stood in concert alone on the stage of the great Teatro Colon, wondering as I sang why I was not in *Tosca* costume backed up by orchestra and operatic *décor*. Senhora de Anchorena came to me during intermission, saying "You are a great surprise. We are so delighted. We look forward eagerly to hearing you here in opera"; later, luncheon at Senhora de Anchorena's, whose family founded *La Prensa,* the country's leading newspaper, where we all discussed politics. How intensely political the Argentine playboys, who once spent all their money and time on the famous Parisian beauties and the ladies of Biarritz, had grown! Now they are home, turning their passionate, ferocious interest towards their country and its political destiny. Norman Armour, our ex-ambassador, who with his wife organized the charity concert for British War Relief and the Argentine newsboys at the American Embassy, when the few seats in the ballroom netted several thousand dollars. Good-by to the Argentine. And then the snow and ice twenty-two thousand feet above in the Andes.

Santiago, Chile, where crowds, forgetting internecine political strife, jammed the theater to hear music and song by the "Singing Ambassadress of North America," as they called me. First glimpse of the startling beauty of Peru at a stopover at Arequipa, where Tia Bates runs her glorified boardinghouse—unexpected dinner there with Jo and Florence Davidson and Aaron Copland. Peru with its marble palaces and black wood grilled balconies where President Prado (chic, good-looking Bond Street don) and his charming wife invited us to tea in a room overlooking.a garden where baby llamas grazed. In Lima, Hector Boza, Peruvian gallant, old friend of Neysa and Jack Baragwanath and a beau of mine from Music Box days, was my supper partner when Vice-

President Larco Herrera, noted for his hospitality to visiting North Americans, treated us during supper to an extraordinary performance given by Inca Indians in native dress. Romantic and primitive, their ancient musical instruments a background for the soprano voices that sang songs-without-words in the highest range of voice I ever heard—an effect almost Oriental, weird, melodic.

I cannot tell the story of that Latin-American tour without including my memories of Mexico, on a visit which preceded it. I was singing with the Minneapolis Symphony on Easter Sunday and dashed over to the airport, where I changed from my concert clothes into a traveling suit in the ladies' room and caught the plane to Mexico City. Jean Dalrymple, successful publicist, charming woman, and devoted friend whom I love dearly, accompanied me on the whole South American tour. We were a little entourage of four—accompanist, manager, Jean, and I.

All through our South American tour we found a revival of *One Night of Love* preceding us, with 24-sheet posters facing us everywhere! The most enormous poster of the most enormous smile that's ever been photographed, with arms outstretched, grabbing for the whole world! Finally, in Peru, Jean turned to me with a tired expression and said: "When Iturbi and I toured South America in 1935 we found these same posters everywhere. Iturbi never said a word, but when we got to Peru and he opened the shutters of his hotel window and looked out on the same poster, he threw his hands in the air and screamed, '*Mon Dieu, toujours le printemps!*'"

In Mexico City we were greeted enthusiastically, and even though we arrived on a later plane than the one originally scheduled, the crowd was there waiting. We were assigned a police escort, young men who all looked like Rudolph Valentino, were driven to the Hotel Reforma, and found beneath our windows another crowd that serenaded us with guitars. (I'm never off balconies in movie life or real life. I'm eternally leaning over them, waiting for a serenade!)

I had no sleep, having sung the day before, and was upset by

the fact that my trunks hadn't arrived. Furthermore no one knew
when they were expected. In the midst of this personal jitteriness,
accentuated by the high altitude, we received an invitation for
a Pan-American Reception at the palace of Ezequiel Padilla,
Mexico's Minister of Foreign Affairs. I didn't want to go. I
wanted to find some quiet little restaurant, where both the food
and music were good, and where I could sit back and relax. In a
spasm of childishness and fatigue I locked the door of my room
and refused to come out. Soon my conscience got the better of me,
and opening the door of the bedroom enough to peek out I saw
Jean Dalrymple, Isaac Van Grove, my accompanist-conductor
(whom I inherited from Mary Garden), and Ernesto de Quesada,
the manager, sitting like a trio on the mourners' bench, their faces
all puckered, worried about starting off the tour on the wrong
foot. They looked so discomfited, so sad, that I burst into laughter. "Oh, all right," I said, "if you think it's so important, let's go."

We found an electric iron, pressed the top part of one evening
dress and the skirt of another, and I set off in great style for the
green marble palace of Padilla. Josephus Daniels, then American
ambassador, and his late beloved wife, my personal friends,
were there to greet me. The Daniels were much loved and respected throughout Mexico and had turned the embassy into a
congenial meeting place for all Americans, North or South. Mr.
Daniels presented Señor Padilla, a tall, olive-skinned handsome
Mexican with the great distinction and exalted look of his own
race.

All of Mexico's diplomatic society was there that night, as well
as the leading singers and dancers of Mexico City, who turned
the marble hall into a gay Mexican street scene at fiesta time.
Gone were the fatigue and the worries about high altitude. I
loved every moment of that evening. As I was leaving, Padilla,
the eternal poet, said to me in front of a group of friends, "Good
night, Doña Grace. We are so honored to have you in Mexico
that even the earth will tremble in your honor." The next day
the mightiest earthquake in twenty-five years shook the earth of
Mexico. Señor Padilla was indeed a prophet!

Padilla is a great diplomat, as he later proved at the famous Rio Conference, when through the sheer power of his rhetoric and his personality he was able to sway the Conference away from consideration of Nazi alliances. I was proud to repay, in part, the debt of courtesy he extended to me in Mexico City when he was in New York the last time. There I gave a luncheon in his honor, where he made a tremendous impression on all who met him. He is undoubtedly a major statesman and one of the shrewdest exponents of democracy in this hemisphere. Completely opposed to the Nazi controls that have sometimes extended themselves south of the border, he is a brilliant champion of co-operation with the United States and is talked of down in South America as "The American Man of the Future." I think of Padilla as a mirror of his country. Mexico has become a frontier of freedom, and Mexico City a miniature Paris, an assimilation of new and old cultures. One feels the sense of a great civilization, just coming into its own. It is full of young inspiration, with a terrific national pride that is just learning how to assert itself. A trip across the border into Mexico is the most enlightening experience and immediately quashes our common provincial use of the word "American" in the sense of limited only to citizens of the United States. I left Mexico the proud possessor of the Medal of Honor of Mexico City and of the Aztec Eagle, highest honorary awards that can be conferred.

The Latin-American tour was over. I came back with a sensation of how vast, yet how integrated, this Western Hemisphere is, and what a future there is in it for all of us.

After my concert in Cuba, a place that bubbles with gaiety and love of music, and where I was presented the decoration of "Carlos de Céspedes" by President Batista, I received a letter from Mr. Messersmith, our representative at the American Embassy in Havana, which underscored clearly to me the importance of my whole south-of-the-border experience. I quote from it:

I need not tell you that your performance here was a magnificent success. I have seldom seen an audience so captivated as you had yours here last week. I felt very proud and happy for many reasons. It was a personal triumph for you, and you know how critical Latin-American audiences can be with respect to an artist from our own country. It was, therefore, I think a great tribute that an American artist should receive such a completely enthusiastic and thoroughly understanding reception by a Latin audience.

I sometimes think that a great artist can do more for the development of good relations in a few hours than an ambassador through a whole year of hard work. In any event we are all deeply grateful to you for what you did here, and your concert will be long remembered. You may be sure it has added much to the understanding of American culture and art.

The past years have been spent going from coast to coast, on extensive concert tours. In between concerts I have sung at camps and bond rallies everywhere, when I found that a simple little song was the best farewell one could give the boys who were setting out for destinations unknown. Everywhere at hospitals and at convalescent centers music has been a great morale builder. I inaugurated, at my public concerts, when I couldn't visit the camps, the now popular custom of inviting music lovers among the uniformed men and women to be my guests of honor on the stage. Their presence not only stimulated me as an artist, but I felt the audience come closer to the music itself as it sensed in it an integral answer to personal emotion.

Down in New Orleans, where I opened the season with the New World Symphony Orchestra, I met the fabulous Higgins family. Andrew Higgins is a kind of Paul Bunyan of the South— big physically and in vision, an Irishman who started out as a lumberjack and now can point with justifiable pride to the American soldiers who land throughout the globe on Higgins barges. Mrs. Higgins is just as fabulous, handsome and irresistible, like a frontier wife. When the two of them recently went up North to see President Roosevelt, they remained to chat with him while ambassadors and secret agents of state waited. As she later described the interview, "Where Andrew left off, I took up, in talking with Mr. Roosevelt."

Since the bad must be told with the good, there was that unfortunate concert in Philadelphia back in 1935 or 1936 at the Academy of Music, where the event was sold out so heavily in advance that three hundred people were seated on the stage. In the face of this fanfare of advance publicity, fans, and flowers, I managed to sing one of the worst concerts of my career. If one ever has any right to offer an alibi, mine was that, because I had to sail immediately after for engagements in Europe, I had recorded for six hours the day before the concert. I thought I should just be warmed up the next day. I was not warm. I was as cold as cold turkey. "Grace Moore Saw, Sang, but Failed to Conquer," said the newspapers, throwing in the extraneous remark that I had demanded a piano that was in tune for rehearsal. Well, what is so outrageous about a well-tuned piano? Is it supposedly esoteric? The Philadelphia *Inquirer* had the grace to run a letter the next day from an unknown champion who said: "Another crack was taken at Miss Moore for desiring a piano which was in tune, rather than the out-of-tune piano used by Rotary and Lions clubs. Why should a request like this draw sarcasm? Anyone with a modicum of musical intelligence can appreciate the necessity and value of a good piano, well in tune, for rehearsal purposes as well as concert use." Thank you, unknown fan. Every year since has been a slow but sure vindication of l'affaire Philadelphia!

One of the diversions of a concert tour is the amount of sociability that goes with it. On such an occasion one may be graciously invited to partake of "something light"—or the entertaining may be done on the large scale. If we are in a city for the first time, my manager plays safe and sends a supper menu to my hostess! There are those rare and delightful occasions, like my recent visit with Evalyn Walsh McLean at her huge, friendly mansion so appropriately named Friendship. She gave one of her more intimate parties, as she called it, with supper tables seating 125 and a gold table service. The Hope Diamond cast its brilliance over the assembly.

Again I remember another concert after which I was asked to

stand up and say hello to hundreds of people. Then someone handed me some lady-fingers and a demitasse.

"Thank you," I said, "but I'm always hungry after a concert because I never eat before. I'll save these lady-fingers for *after* supper."

"I'm sorry," was the reply, "but this *is* supper."

Concert tours remind me of the never-to-be-forgotten one at Chautauqua, when I slept all night in a deserted railway station until Humphrey Doulens could flag the Knickerbocker Express. I had a small suitcase for a pillow and was covered with newspapers to keep warm. I had come to this rather than stay one more minute in that awful house where we had been lodged, and where no one spoke during the meals except the domineering mother, who took me out and showed me every tree and bush and flower on the place, and where the henpecked sister took pills constantly and never opened her mouth the whole time we were there.

Then there was the time I was cooking artichokes on the electric stove in the aristocratic old Blackstone Hotel in Chicago and blew all the fuses in the whole hotel. They traced the break to the smell of artichokes, but I had put the pan out on the window sill and the stove under the bed and looked bland as peanut butter when the threatening knock came on the door.

In Chicago I always look forward to seeing the Charles B. Goodspeeds. "Bobsie" Goodspeed, who is a lovable and loyal friend, does more for music and the arts than almost anyone else I know there. She has turned the Chicago Arts Club into an important institution for the introduction of new and interesting singers and lecturers and as a center for exhibitions of the best in the world of painting. "Bobsie" is a friend of Mary Garden's, an amateur painter of unusual talent whose life revolves around important friends. Her home is a center of brilliant hospitality; each year for Christmas dinner she has the Ballet.

I remember, in my concert tours across the States, the time I traveled for miles in an air-conditioned train and found on my arrival, when I was being interviewed by the press, that I had completely lost my voice. Later I issued a scathing interview against air conditioning to a newspaperman and my manager, Jo Dwyer, whose father turned out to be the vice-president of the railroad.

I always look forward to my Texas engagements. The people there love music like Latins. On one visit I was made a Texas Rangerette and an honorary chief of police in San Antonio. John Rosenfield, the eminent critic of the Dallas *News,* last year came over to review the opening of the splendid San Antonio Symphony season when I was soloist with the orchestra. His eloquent music criticism was combined with the story of our supper party afterwards, when we sat in a little Mexican restaurant while fifteen guitar players serenaded us. He said I was the only prima donna he had ever known to rate a serenade of fifteen guitarists. It was very unlike the elegant reception Ann and Dick Harrison gave me there recently, but both in their way are San Antonio high lights in my memorabilia.

I have canceled few engagements in my long professional career, but each time I do, it is turned into a major scandal. Recently, when Freddie Schang, my manager for the past twelve years, went into the Army, where he is now commissioned a captain, I changed managers, going with the organization of Colston Leigh. Freddie Schang and I retain the unique and loyal friendship of long association. He was the devoted live wire of my career. Leigh, the lecture impresario, has recently turned to the musical world, signing me up as the first name of the concert circuit. When I made announcement of the change, rivals circulated the rumor that I would never appear on schedule. Leigh has set out as the lone wolf, not only to put his own artists across, but to break up the narrow-mindedness and highjacking of musical combines, and to open up and develop new outlets for music even in the small cities of America. He has imagination and drive and brings to the concert world a much-needed flair.

For a year in 1941–42 I took over the management of my own career. There were lifted eyebrows and sarcasm. Being so accustomed to these *faibles* of humanity in the world of music, I shrugged them off. The results in gross receipts surpassed my previous year. But lo and behold!—when Val, my business manager, and James Davidson, our tax expert, figured out the final results, I had saved less because I had no commissions to write off! I had the pleasure of discovering, though, that I had many friends in the business world of music, and that Grace Moore *wasn't* hard to manage, but that often she was tired and harassed by little, unimportant things and wasted priceless energy. Like any artist at such a moment, all I needed was someone to help me laugh the worries away. I learned a lot about myself that year. The work of being a manager was taking time and effort needed for the singing career. So it is fair play to pay a nominal percentage to any manager who guides the destinies of a human being who also has a box-office value. The public thinks the fees paid to artists are exorbitant. But, believe me, when taxes, secretaries, publicity, living expenses, and Valentina or Hattie Carnegie dresses are paid for and charity donations are made, there is little left over from a singing career, which, because it depends on a voice, is the most precarious career of all.

I have sought and gained valuable experience in a variety of fields, each of which has aided in the mastering of communications. When in 1942 I closed my season in *Louise* at the Metropolitan and accepted a personal-appearance engagement at Roxy's in New York at the highest fee ever paid a singer on the four-a-day, some of the musical stuffed shirts said, "Unless it's for financial reasons, why does she do it?" Well, I love to sing for people, that's all, no matter where. A Roxy audience was new to me, and to many of them I was new. I realized that a wartime audience had sprung up in New York, an audience which might never go to the Metropolitan but would love the operatic arias if opera came to them. I reasoned that the Metropolitan was a democratic institution and that it could gain strength, rather than lose it, by the acquisition of new friends. In spite of all the lifted brows I knew that if I could stand on the stage at Roxy's and reach out to the vast audience so that they liked what they heard, it would be a great "come-up" not only for me but for opera. The letters that poured into the management proved that they wanted more of Puccini, more of classical melodies. They were music-hungry. And there has certainly been plenty of tradition for what I did. Mr. Balaban and his associate, Mr. Jack Partington, general director of Roxy's, both lovers of music, lured Schipa, Swarthout, Schumann-Heink, and other artists into the same kind of engagements.

It was a completely happy experience. The stagehands, some of whom were old friends from the Music Box, cheered me on. I had a constant stream of visitors, lads who had fought in the South Pacific, the *matelots français* who had just come over on the *Richelieu,* boys of the R.A.F. in their handsome gray-blue uniforms, boys down from Camp Dix who had never heard an operatic aria in their lives. And the letters! "Who is Puccini?" asked one. "Where can you hear the whole thing sung out?" asked another. "I never knew opera was like that; I thought it was stuffed-shirt."

The public-relations job was immense. No matter where, a job well done can develop prestige for mass appreciation, and that is what opera needs to get out of the red.

No book about me is complete without a few words on our farm in Connecticut. I have owned many houses, but this is our real home. It was only a little weather-beaten salt-box house, hung over with two great maple trees that towered about the roof, set on a slope that overlooked rolling hills and the valleys of an old and mellowed countryside. Inside there were the typical worn beams, the big open fireplace where the family meals were once cooked, and not a sign of modern improvements. It was so simple, so unpretentious, so completely charming that the moment I saw it I wanted it. We finally persuaded the owners, Mr. and Mrs. George Waldo, great music lovers and owners of the Bridgeport *Post,* to sell it. Their only consolation in parting with it was my sincere appreciation of its quality.

The house, which came with its own name—Far Away Meadows—is more than two hundred years old and had once been a store. We found old account books written in beautiful English script that suited the names of the clients—Reuben Spring, for instance, one of my favorites. Much of the house had been beautifully restored; especially the three-way fireplace with a big opening which services the main hall, the dining room, and the front parlor. Val and I first built a little guest house while the repairs were being made in the main house and the steam heating installed. Then we attached a new wing to the old house itself, which included a large blue music room where I can work as I look out over our flower garden.

The place is filled with souvenirs of my career, and I intend to go on adding to them. I love my little front parlor, which I have done in a kind of distilled Victorian fashion—with a little harmonium I picked up for twenty-five dollars on Cape Cod, yellow-rose wallpaper picked up in Chicago, a yellow-rose carpet from New York, a long needlepoint footrest, chairs of mint-green stripes, fuchsia cushions, and treasured Victorian bibelots. I love the hilltop from which Val and I can see the changing moods of the weather and the earth for miles around. I love the apple trees in front of the house, and the red barn and the henhouse, and the kitchen where I hung pots and pans from France, and where I can go on a culinary spree with the hundreds of recipes I have picked up along with my other souvenirs.

Val has worked so hard on the place, breaking up the fields, building new stone walls and repairing old ones. Our other "day laborer on the Parera farm," as he likes to call himself, is Van Truex, head of the American School of Design in Paris and head of Parsons School in New York. Van, who lives more charmingly and with more grace than anyone else I know on his modest means, is a constant beloved visitor at Far Away Meadows.

This past year our friends—the same old ones we have always had—come to visit us in new ways. They "bus" from the Bridgeport station, instead of rolling in in the station wagon. Elsa Maxwell continues to be the lady of largesse, when she flings away a full month's worth of ration points on one ham which she brings as her week-end gift. The Gilbert Millers, who live on a neighboring farm, "pool" wedding anniversaries with us and we give our party jointly. This last summer my little Spanish-looking niece, Grace Moore the Second, daughter of Jim and Marian Moore, came to visit and piped out, at the age of three, her repertoire of six songs in a high perfectly placed voice that rang out over Far Away Meadows like a prophecy. Another Grace Moore to plague the public?

It has been a good life so far. I've liked living it, and look forward to more of the same. One thing is certain: life never stops on page XYZ, even if a book does. Writing this while I am still singing, still working, still planning makes it even more difficult to know when to say "the end." If I were retired, at least the career part would be over with and I could enclose it in a neat little nutshell labeled, "Her Life and Times, Beginning and End." I can't do that—not at the moment.

This, then, is for today. As for tomorrow and tomorrow—who knows?

Opera Biographies

An Arno Press Collection

Albani, Emma. **Forty Years of Song.** With a Discography by W. R. Moran. [1911]

Biancolli, Louis. **The Flagstad Manuscript.** 1952

Bispham, David. **A Quaker Singer's Recollections.** 1921

Callas, Evangelia and Lawrence Blochman. **My Daughter Maria Callas.** 1960

Calvé, Emma. **My Life.** With a Discography by W. R. Moran. 1922

Corsi, Mario. **Tamagno, Il Più Grande Fenomeno Canoro Dell'Ottocento.** With a Discography by W. R. Moran. 1937

Cushing, Mary Watkins. **The Rainbow Bridge.** With a Discography by W. R. Moran. 1954

Eames, Emma. **Some Memories and Reflections.** With a Discography by W. R. Moran. 1927

Gaisberg, F[rederick] W[illiam]. **The Music Goes Round.** 1942

Gigli, Beniamino. **The Memoirs of Beniamino Gigli.** 1957

Hauk, Minnie. **Memories of a Singer.** 1925

Henschel, Horst and Ehrhard Friedrich. **Elisabeth Rethberg:** Ihr Leben und Künstlertum. 1928

Hernandez Girbal, F. **Julian Gayarre:** El Tenor de la Voz de Angel. 1955

Heylbut, Rose and Aimé Gerber. **Backstage at the Metropolitan Opera** (Originally published as **Backstage at the Opera**). 1937

Jeritza, Maria. **Sunlight and Song:** A Singer's Life. 1929

Klein, Herman. **The Reign of Patti.** With a Discography by W. R. Moran. 1920

Lawton, Mary. **Schumann-Heink:** The Last of the Titans. With a Discography by W. R. Moran. 1928

Lehmann, Lilli. **My Path Through Life.** 1914

Litvinne, Félia. **Ma Vie et Mon Art:** Souvenirs. 1933

Marchesi, Blanche. **Singer's Pilgrimage.** With a Discography by W. R. Moran. 1923

Martens, Frederick H. **The Art of the Prima Donna and Concert Singer.** 1923

Maude, [Jenny Maria Catherine Goldschmidt]. **The Life of Jenny Lind.** 1926

Maurel, Victor. **Dix Ans de Carrière, 1887-1897.** 1897

Mingotti, Antonio. **Maria Cebotari,** Das Leben Einer Sangerin. [1950]

Moore, Edward C. **Forty Years of Opera in Chicago.** 1930

Moore, Grace. **You're Only Human Once.** 1944

Moses, Montrose J. **The Life of Heinrich Conried.** 1916

Palmegiani, Francesco. **Mattia Battistini:** Il Re Dei Baritoni. With a Discography by W. R. Moran. [1949]

Pearse, [Cecilia Maria de Candia] and Frank Hird. **The Romance of a Great Singer.** A Memoir of Mario. 1910

Pinza, Ezio and Robert Magidoff. **Ezio Pinza:** An Autobiography. 1946

Rogers, Francis. **Some Famous Singers of the 19th Century.** 1914

Rosenthal, Harold [D.] **Great Singers of Today.** 1966

Ruffo, Titta. **La Mia Parabola:** Memorie. With a Discography by W. R. Moran. 1937

Santley, Charles. **Reminiscences of My Life.** With a Discography by W. R. Moran. 1909

Slezak, Leo. **Song of Motley:** Being the Reminiscences of a Hungry Tenor. 1938

Stagno Bellincioni, Bianca. **Roberto Stagno e Gemma Bellincioni Intimi** *and* Bellincioni, Gemma, **Io e il Palcoscenico:** Trenta e un anno di vita artistica. With a Discography by W. R. Moran. 1943/1920. Two vols. in one.

Tetrazzini, [Luisa]. **My Life of Song.** 1921

Teyte, Maggie. **Star on the Door.** 1958

Tibbett, Lawrence. **The Glory Road.** With a Discography by W. R. Moran. 1933

Traubel, Helen and Richard G. Hubler. **St. Louis Woman.** 1959

Van Vechten, Carl. **Interpreters.** 1920

Wagner, Charles L. **Seeing Stars.** 1940